TRANS-EUROPE EXPRESS

OWEN HATHERLEY
TRANS-EUROPE EXPRESS

Tours of a Lost Continent

ALLEN LANE
an imprint of
PENGUIN BOOKS

ALLEN LANE

UK | USA | Canada | Ireland | Australia
India | New Zealand | South Africa

Allen Lane is part of the Penguin Random House group
of companies whose addresses can be found at
global.penguinrandomhouse.com.

Penguin
Random House
UK

First published 2018
001

Copyright © Owen Hatherley, 2018

Set in 10.8/13 pt Dante MT Pro
Typeset by Jouve (UK), Milton Keynes
Printed in Great Britain by Clays Ltd, St Ives plc

ISBN: 978–0–141–98832–0

www.greenpenguin.co.uk

Penguin Random House is committed to a
sustainable future for our business, our readers
and our planet. This book is made from Forest
Stewardship Council® certified paper.

To both of my parents, for different reasons

'What have I told you!' says W., as we board the train in Frankfurt. 'This is public space. Pub-lic. That means outside your head.' He points to my head. 'Private'. And then out to the world. 'Public'.

W. is a great upholder of this division. Abolish the public/private divide and you abolish civilisation, W. always says. He looks around him contentedly. – 'See how quiet it is in Europe?' It's civilised,' he says, 'not like you.'

Europe makes him gentler, better, W. says. It improves him. It's the public spaces, he says. They're so quiet in Germany. So calm.

Lars Iyer, *Spurious*

CONTENTS

CONTENTS

Contents

Europe in 2018

Randstad
Meuse–Rhine Euroregion

| | 300 miles |
| | 500 km |

FINLAND
•Vyborg
Narva• •Ivangorod
•Stockholm
ESTONIA
SWEDEN

LATVIA

Baltic
Sea
LITHUANIA
RUSSIA

BELARUS

NY
POLAND
•Leipzig
•Łódź

RUSSIA

UKRAINE

CZECH REP.
SLOVAKIA
•Lviv

STRIA
HUNGARY
MOLDOVA

SLOVENIA
ROMANIA

CROATIA
BOSNIA &
HERZEGOVINA
Split• SERBIA
BULGARIA
Black Sea
MONTENEGRO
•Sofia
ALY
Adriatic Sea
•Skopje
ALBANIA MACEDONIA
T
•Thessaloniki
U
R
K
E
Y
GREECE Aegean
Sea

•Athens

MALTA
•Nicosia
CYPRUS

Introduction: What is a European City?

A couple of days after the result of the referendum on Britain's membership of the European Union, I visited Southampton, a medium-sized port city on the south coast of England. It had, to my surprise, voted 'leave', and by roughly the same margin as the country as a whole – a little bit over 50 per cent. A rainy walk ended at Ocean Village, a development built in the mid-1980s on a small derelict part of the city's docks, which are – unlike those of Liverpool, Bristol or London – mostly still in use. Formerly on the site was the late-1940s Ocean Terminal, a streamlined design for the luxury travellers for whom Southampton was a more long-winded precursor to Heathrow, but that was demolished without a second thought in favour of a miserable collection of introverted, pitched-roofed housing complexes in cul-de-sacs and vaguely Postmodernist office blocks surrounded by car parks, with an exurban American-style multiplex cinema and a shopping mall. This latter was one of several car-centred, big-box malls built in the city centre between the 1980s and the present day. The mall was demolished after less than twenty years of existence, and replaced with a skyline of extremely dense 'luxury flats' along a boardwalk, the apartments packed tightly together so that every single inch of rent could be extracted from the site. If you look at the site on a map, you can see a peninsula jutting out into Southampton Water, the estuary that leads to the Solent. But there's no view of the estuary here in any publicly accessible space. Amazingly, the designers of the executive housing estate here managed to create the same sort of insularity you'd normally find on the outskirts, near an Asda on the M27. There's one place you can see out to the sea and contemplate the world beyond – a hard-to-find corner, through a fence marked 'RESIDENTS ONLY'. You can still see through the gates, just about.

In 1997, a new building was opened there, called Harbour Lights. I can still recall the excitement. Here was a building that was elegant, confident, oriented towards the water rather than to a parking space, and, most of all,

Ocean Village, Southampton, gateway to the Empire

a building that felt *European*, as much so as the fare of sub-titled arthouse movies it served up to the greedy consumption of myself and my friends. It was, I later realized, one of several buildings, often on watersides, that were the harbingers of a 'Europeanization' of urban space in Britain. Bradford would be an Italian hill town, Gateshead would be the new Bilbao, Salford would become as outward-looking as Rotterdam, Sheffield would model its public spaces on Barcelona. Each one of these towns and cities voted in the majority to leave Europe. What went wrong?

It is hard to recall how insular and grim mainstream British architecture was in the 1980s. Yes, a few spectacular or at least original buildings were realized by the likes of Rogers, Stirling or Foster, and, yes, some conservation of nineteenth-century architecture was probably necessary. But the urban redevelopment schemes of that decade, well up until the late 1990s, were pinched and anti-urban, defined – no matter how central or dramatic the site – by cul-de-sacs, squat mock-Victorian offices and endless surface car parks, all of it based on a paranoid and misanthropic notion of 'defensible space'. This philosophy spanned both left-wing councils and Thatcherite developers. It is astonishing that the architects of Ocean Village didn't think that it was worth bothering to emphasize the bridges, ships and silos of Southampton Water, either for residents or for visitors, but this was the norm at the time. You could find similar stuff in Salford Quays, inner-city Liverpool, London's Docklands, or along Bristol's Floating Harbour. The contrast with European architecture of the same decade is remarkable. There was a reaction to Modernism everywhere on the continent, East, West, North and South, in terms of its aesthetic and the blocks-in-space approach to planning, but the way this reaction was manifest seldom took the British approach. On the contrary, in Berlin's IBA, in Palomeras in Madrid, in late-Soviet Riga, in the inner suburbs of Paris, in Södermalm in Stockholm, the decision was to turn to the nineteenth-century city-block structure, with shops and cafés on the ground floor, flats above and intelligently planned semi-public courtyards in-between. The results were modern and urban, if not 'Modernist' in the ideological, post-war sense.

At some point in the 1990s, British politicians – mostly, if not exclusively, Labour – noticed the enthusiasm that British planners and architects had acquired for the European city. From their visits to Barcelona and Copenhagen sprang a thousand pavement cafés, gamely placed on drizzly street corners. In emulation of François Mitterrand's *Grands Projets*, the Arts Council, armed with ill-gotten gains from the National Lottery, lavished cash on the likes of Southampton's Harbour Lights. Designed by Burrell Foley Fischer, the building was a shift to the modernity that the city had otherwise abandoned in the 1980s. Glass, steel and wood, jutting out in vaguely nautical fashion to provide public views, it was also a very rare new building for 'culture' in a city which had otherwise devoted itself to becoming a giant out-of-town mall for Hampshire suburbia. In many places you wouldn't look twice at it, but here it seemed to suggest a different kind of city. I'm sure there are thousands that would say the same about their rather more famous cultural buildings, built in the New Labour decade, even given its high-profile disasters (of which there were many;

to name but a few: Manchester's Urbis, West Bromwich's The Public, Sheffield's National Centre for Popular Music, all closed and then given new, less arty functions in less than a decade). Yet the new high-rise luxury flats, going up at the time of writing at the other side of Ocean Village, tell the story of why this vision was rejected.

In 1992 Penguin Books and the Labour Party co-published *A New London*, a collaboration between the then Labour shadow minister for arts and media, Mark Fisher, and Richard Rogers. On almost every page, Britain's dilapidated streets and petty new developments were contrasted with a given European example of openness, cleanliness and experiment. This was the blueprint for everything the Urban Task Force would do under Rogers from 1997 to 2010, promising nothing less than an 'Urban Renaissance'. Yet

The European-style Ocean Village

even in that 1992 manifesto, the authors noted that the social housing planned in the Barcelona Olympic Village couldn't be realized because of the funding structure. What Rogers and his ilk missed was that, already in the 1990s, Europe was becoming more like England, privatizing and paring back its public commitments under the soft-neoliberal commands of the Maastricht Treaty – only it was doing it much more slowly and peacefully, maintaining a level of quality control and order in the process. The new 'Europe' built under New Labour was a façade, and it never really made it into everyday life, into council estates and suburbs, except when the former were demolished to make way for something more 'aspirational'. If the centre of Manchester became like a cheaper, rainier, PFI version of Barcelona, its suburbs and satellites stayed resolutely part of 1980s England, with all the retail parks, exurban developers' housing, crap jobs and elimination of alternatives that entailed. Lottery-funded arts complexes never replaced, and couldn't replace, skilled work, secure housing and a sense of purpose. In Britain, the experience of 'Europe' has been for the lucky few. Like so many adoptive Londoners, I find the Britain promised by Brexiters quite terrifying – xenophobic, paranoid, enclosed, pitifully nostalgic, cruel. But in much of the country that landscape never went away.

On that visit to Southampton, I got into a passionate argument with my mum, who had been one of the 54 per cent of people in the city to have voted to leave the EU. She works in the National Health Service, but she was not at all convinced by the dissembling 'Leave' campaign's promises that the money 'we' spend on 'Europe' would be spent on the NHS once Brexit had been achieved. She had no desire to see anybody deported, nor to see controls on immigration. Rather, she couldn't bear to vote for membership of the 'bosses' club' that is the European Union, especially after what it had done to Greece, memorably described by its finance minister as 'fiscal waterboarding'. She believed, not entirely inaccurately, that the EU's clauses enshrining balanced budgets and in favour of 'competition' made any left-wing programme impossible. I was and remain unconvinced by these arguments for leaving the Union, and I continue to believe that a European superstate should still, despite everything, be a left-wing demand, and not only given the history of the angry little nation-states crowded into this subcontinent. Britain is one of the few countries that would have a more just social settlement within the EU than out of it, as is now evidently proving to be the case. But at the heart of my own response was something quite irrational. That is – the reason why I wanted to stay in the European Union was architectural. The previous year, I'd been on a commission at the *Architects' Journal* to write about contemporary European cities in the lead-up to the referendum. Many of them were of the same sort of size as Southampton, with similar histories and similar economies to it. Yet I have still not seen anything quite like Ocean Village in continental Europe. In most of Europe, a medieval and multicultural city, with a varied and interesting architectural heritage, two universities, an affluent, educated population (Southampton is and has all of these) would never have imagined building something like this.

I have never seen in continental Europe an example of planning failing so utterly, the natural assets of sea and historic city wasted so totally, a visual sense atrophied so completely, and urban qualities ignored with such aggressive philistinism. Despite rather than because of the 'waterside regeneration' showcased by the cheap new high-rises going up on Ocean Village, I held on to the belief that, if not by institutional osmosis, then perhaps through ease of travel to France, the Low Countries, Spain, Germany, the Baltic, we might have seen just a little of these ideas, and that ease at living in cities rather than in parodies of the countryside, gradually become the norm here. There are a few places where I've most felt 'Ah, this is Europe, and this is better.' They would include the 'Islands' in Lyons, where the quays at the confluence of the Rhône and the Saône are now lined by modern, elegant apartment buildings, with chic public spaces and

Lyon's Ocean Village

even, that shocking thing, a well-designed shopping mall; the centre of Zagreb, with its horseshoe of parkland looping around turn-of-the-century buildings fading with just the right amount of battered grandeur; the seafront at Trieste, a sort of anti-Southampton, with everything looking right out at the water. The list could go on.

I could construct a composite description of the 'European City' that would encompass the aspects that make it seem like a relative exemplar – in an era that is generally lacking in such things – for British towns. Pulled together from things that are routine to varying degrees in Germany, Austria, Scandinavia, the Low Countries, Spain, Italy, France, even to a degree Poland and Estonia, it would entail a housing system where property ownership does not dominate and decent social housing is normal, accessible and cheap, a lively culture of architectural debate that has long since moved on from tedious polarities of 'trads versus Modernists', urban public transport would not be a matter of creaky privatized buses but of integrated, publicly owned networks of tubes, S-Bahns, trams and trolleybuses, with elegantly designed stops, stations and carriages; there would be a relative equality of income; a response to deindustrialization more about research and training than de-skilling and casual work; an integration with trees and nature under strict manners; cycle paths as a basic good, with cars banned in some central areas and strongly curbed everywhere else; a free education system, universal child care, universal health care; an approach to the buildings of the past that is based on conservation rather than conservatism; a decentralized system of local government, whereby provincial cities and regions don't have to go cap in hand to the capital whenever they want to electrify their railways or build a tram line; it would have streets and spaces which flow easily into each other, making walking a pleasure, rather than breaking them up with fences, spikes and CCTV cameras. This is a pick and mix made up of little pieces of, say, the Rhine–Ruhr region, Lyons, Porto, Tallinn, Bologna, Warsaw, Leipzig, Maastricht, Copenhagen, Helsinki. It leaves out various less attractive things about urbanism in the aforementioned countries – a less comfortable relationship to multiculturalism than London, Birmingham or Manchester, high unemployment, and the appalling delusion on the part of each of these countries' 'centrist' politicians that Britain's culture of deregulation and abuse of the public sphere is in any way worth emulating. However, when you make *Europe* into an exemplar – even if the intention is to juxtapose it with how things are done in Britain, the United States or the Antipodes – you're always connecting yourself with a long and disreputable history of exceptionalism. As soon as you venture much further out of the places that have their entries in the listicles of 'Most Liveable City', you'll find another side to the continent and the cities. The 'European' city is not merely the 'social city', dense, historically rich, egalitarian, clean, walkable and dominated by public transport, it is also the city of the ' nation-state', a European invention which has caused countries all over the world to reshape themselves – or be forcibly reshaped – in its image.

To Each Their Own Athens

Every country in the European heartland has its own little racist quip about where 'they' start, and where civilization ends. For the French, 'Africa begins at the Pyrenees'; for the British, 'the wogs start at Calais'; for the Cologne-based West German Chancellor Konrad Adenauer, the 'Asian steppe' began at the Elbe river, leaving Berlin deep in Asia. Europe, geographically, is a fiction – not an easily definable continent in the way that, say, Africa and Asia, or North and South America, are physically distinct from each other. It's an odd-shaped protrusion at the West of Asia, strictly more of a subcontinent. Its borders make little sense – the Urals, the alleged north-east border, define little, being a shallow range of hills dotted with Soviet industrial towns on each side. In fact, historically, that border has shifted constantly, from the Dniester to the Volga, only settling on the Urals in the nineteenth century. The southerly borders like the Bosphorus or the Straits of Gibraltar have a bit more of a pedigree, and of course there are the political definitions. The European Union can't serve to describe 'Europe', given that Switzerland, right in the Western affluent centre, isn't inside, nor Norway – and nor, possibly, by the time you read this, Britain. The Council of Europe's definition is a little more capacious, in that it includes Turkey and Russia, which contain within themselves Europe's two largest cities (that is, Istanbul, with 14 million inhabitants, and Moscow, with 12 million; London's 8.5 million is a distant third, St Petersburg's 5 million fourth – with Berlin's 3.5 million,

11

the EU's biggest city when Britain leaves, an even more distant fifth), however much most of their national mass is in unquestionably 'Asian' Anatolia and Siberia respectively. Geography and politics can disconnect in interesting ways: the rules of admission for the Council of Europe exclude Belarus, because of its use of the death penalty – and, if the Urals, Portugal, Iceland and the Bosphorus really are the four corners defining Europe, then the continent's centre is in either Belarus or Lithuania, depending on where the line is exactly drawn. One alleged border of Europe is the Caucasus mountains, which apparently separate Russia from Iran. But south of this border, placing them in Asia, are three countries which are in the Council of Europe – Georgia, Armenia and Azerbaijan. The European Union even includes Cyprus, a country far closer to Damascus than to Athens, and some distance east of Ankara, let alone Istanbul. And now not only Israel but also Australia are in Eurovision (after all, both nation-states were founded by Europeans).

The inclusion of these countries in conventional definitions of Europe makes clear that this is not a matter of geography, but of politics, and of 'shared history'. The origin myth of Europe, by now somewhat knocked about, is the 'Graeco-Roman' heritage, whereby a rational civilization with equality before the law, advanced technology, mathematically precise architecture, individualist literature and realist art gradually – after a Dark Age, anyhow – became the Europe we know. This has a little basis in the way that the Greek city-states defined themselves against the 'barbarians' of Persia, a stronger and richer state with a more authoritarian system of government, but Europe today bears only the vaguest relation to the Greek or Roman world, concentrated as it was on both sides of the Mediterranean, with North Africa and the 'Middle East' far more important, developed and wealthy than imperial peripheries like Britain or Spain, let alone places outside the empire altogether like most of Germany or all of Scandinavia. Histories of Western architecture have a conventional narrative, one never quite shaken by the reaction against the 'Whig interpretation of history', an easily explicable narrative of progress: Romanesque architecture, or Norman, as we call it, with its round arches, blunt towers and heavy stone; Gothic, in its many variants, with its expanses of coloured glass, the 'flaming line' of its tracery and the vaulting structures that keep it up; the Renaissance, when Roman architecture's principles of rationality and order were rediscovered; Baroque, where they were manipulated and distorted; Neoclassicism, in which the 'purer' architecture of the Ancient Greeks became the new model; and Eclecticism, whereby some or all of the above were mixed and remixed, mostly in the nineteenth century, as it stumbled around for a new style. These were followed by Modernism, when an aesthetic borrowed from engineering and abstract art created a totally new Western paradigm ready for export, which then became the 57 varieties of modern architecture – Brutalism, high-tech, Deconstructivism. Naughtier narratives might make more space for the many deviations from this – a less moralistic liking for nineteenth-century pomp, or an emphasis on industrial architecture's neglected role, or of the later influence of America, both in the various attempts at skyscrapers from the 1910s onwards and in the sprawl of malls and suburbs.

Classicism – Temple of Hephaestus, Athens

Gothic – Lincoln Cathedral

Renaissance – Konopnica House, Lublin

Baroque – St Andrew's, Kiev

Along with this narrative comes the gradual development of conscious town planning, in which the city is formed into a machine-like apparatus for the circulation of goods and traffic: shaped, rather than allowed to emerge gradually through precedent. With this comes the belief that the architecture in such a city should be planned in such a way as it forms a coherent whole. This is not untrue in and of itself, but it usually ignores the fact that the eastern Mediterranean was, until the early modern era, in most respects richer, more educated and more 'civilized' than North-Western Europe, something reflected in the complexity and structural ingenuity of Umayyad or Ottoman architecture, and something of which both Gothic and Renaissance masons and architects were well aware. Similarly, precisely calculated

Neoclassicism – Berlin

Modernism – Waldsiedlung, Berlin

Expressionism – Tonhalle, Düsseldorf

Brutalism – ČEZ Aréna, Ostrava

formal squares and wilfully planned and replanned cities could be found in Isfahan or Samarkand, sometimes before they could be found in Florence or Rome. But the 'story of European architecture' as it is usually told still leaps from the Graeco-Roman achievements – in which may or may not be included the great dome of Hagia Sophia in Constantinople/Istanbul – to their several rediscoveries: first in the 'Romanesque' architecture that developed after Charlemagne brought some political stability back to Western Europe in the ninth century (although this architecture is equally an emulation of the still-extant Roman tradition then in use in the Byzantine Empire, the buildings of Ravenna or Istanbul); then, after the strange interlude of Gothic, comes the 'real' rediscovery of Roman principles in the Renaissance, then the 'scholarly' return of the Greeks in eighteenth-century France, Germany and Britain.

After centuries of familiarity, it's quite hard to appreciate just how strange an argument this is: a historical melange, a totally modern construction that came along with the scientific, technical and military innovations that helped Europe to preside over the rest of the world with extreme ruthlessness. At the turn of the nineteenth century, cities in places that had been the Roman Empire's distant periphery, like Budapest or Munich, or outside the empire altogether, like Berlin, St Petersburg or Edinburgh, totally reconstructed themselves on the basis of their understanding, based on the examination of ruins, of what architecture had been like in Athens in the fifth century BC. This can be seen probably at its most bizarre and most beautiful in Edinburgh. The notion – still indulged by some architectural traditionalists – that architecture before Modernism is a matter of locality, place, the 'vernacular', is magnificently contradicted in the Scottish capital, where the irrational tangle of tall tenements and stinking alleyways that history had bequeathed it were supplemented by a town extension laid out like a mathematical graph, its precise terraces and tenements dressed with decorative motifs borrowed from ornaments on broken bits of stone found discarded in Attica or the Aegean. Here, public buildings in the age of electricity were designed according to methods that a slave society devised in order to emulate wooden construction in stone, over 2,000 years earlier.

This idea was then imposed upon Athens itself. Athens had for centuries been a small, Greek Orthodox provincial town in the Ottoman Empire, while the centres of local power and culture – not just Turkish, but also Greek culture, art and authority – had long relocated to Salonika – now Thessaloniki – and Istanbul, and further afield to Alexandria or Trabzon. When in the 1820s a large part of Greece won its independence from the Ottomans, with significant British, French and Russian military assistance motivated by a combination of historical romanticism and cold geopolitics, the new country moved its capital from Nafplio, where more people actually lived and where the independence struggle was centred, to this once-important provincial town. British, French and German archaeologists had already ransacked the Acropolis to take its artefacts back as booty. The British architect James 'Athenian' Stuart, who had published some of the first accounts of the city's relics, once paid an actual Athenian to demolish the house he lived in, so that it wasn't in the way of the ruined temple Stuart was sketching, a remarkably clear image of the physical destruction of the 'real' and existing city, with all its accretions and everyday lives, for the glorious ghosts of its past. The results of the activities of 'Athenian' Stuart and those like him would became pattern-books for the replanning of Paris, London, Edinburgh, and especially Munich and Berlin. With Greece's independence, the new nation-state invited a branch of the German aristocracy to become the Greek royal family; German architects, basing their ideas strictly on their interpretation of Athens's newly uncovered monuments, designed the civic buildings of the new Athens: the new Academy, the National Museum, the National Library and the Royal Palace (now the Parliament) on

Syntagma Square, among others. Orthodox Christians in Greece, who had called themselves 'Romans' for centuries, symbolically renamed themselves with their classical name of 'Hellenes'.

It is uncontroversial that a history so extraordinary should become a source of pride to modern Greeks. More to the point here, it is logical that the newly scientifically endowed states of Europe, with their ability to build and measure with unprecedented precision, would embrace Ancient Greek architecture, through the style they called Neoclassicism. As one hostile observer, William Blake, put it: 'Grecian is mathematic form, Gothic is living form.' This rationality also goes toward explaining the devout, anti-Rationalist reaction that helped power the Gothic revival in Northern Europe, at least at first: not only was Greek architecture pagan architecture, it was a mean and

The University of Athens

calculating form of design appropriate to the age of the workhouse and the cotton mill. But in Athens Neoclassicism's hegemony entailed a massive act of erasure. A little of this had been achieved already, before independence, not so much via 'Athenian' Stuart's house demolitions, but via the results of bombardments in the war of independence, and most of all through an integral part of the Parthenon being broken off and stolen by the English diplomat Lord Elgin. But, beyond that, the new independent Greek regime decreed that the Acropolis had to be cleared of all the accretions that had grown on the site since the end of the classical era. Not only was it full of warehouses and other unacceptably everyday things, but the Ottomans had actually insulted the site by *using* the buildings: the Parthenon, for instance, had been repurposed as a mosque, with a minaret in the middle. A huge swathe of the city centre, the ancient Agora, would later have any living trace removed, in order to discover the older, deeper traces of the marketplace where Socrates, Pericles, *et al*. had all once walked and reasoned.

Greek speculators and developers then built a rather lovely, modest, Neoclassical city around these, one that is notably a lot less implacably straight-lined and spacious than such Athenses of the North as Edinburgh or St Petersburg; and in the twentieth century a dense, unsentimental concrete city was built around that. One result of this is the cognitive dissonance when you find a fragment of the Ottoman legacy still left in modern Athens. Opposite Monastiraki Metro station, a Neoclassical pavilion of 1895, is the Tzistarakis Mosque, designed in 1759. If you believe that historic civilizations are about continuity rather than sudden, modern breaks, then this building represents the 'real' recent history of Athens, a minor but attractive structure with three little domes around one great one, and a pointed-arched colonnade. Its plan and structure are very clearly descended from the Pantheon and Hagia Sophia, but the style has become folksier as time has gone on and the city declined in importance. Any argument that this was the 'authentic' Athens and classical Athens just an antiquarian fake would inevitably meet with anger and scorn, along the lines of the mosque being an expression of the colonial architecture of the Turkish occupiers, who had sought to eradicate the 'true' architecture of the city and its 'real' culture. Even now, the resulting 'historic' landscape has to be extremely

Tzistarakis Mosque

Maintaining the Acropolis

carefully maintained. At the time of writing, the Acropolis is a high-tech place, with cranes, gantries and massive teams of scientists maintaining the condition of the citadel built under Pericles' rule and to Callicrates' design. German journalists decrying that they have to bail out the lazy, epicurean Greeks (who in reality work among the longest hours in the EU) have recently argued that these aren't the 'real' Greeks anyway, but some Ottoman-Albanian aberration who just happen to occupy the same place and use the same language – something that the German press should be wary of, given Hitler's view that Germans were the *real* heirs of the Ancient Greeks.

These acts of definition and erasure in Athens are a useful reminder that while Europe has its 'Other' outside its own self-definition – the Middle East most of all, the Far East more vaguely, and more recently the more modern barbarism of the United States of America – the Other is also within, in the form of Central–Eastern Europe, tainted by Communism; in Greece, Russia, Ukraine or Romania, home of the 'Eastern' Orthodox Church; and, especially, the Balkans, tainted by the Ottomans, Orthodoxy *and* Communism. This makes using 'Europe' as a neutral term extremely difficult – there simply isn't a definition of it that isn't in some way racist or colonial. For all that, I've often not been able to help but reach for 'This isn't what would happen in *Europe*' when visiting certain places that don't live up to the standards described above. Sometimes, this is quite an exciting feeling, as in Naples, where the friction between several attempts to plan the place – under King Vittorio Emanuele, ploughing boulevards through it in the nineteenth century; or the desolate, failed high-rise central business district built under the direction of the Japanese architect Kenzo Tange in the 1970s – creates a thrilling contrast with the high-tension tenement city crammed into the Ancient Greek grid-planned centre, and the tangle of speculative apartment blocks shoved as if at random into the hills. 'Not Europe' sums up the mess of somewhere like Birmingham or Bristol, where several attempts to plan Georgian-Grecian 'improvements', Parisian 'corporation streets' and Le Corbusier 'radiant cities' have run aground on greed and graft, leaving a chaos whose explanation you can piece together yourself, if you don't mind running up against some of the cheapest and nastiest of townscapes in the process.

Emptiness amid density, Naples

It is also what comes to mind in Kiev, where the ordered, axial city built by the Soviets has been transformed through epic levels of corruption into a multilayered metropolis of brutal commerce, where every underpass and Metro station entrance in the city centre has been extended into one discontinuous underground mall, classifiable into the luxury boutique underpasses, the Western brand underpasses and the destitute-people-selling-Chinese-goods-or-their-own-possessions underpasses. Elsewhere, the 'not Europe' problem is not one of architecture at all. St Petersburg, for instance, is very closely comparable to Paris or Stockholm, in terms of the size and height of its buildings, the width of its streets, the promenades along its river, but it has strikingly little of the easy street life you can find in those cities, stuck instead in a petrolhead car culture barging down streets that elsewhere would be full of bicycles. An aggressive governmental philistinism sees the tolerance and ease that some Western European metropolises manage to encourage as just another facet of a decadent 'Gayropa'.

Sometimes, though, the 'this is not *Europe*' reaction comes when you're in somewhere trying to make itself *more* European. One example that comes to mind is the combination, in Belgrade, of a 'Berlin-style' hipster district of low-rise blocks and warehouses about to be erased for the construction of a UAE-funded skyscraper district based on principles of 'walkability' and 'sustainability'. You know, usually, if you're in somewhere uneasy about how European it is, because it has lots of things with

St Petersburg: cars where cycles would be

'Europe' in the name: European Square, Kiev; the Hotel de l'Europe, Minsk; European Union Metro station, Sofia; and it is no coincidence either that it is so often in these states that nation building is neverending, with the search for a useable past constantly repeated. For 'Eastern hands' in the media and the Foreign Office bureaux, Ukraine's or Belarus's failure to become 'normal European countries' must be because they've not become real 'nations', something which can only be achieved by finding the purest, most inflammatory form of nationalism, most likely to alienate the neighbours and consolidate the faithful. Recently Ukraine underwent *Euromaidan*, a popular insurrection, after its president was coerced into rejecting an Association Agreement with the EU, something that was seen as denying Ukraine a chance to follow, say, Poland, from the 'Second World' into the 'First'. This was optimistic, given that other countries which have such an agreement include Jordan, Algeria and Egypt, and this hasn't catapulted them into peace and prosperity. One surely unintended consequence of Russia's subsequent invasion of Crimea and Donbass was the recalibration of Ukrainian history around the alleged centrality of a band of vicious, unpopular far-right guerrillas of the 1940s: given that they were not Soviet, it apparently follows that they must have been European. In Belarus, conversely, Europe = civilization has been a hard sell. As the Belarusian liberal Andrey Dynko has put it, 'until recently, an ordinary Belarusian above all associated Europe's *mission civilisatrice* with "Hitler the Liberator" posters. It was hard for a person who had gone through experiments in amputation without anaesthesia in the Nazi death camp

at Auschwitz to agree that Europeanness means civilization.' Only the truly European countries, like Britain, a
rich imperial centre for 500 years, have the luxury of
choosing not to consider themselves 'European'. Our use
of 'the Continent' to define the rest of Europe is a constant source of amusement to everyone else in it.

Another urban European myth, perhaps rather surprising given all this history, is that Europe is a uniquely
multicultural continent. This may be true in terms of the
diversity of languages and nations crammed into this subcontinent, though they are usually predicated, explicitly or
otherwise, on the fitting of each one into a bordered box.
In Europe's historic cities, multiculturalism can often be a
melancholy presence. In one square facing the quays of
Trieste, where a dodgy statue of James Joyce leers on a
bridge at the passing girls, a Palladian Catholic church
and a Byzantine Serbian Orthodox church face each
other, these 'Western' and 'Eastern' styles that are conventionally thought to cancel each other out managing to
complement each other in their contrasts, something
made possible by how smooth and pleasant the surrounding townscape is, a feeling created through cared-for,
generously planned streets, well used. Just behind this
square is what looks like a mosque, with a tall bulbous
minaret, but this is deceptive – it's actually just an unusually experimental Catholic church, a product of the
surprisingly eclectic architectural culture of Italian Fascism. A bit further out from this central quayside space is
one of the largest synagogues in Europe, a staggering
cubic behemoth, a massive vindication of pride and presence of the most persistently persecuted group in Europe.

Trieste, Palladianism and Orthodoxy

Nearby is a particularly beautiful structure built as the cultural centre of the Slovenian community, in a very late-Hapsburg experiment in rationalized Art Nouveau. You can find similar signs of multiculturalism (or rather, multi-confessionalism) easily enough if you look around places in this book such as Lviv or Thessaloniki. But all these are signs of a *vanished* multiculturalism, with the real thing mostly destroyed by nationalism, post-war 'population transfers', and, most of all, by the Holocaust; these cities all became largely homogeneous in the second half of the twentieth century, after a history that had up until then only ever been multicultural. Trieste has multi-cultural architecture; it does not – except in the case of very recent migrants, about whom there is an unseemly panic – have a multicultural present.

The really existing multiculturalism that you can find today in, say, Berlin, Paris, Rotterdam, Brussels, Stockholm or London, dating mostly from the last fifty years, has left much less architectural evidence, at least in terms of 'high architecture' and permanent buildings, though the effects have been huge in the subtler textures of urban life. In this respect, Woolwich, south-east London, where I wrote this book, is fairly typical. Two Art Deco cinemas of the 1930s, which have been bingo halls for most of their working life, have more recently become West African evangelical churches. In one case, this is rather fitting: the old Woolwich Granada has an auditorium designed by the Russian émigré theatre designer Theodore Komisarjevsky in a free improvisation upon Gothic guildhalls and cathedrals, executed with bargain bin materials and a consummate spatial flair. It is now the Ebenezer Building, the Christfaith Tabernacle Cathedral. Nearby, a dour, brick Neoclassical 'prayer box' built for dissenting Protestants at the start of the nineteenth century is now the Gurdwara Sahib. The only *new* building that is a direct consequence of this new multiculturalism is the Greenwich Islamic Centre, also known as Plumstead Mosque; it is a drab red-brick building with a hurried-looking gold dome, its dull and tacky design the not particularly edifying consequence of two architectural traditionalisms meeting. Other places, however, have not even been this enlightened. Switzerland voted against its townscape chocolate boxes being defaced with minarets. Greece, much of which was still the colony of an Islamic empire as recently as the 1910s, has various prohibitions on Islamic architecture returning to its cityscapes:

the aforementioned Tzistarakis Mosque, now a folk art museum, has long been denuded of its minaret.

Some Capitals of Europe

Arguably, the city which has developed the greatest level of anxiety about its own multiculturalism is Paris. Possibly because of the preferences developed as an adoptive Londoner, on my few visits to the French capital I've found it alienating and baffling. The coexistence of different time periods, architectural moments, clashing forms, clashing ideas about city planning that you can find in the centre of London (although often underpinned by an underlying Rationalist Georgian grid) appear, at first, to be absent in Paris, replaced with a mandatory limestone speculative neo-Baroque, thrown up in a few decades. The grand public buildings, particularly but not exclusively the horrible Louvre, are often flatulent and graceless. What is so frustrating about the French capital is the incessant praise it has received both from conservatives – who can be expected to love a city where you can walk for miles without seeing a single piece of twentieth-century architecture, and where both modernity and multiculturalism are strictly kept to reservations – and from political radicals, for whom the revolutionary history of the French capital, the tedious litany of 1789, 1848, 1871, 1968, means that they can enjoy the most perfectly elegant bourgeois streets by kidding themselves that what they're really enjoying is the fact that a gang of marauding artisans and prostitutes once hauled the red flag up from the roof of what is now a luxury antiques emporium. The quality of life compared with London may be enviable, but not much else.

When I first visited Paris, I found this disconnect deeply weird, having read about the place for many years beforehand. Walking along the eighteenth-century lanes of the Marais, I could only be puzzled as to why what to my eyes looked like one of the more boring corners of St James's or Belgravia was considered to be of such world-historical importance and intrinsic interest. The monolithic streets of Haussmann's Paris, meanwhile, reminded me most of the Stalinist boulevards of Moscow, or at best the tenemented streets of Glasgow, neither of which are anywhere near as celebrated; neither considered remotely romantic. In fact I found it all rather disturbing, all these white boulevards full of solely white people, with their trees filed down to a neat point along militaristically measured counter-insurgency free-fire zones, with a feared multicultural suburbia forming a doughnut around them. Even the tube appeared to be segregated according to class and race: the RER for the proles living in the 10-million-strong Paris conurbation, the Metro for the 2 million inhabitants of 'Paris'. Reaching the Centre Pompidou, that prototype for the peculiar mix of modern art and tourism that later created the Tate Modern, was a massive relief. For all its jugglers, Rogers' and Piano's edifice came to me as a great exhalation, a vindication of modernity, action and openness, of emphasized workings over trimmed façades, which I could happily stare at for hours.

Of course, this is an exaggeration, as I gradually realized. To the north and east, this tight-arsed cityscape shakes itself out into looser spaces, especially as you cross the Place de la République, where districts such as Ménil-montant, Belleville and La Villette can rival Whitechapel or Deptford in their diversity and liveliness, and in the surprises and shocks to be found in their cityscape. Rummage around a little here, and you can even find some excellent Modernist buildings, usually either legacies of the Communist Party of France's one-time dominance of working-class Paris – Oscar Niemeyer's flamboyantly futuristic PCF headquarters, or housing estates such as the wild Orgues de Flandre, an eruption of concrete aggression into the endless limestone – or legacies of François Mitterrand's *Grands Projets*, such as Bernard Tschumi's marvellously flawed, charmingly dated neo-Constructivist theme park at La Villette, a 1980s idea of the three-dimensional city, walkways and jagged multi-coloured shards, like living in the old Channel 4 logo. However, the Paris/*banlieue* divide is incredibly strong, and only reinforced by the clichés of Parisian radicalism. Nanterre, a suburb built in the 1960s and 1970s, near to the new skyscraper business district of La Défense, was always regarded with horror by the 1968 'revolutionaries'. Many of them studied at the glassy university there, which was then surrounded by North African shanty towns. When I went for a walk there in summer 2014, I headed for the Tours Aillaud, an estate described by the late art critic Robert Hughes as 'social scar tissue'. It is certainly whimsical – tubular high-rises with windows the shape of the patches on cows, coloured green, yellow and blue, with little pyramids on top and with the pavement landscaped into little circuses and hillocks, detailed in cobbles. Dozens of people, most of them of second-,

Monolithic Paris, approaching the Panthéon

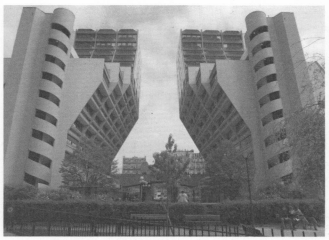

Orgues de Flandre, north-east Paris

third- or fourth-generation Maghrebian or sub-Saharan descent, were sat around chatting with prams, enjoying drinks and cigarettes, with an informal casualness most unlike that infuriating Parisian 'Look at me as I enjoy our traditional café culture' look. Crowds of school-children leapt about the artificial hills. This is the sort of working-class life seldom seen in Paris proper, but because this and places like this are remnants of the 'planner state', the Integrated Spectacle of Keynesian capitalism, of Gaullist–Stalinist *dirigisme*, their usual natural defenders are obliged to despise them, and prefer instead the streets shaped as revolution avoidance by Napoleon III and Baron Haussmann.

There are many other cities like this, and they are often the most praised in Europe. One is Venice, which

Social scar tissue in Nanterre

has faced a decline of its population usually only seen in such notorious urban disasters as Detroit or Cleveland, becoming a dream-archipelago mainly inhabited by tourists, with most of the Venetians long since moved to Mestre and Marghera, something which owes as much to the degree of historical preservation as it does to subsidence. Another, in visual terms, is St Petersburg, where the districts move out in consecutive historical arcs – the ideal Enlightenment despotic metropolis in the middle, then one circle of a nineteenth-century industrial city, another circle of a Constructivist and Stalinist urban experiment, then another circle of prefabricated highrises. In St Petersburg's Vasilievsky Island, you can see almost everything that has ever happened in European architecture for the last 300 years, from Mancunian textile engineering red-brick mills to Brezhnev-era angular Brutalist towers along canals. You will very seldom find them in the same place, but rather in discrete, distinct districts. Here, though, the class division is not so stark – in fact, until recently, the outskirts' centrally heated, large, prefabricated flats were more likely to be comfortable than the subdivided nineteenth-century flats of the city centre.

It is most instructive to see 'Paris' applied as a method to cities of a different sort, like London or Berlin. The German capital's tortured history has given it an incredible architectural and spatial richness, with every single important architectural and planning movement doing their best work here, often in the city centre, with a notable lack of coherence, visual repose or elegance, but with a quantity of spatial thrills Paris can't rival. The city as reshaped under the direction of the Social Democrat town planner Hans Stimmann since the 1990s and the fall of the wall has been based on trying to replicate the discipline which the city once had 200 years ago, in the age of great Neoclassicists like Schinkel ('Athens on the Asiatic Steppe'?), and which has long been enforced upon Paris. Buildings were to be of a uniform height, with a uniform window shape (and no Modernist ribbon windows!) and to be clad in something at least resembling stone. The success of Berlin in the last fifteen years, as a sort of unofficial European hipster capital, has managed to do what capitalist cities are meant to (that is, it has encouraged rising property prices and the in-migration of middle-class professionals), but this has if anything been despite Stimmann's effort at homogenization, with incomers preferring areas scarred by war and Modernism such as Friedrichshain, Mitte and Kreuzberg. To declare that a city like this, with its large Turkish population, its lively political left, its artistic and musical avant-garde, should respect the architectural principles of the eighteenth century is perverse.

Perverse but influential. Similar principles have been embraced in London, in recent years. They had, as defenders of them correctly pointed out, saved Berlin from the worst, from the hideous riverside yuppieville London and Manchester devolved into. Because of this increasingly evident contrast, the response from the British capital has been to invent its own new set of rules, mandating Georgian window proportions, flat roofs and brick or masonry cladding. After the likes of Ocean Village and Salford Quays illustrated what the unplanned, uncoordinated

'Anglo-Saxon' alternative looked like, it is unsurprising how this Georgian vision has swept all before it. Now, London – if not other British cities – is suddenly full of cheap but earnest developers' versions of modern Amsterdam, Berlin or Porto. King's Cross Central, the area immediately around the Eurostar terminal, which can take you quickly to Brussels, Amsterdam, Eurodisney or Paris, is the exemplar. The housing by MaccreanorLavington is Dutch, richly decorated with textured and patterned clinker brickwork, in a German Expressionist craggy skyline; alongside, the office blocks by David Chipperfield, with their rows of colonnades, are Italian Rationalist, icy, airy and precise; Stanton Williams's Central St Martin's is Spanish or Portuguese classicized modern, a severe concrete cube on a stark yet sunny waterside square. You will find their originals in this book.

For Perry Anderson, not on the whole a particularly sympathetic critic of the institution, the European Union is the 'last great achievement of the bourgeoisie'. In terms of the scope of its ambitions and the complexity of its apparatus this has an element of truth, however much the EU wilfully organizes itself as a deeply unromantic and strictly limited technocracy. So we ought, if this is so, to be able to see in the cities of the European Union some of the flair and élan for town planning and co-ordinated architectural ensembles that were seen in the creation of, say, Munich, Edinburgh, Rome, Florence, St Petersburg, Bath, all those great cityscapes formed by the happy intersection of the Enlightenment tradition of visual planning and organization, and the capitalist operation of property speculation and rent seeking. This has

King's Cross crossed with Rome

been much of the appeal of European cityscapes since the late 1990s, particularly when marketing themselves abroad – as much as they are going to see history, visitors to Bilbao, Barcelona, Amsterdam, Rome or Berlin are also going to see the modern ensembles of the last twenty years, the new riverside districts, the Guggenheim museums, the skyscraper skylines, the bridges and railway stations of Santiago Calatrava. Many of the places we will come across in this book are major human achievements, and, as someone who seldom finds enjoyment in recent architecture, it gives me great pleasure to be able to praise them.

However, two cities which are unlikely to be common destinations for the 'European City Break' are each an exemplar of why the European Union has had such problems in selling itself. Brussels, where its governmental power is situated, and Frankfurt, citadel of its financial might, are not notably picturesque, and the European Union has, famously, failed completely in creating an architectural image that would provoke any kind of identification. Frankfurt gets around this by having, in front of the European Central Bank, a giant sculpture of the Euro sign, a gesture of such crassness that even American capital would find it kitsch (imagine a giant dollar sign sculpture in Wall Street). Frankfurt is, though, one of the cities where there has been some sort of explicit rejection of the zoning of business districts that puts the skyscrapers on the outskirts of Paris, Munich and Madrid. This gives it a certain impressive vigour, to be sure. The railway station is one of those terrific steel cathedrals, akin to those in Hamburg or Cologne, or to Berlin Ostbahnhof: a clangorous hangar, not wildly dissimilar to the likes of St Pancras or York, but harsher, spiky and unsentimental. The streetscape outside is peculiar. I stayed, on my one visit to the financial capital of the European Union, in a Russian-run hotel in a largely Turkish district, and on a short walk towards the skyscrapers discovered the interesting fact that the red-light district is right next to the central business district, something which couldn't possibly be solely coincidental: 'AMERICA PEEP SHOW', in front of the tubular shaft of Westendstrasse 1, designed by the American firm Kohn Pedersen Fox for DZ Bank.

American as it may all look, the city runs on public transport, with Germany's routinely beautifully designed tram, U-Bahn and S-Bahn networks. The skyscrapers are, as in the City of London, shoved in every which way,

The New New Frankfurt

unregulated, creating exactly the sort of jagged, unstable aesthetic that planners in Berlin or Munich have been desperate to avoid. The implication is that financial power and the sort of careful preservation and dogmatic overall planning that make European cities distinctive are mutually exclusive; certain cities have to take up the slack. The result, best viewed from the café of the Staedel Museum on the other side of the River Main, is a tad bleak, with all the glass volumes outlined wanly against the slate-grey sky. London, for a time, tried to resist this skyline happening to it – Frankfurt's Commerzbank, designed by Norman Foster Associates, is based on a rejected proposal for the City. This has long since ended, but while London skyscrapers are forced into whimsy and shapemaking by the need to keep out of protected views of St Paul's, the architecture of Frankfurt's financial might is devoid of such patronizing japery: its towers are cold, hard, unromantic. The other side of the city can be found if you take the U-Bahn out to Römerstadt, home of the 'New Frankfurt', a Modernist experiment of the Weimar Republic, when the Social Democrats tried to replan it as a social machine.

The chief architect, Ernst May, had a background in the Arts and Crafts movement, and had worked in Britain. These are, strange as it may seem, analogues of Wythenshawe, Becontree or the interwar suburbs of the West Midlands. From 1925 onwards, May laid out a series of garden suburbs and had them built using Fordist methods of mass production, using assembly lines and reinforced concrete. As in Britain, these are low-rise, single-family houses with gardens, cousins of Letchworth, Welwyn Garden City and Hampstead Garden Suburb. Yet, unlike the English garden suburbs and cottage estates of the same period, there's no concession to history in the architectural form, all cubes, right-angles and flat roofs – a lack of sentimentality that has endured ever since. If you go to the 'New Frankfurt' now, you can take a tour called the 'Forward Route of Social Democracy'. In the skyline visible just over the horizon of German financial power, able to dictate the policies of Greece, Spain, Portugal, Italy, is a vision of where that forward route eventually ended up. The New New Frankfurt is the seat of a trans-national financial power

The Old New Frankfurt

run by a partly Social Democratic government which legislates against the possibility of other governments implementing social-democratic programmes.

Brussels is even weirder. Historically, it is deeply bourgeois. So bourgeois that brief residents Marx and Engels despaired of this most industrialized part of continental Europe ever becoming revolutionary, and hence the perfect place for the headquarters of both the European Union and NATO – a safe metropolis at the crossroads of the Germanic and Francophone worlds, a sense of safety which only recently has been shaken by a small group of terrorists in inner-city Molenbeek. Yet, in making Brussels the capital of Europe, combined with the linguistic and tribal chaos of Belgian politics, the EU managed to accidentally create a highly diverse, complex and strange city. In doing that the weirdness already at large in the capital is positively amplified. This may sound counter-intuitive, in that Brussels is usually considered an urban planning disaster – the term 'Brusselization' was coined as early as the 1960s to define the destruction of historic townscape by unplanned speculative office blocks. However, except for a brief attempt to beef the city into an imperial capital, which we will come to, the city has always been basically unplanned, at the mercy of the whims of its burghers to a degree that often recalls Britain. One result of the radically bourgeois architecture of the capital of Europe has been a few sporadic attempts to make it less bourgeois, with a surprisingly extensive history of buildings for the labour movement to be found in among the endless speculative townhouses.

Due to an ordinance which made the repetition of buildings practically illegal, apparently more because of a rash of lawsuits between Belgian architects, rather than a disdain for uniformity, any Belgian street looks vastly different to any English, German or French street. You don't get uniform terraces either of houses or of tenements, you don't get semis, and hence you don't get repetition. This doesn't actually lead to the riot of ideas you could naively expect, and in poorer areas like Schaerbeek and Molenbeek the same architects would hang minor variations of brickwork details on what are essentially normal tenements and terraces. Even in the best instances, the apparent uniqueness of the Brussels street is a matter of small details and dressings rather than fundamentals. In practically every case, we're dealing with three- and upwards storey townhouses and flats, without

Brussels suburbs

gardens, clinging to the streetline, with very few experiments at anything other than the level of style, design and placement of balconies and facing materials. So although it almost never looks like the 'great European cityscapes' of the Paris sort, Brussels street design is especially bourgeois in that there is much ostentatious individuality, but nothing truly nonconformist or revolutionary. Yet, if you take the view that architecture is for looking at rather than treating as a backdrop, this is not necessarily a bad thing – there is lots and lots to see.

Brussels is where the late-nineteenth-century experimental architecture known alternately as Art Nouveau (here and in France), Modernism (in Spain and Russia), *Secession* (in the Austro-Hungarian Empire) and *Jugendstil* (in Germany) was first 'invented'. A typical street in the affluent west of Brussels, around the Koekelberg Basilica, will support the idea once common among historians that Art Nouveau was just architectural frippery, an irrelevant detour from the true path of Modernism. Everywhere you'll find the twisting, whipping iron ornament, decorative tiles, plate glass windows and whimsically emphasized gables. From the 1920s on, Art Nouveau shifted into the less twisting lines of what was retrospectively called Art Deco, but at the time usually called Moderne or modernistic architecture. This stuff is still a matter of small details – the fronts of doorways, the edges of balconies, odd little ornaments – but this time the lines are cleaner, the materials more obviously high-tech, in steel, concrete and often in now obsolete materials like Vitrolite and chrome. The architects of these intriguing houses – Fernand Bodson, Antoine Pompe, Joseph Diongre – are totally unknown outside Belgium. To see exactly what makes Modernism as a *movement* different from this play of styles, the housing estate known as the Cité Moderne can serve as illustration. It was designed in the early 1920s by a team headed, ironically enough, by one Victor Bourgeois. The 'modern city' actually anticipates the work of Ernst May in Frankfurt, though is far less extensive; while the New Frankfurt was a matter of council estates, the Cité Moderne was the product of a left-leaning housing co-operative. There is repetition, but in an enveloping, friendly manner. There is an aesthetic consistency, and there is lots of what Brussels had and still has very little of – gardens. This was at that strange point where it was Modernists rather than their opponents who favoured family houses with gardens over flats. A monument to Bourgeois was added at the estate's

Cité Moderne

centre in the 1950s. Just to remind you of the politics, the streets are called things like 'Co-Operation Road' or 'Evolution Road': the march of progress, together.

Brussels is a city of parts, of pieces. Sometimes these can be complete pieces, untouched by unpleasant additions – one of the defining moments in visiting the capital of Europe is making your way through workaday streets and then suddenly finding, totally unexpected, the Grand Place, one of the most opulent Baroque set-pieces in the entire subcontinent, in all of its glory, the houses of the guilds encrusted with the most extravagant gables, swags and relief sculptures. Though a complete Baroque set-piece, it is not Baroque in the manner of the Louvre, of Dresden, of Rome, where a completely new conception of space and power has been created, based on vistas, emphases and axes – it is just a medieval square that has been rebuilt in the 'style of the day', with the day being 1699. One of the institutions founded in the Grand Place is the Belgian Workers' Party. Victor Horta, the city's most famous architect, was a member, and designed for them the Maison du Peuple, a metal monument this time for the Internationale, housing everything from socialist events and concerts to disputatious conferences between Bolsheviks and Mensheviks. It was demolished in the 1960s, though fragments of its metalwork were saved and eventually became ornaments for a Metro station. Horta's architecture is where Art Nouveau seems genuinely revolutionary rather than reformist, a new world of glass and iron rather than dressings to Beaux Arts houses, with machine-crafted ornament attempting to rival nature in its illogical curves and permutations. Ironically enough, one consequence of the demolition of the Maison du Peuple was a lively conservation movement, and as a way of saving the Art Nouveau public buildings that seldom work properly, Brussels has an agency which restores them and makes them into (usually curiously chosen) museums. A department store by Horta becomes a cartoon museum, and Paul Saintenoy's wonderful Old England department store becomes a museum of musical instruments. The headquarters of the socialist newspaper *Le Peuple*, designed in 1930–32, is now the offices for the government of Asturias, with their flag where the red flag once was.

Within Brussels itself, the important twentieth-century question has been the tension between a bourgeoisie and a proletariat, between Francophone and Dutch, between

Belgian capital and capital of trans-national institutions –
but these conflicts have largely ignored the international
activities that made Brussels rich. In the narratives of
great European cities, enlightened capitalist planning
and twentieth-century social reform can seem like the
only forces that have shaped big cities. The problem with
focusing a book on the European city solely is that you
have to look relatively hard to find the traces of how
the European city managed to become what it is. So one
thing worth remembering in Brussels is that it is a capital
built on mass murder. Its most glorious years, architecturally, the late nineteenth century up to around 1940,
are the years when this tiny country presided over what
is now the Democratic Republic of Congo, where initially, under the personal rule of Leopold II, there existed
a regime straightforwardly characterized by institution-
alized genocide, purely motivated by the extraction of
the country's natural resources for the personal fortune
of the king, and then, after the resulting scandal, for
the enrichment of the country and its capital. What Europeans did in Congo compares closest to the Khmer
Rouge's Cambodia, Stalin's Soviet Union and Nazi
Germany in the extent, scope and ruthlessness of its
violence. Brussels has streets named for, and monuments
to, one of the greatest mass murderers in history, and
appears entirely uninterested in that fact. The oppression
of the Belgians by the Belgians does not even remotely
compare to what Belgians did to the Congolese, but Brussels is nonetheless a city whose very skyline is marked
by the barbarism of Leopold II and his more bourgeois
lieutenants, in the form of the Palais de Justice his

government had built in the 'upper town'. This part of
the upper town was literally constructed on top of the
lower, displacing thousands of slum dwellers. You can
get a lift down to the lower town, which attaches itself to
the palace's ludicrous bulk with an admirable lack of
decorum.

As Neal Ascherson pointed out in his study of Leopold
II, *The King Incorporated*, one professed motivation for Leopold II's transformation of Congo into an extractive
charnel house was the beautification of Brussels, to change
it from the shabby mercantile city that it was then and is
now into something more closely resembling Paris, with
grand boulevards of limestone, great public buildings for
the arts and sciences, great parks and gardens, and of
course a big triumphal arch. Today, these are still an irrup-
tion into the chaos created by Belgian patterns of land use
and speculation, rather than, as in Paris, the defining note
of the cityscape. Two of them, however, are genuinely
dominant: the Palais de Justice and – seen in the distance
from the viewing platform next to it – the Koekelberg
Basilica. This was planned to be the largest cathedral in
the world, with Leopold II laying the first stone in 1905. It
is still one of the largest in Europe, but the design went
through various revisions, it was not consecrated until the
1930s and it was eventually finished in 1969, to a freakish
revised design by the architect Albert van Huffel. It is a
bulging, bulbous mass of blobular domes, Gotham City if
it were more Byzantine than Goth. It is reached by a grandiose ceremonial route named, of course, after Leopold,
and it should be noted that this is roughly the ethical
equivalent of the road to the skyscrapers of Frankfurt

being named Adolf Hitler Strasse or the boulevard to Moscow State University being called Ulitsa Stalina.

The other punctuations on the Brussels skyline are in the northern suburb of Heysel – the Exhibition building, designed in the late 1930s by Joseph van Neck, is like the Futurist architecture that would have developed if the nineteenth-century aesthetic had never really been interrupted, with its steel uprights decorated with figures and ornamentation. Anywhere else it'd be an overwhelming building, but here its position on the skyline is necessarily eclipsed by its giant metal neighbour, the Atomium. This ludicrously literal embodiment of technological mastery – your actual atom, just ready to be split for the purposes of electrical power and/or nuclear Armageddon, is absurdly exciting – to see a massively magnified iron crystal rising hundreds of feet in the air over houses and blocks of flats, as if such a thing were normal, as if we should all be living inside atoms. In front of this is Mini-Europe, a theme park where monuments of the EU are miniaturized and animatronic, several for the countries of the heartland, one each for those that have joined more recently. It is a better image of the EU than its own administrative buildings in the city. In fact, the only things on the Brussels skyline that aren't fascinating (albeit often the product of deeply, deeply unpleasant forces) are the buildings of the European Union itself, in the 'EU Quarter'. The ordinary if inoffensive curves of Berlaymont, the confused Postmodernism of the Parliament building itself, with its fumbling between mirrorglass modernity and a Beaux Arts axis – the less said about these the better; though it is apt, perhaps, that the headquarters of this institution

Imperial and modern Brussels

should be defined, in architectural terms, by a compromise that satisfied nobody. Perhaps this is for the
best. Going on Brussels's own history of monuments, it
could have been a gigantic cathedral that took sixty-four
years to build, a glowering neo-Baroque palace built on a
mound, or a huge and enjoyably silly symbol. Instead, it's
a collection of shopworn office blocks in a diplomatic district, kept low-rise enough for them not even to appear on
the city's skyline – you could traverse the capital of Europe
end to end, and not notice its seat of government. What
you do notice, just at the edge of the EU Quarter, is Leopold II's Triumphal Arches and grand buildings, built with
the proceeds from torture and slaughter. And at the heart
of the EU Quarter is a square called the Espace Léopold.

★

This book is about architecture and cities, but it is also about the forces that made, and make, them. As should by now be obvious, it treats architecture and city planning as a deeply loaded subject, one from which it is easy to read the complexities of European history. In art or literature, this would not be a method that would need much justification, but in architecture it is still oddly controversial to do so. The counterargument to that taken in much of this book is that after a building is built, who built it and what they meant by it is irrelevant – the architectural equivalent of D. H. Lawrence's 'never trust the teller, trust the tale'. There is a great deal of sense to this. Twentieth-century thinking about cities and architecture, while unfairly blamed for all manner of absurd sins, is culpable for a strange moralism that has often had terrible consequences – a particular area of buildings has poor people in and is a slum and hence is dirty and hence ugly and hence must be destroyed. More generally, the arguments of nineteenth-century neo-Goths about morality and architecture now seem faintly absurd: the notion that Gothic brought the community in question closer to God.

Similarly, with the remnants of the many hideous, murderous movements that have criss-crossed Europe. Enjoying the buildings of Augustus, Henry VIII, Stalin, Hitler, Mussolini, Leopold II and Lord Palmerston does not make you into a defender of slavery, a Stalinist, a fascist or an imperialist. However, if you extract these elements from these buildings and treat them purely as form, you lose a huge amount of what makes them interesting, and what motivated their designers. A Gothic cathedral can be appreciated as a pure work of craftsmanship and structural engineering, and you can experience a certain amount of what it was built for, if you take it in this manner. But the masons who built it would have been baffled by your reaction, as they considered their work to be their tribute to God. In what they did in order to bring themselves closer to their God, you can learn enormous amounts about the civilization they lived in, and the role that art, architecture and belief played in it. Form does not instil values or politics, but they are very often among the reasons why a particular form is chosen, and those reasons are worth taking seriously. This is not a book about European architecture in and of itself, but of how the idea of such a thing has been formed, about how European history can be read in architectural space. This is by no means the only way one can look at these cities and these buildings, and my accounts of them are in no way intended to be definitive – rather, they are subjective and argumentative.

In what follows, the definition of 'Europe' is somewhere between those of the EU and the Council of Europe – so, with Cyprus and Russia, but without Turkey, Georgia, Armenia or Azerbaijan. I have made a fairly arbitrary division of Europe into several discrete regions, partly in order to avoid the conventional definitions of East and West, and more recently, North and South. Instead, I've put places under six quasi-geographical headings. Most of these are based on the bodies of water the cities roughly face – the Atlantic, the Mediterranean, the Baltic, the North Sea, with one based on the political concept of 'Central Europe' (here, roughly used in its original meaning of the territory of the German and Austro-Hungarian

Empires), and one on the Balkan peninsula. One way of doing this was as a way out of the divisions of the Cold War, which made tiny geographical distances (between Finland and Russia, Bulgaria and Greece, Saxony and Bavaria) into highly militarized borders. My own definitions are inexact in their own way – Madrid is a long way from the Med, the Meuse–Rhine Euroregion does directly not face the Atlantic either physically or politically – but their intention is to place areas next to each other that have physical proximity but very different histories, as a means to undermining the stories these places tell about themselves, and that each nation tells about its own inviolability.

Within these, I've tried to take each city as an example of a particular corner of the (sub)continent, often at the points where one conception of 'Europe' and 'European values' rubs up against another. The cities include some capitals, several ports, a few industrial cities, two conurbations, one of them trans-national, one village, and one city divided by a UN-patrolled wall. Most of these are in the European Union, but some are not – North Nicosia in 'North Cyprus', Lviv in Ukraine, Vyborg in Russia, Skopje in Macedonia, Bergen in Norway, and possibly, by the time you read this, Kingston upon Hull in Britain. I've tried to keep the pieces short, deciding on geographical scope rather than minute detail, which means that many of them are meant to work as snapshots, immediate first-impression reactions to new places that I hadn't set foot in before – so some, such as Vyborg, are based on brief acquaintance, in towns that you can walk from end to end in a day; others, such as Madrid, are necessarily condensed accounts of certain aspects of huge cities which could easily be written about at the length of this entire book. Some are cities I know well and where I have friends – Łódź, Stockholm, Dublin – others where I was invited to lecture, and many just places that I thought would be interesting. The pieces can be read in any order, although I hope that this Introduction will be read first, and the last chapter last.

1 Atlantic

Le Havre, Normandy's Concrete Manhattan

When I was growing up in Southampton I was fascinated by the knowledge that my town had a 'twin' somewhere in France, as if there were an exotic branch of the family I hadn't met. We had a tower block named after Le Havre, and they had a quay named after us. While the process of creating twin towns might not always be exact (introduce Sheffield to Donetsk and Düsseldorf to Reading and they may not notice the resemblance), these two cities are genuinely close relatives: historic entrepôts favoured for their proximity to the capital, industrial, bombed to smithereens and rebuilt as 'concrete jungles', usually passed through by car en route to somewhere else. Both boast working container ports and large empty spaces to redevelop. So it would be interesting to set these two against each other, like a UEFA Cup version of Ian Nairn's *Football Towns*. Who comes out better, in terms of town planning, architecture, public space, of these two closely comparable, wealthy, historically linked Northern European cities? How different is the same sort of town when in northern France to when it is in southern England?

The first contest, the railway station, is easily won by Le Havre. Southampton Central is an unattractive bolting together of a cheaply renovated streamline Moderne pavilion of the 1930s and a dull 1960s office block. Le Havre's station combines a nineteenth-century iron and glass hall with a clear, Neoclassical concourse, with glass bricks set into the roof and stylish maps of the city and port set into the walls. Outside Southampton Central you have a bombsite, one of the best Brutalist housing complexes in Britain, huge exurban retail sheds and awful speculative architecture of various eras, with no clear path to the centre. Outside Gare du Havre, you find a well-integrated new tram system, a decent new hotel and a straight line to the centre, clearly signposted. The first part of this, the Boulevard de Strasbourg, is fairly normal Empire-style pomp with shabby red-brick tenements behind. There's a diverting variety of minor civic buildings, some with new tenants – 'CHINA SHIPPING', reads the cap above the curved bays of one interwar edifice. Then you come to something different. A strongly rectilinear block of flats, with lower street-facing tenements enclosing a tall tower, with shops on the ground floor, all hewn from reinforced concrete, treated in a variety of textures, smooth and stubbly, almost golden in colour. The repeated window module is strongly vertical, like in a Georgian terrace. A lot rests on your opinion of this module, as nearly the entire city centre is built out of it.

The reconstruction of Southampton as, in Pevsner's and David Lloyd's words, 'a Middle West town . . . if there had been planning control and Portland Stone' provides the most unflattering contrast to Le Havre's remarkable decision to rebuild itself as a rationalized ferroconcrete Manhattan. After the centre of Normandy's largest city

Quai de Southampton

was almost totally destroyed by the Allies in 1944, the reconstruction was entrusted to Auguste Perret, who designed the major civic buildings and developed, with his disciples Jacques Tournant, Jacques Poirrier, Pierre-Edouard Lambert *et al.*, the principles – and concrete modules – that would govern the city until the late 1950s. They define it to this day. The Boulevard de Strasbourg leads to the Place de l'Hôtel de Ville, which is unlike almost anything else in Western Europe of its date. Claimed at the time to be the largest square in Europe, it is a geometric puzzle of extreme regularity and rigidity. From the stairs of the town hall, the gardens step down to precisely arranged ponds of brown, stagnant water, from where you can see the identical high-rises that define this part of the city centre, in parade-ground lockstep. The town hall itself is, like the rest of the centre, in a unique style that was at the time extremely unfashionable – monumental, modular and made out of the loveliest, most carefully tended concrete, as subtle and warm as the best ashlar. The street furniture of benches, lamps and pavements, remarkably all still in place, is similarly strong; the new tram lines fade into the background, something Mancunians might want to take note of when appraising their Metrolink.

This reconstructed centre is on the UNESCO World Heritage List – justly, given the exceptionally high quality and thoroughness of execution, but in the 1950s architectural critics might have expected that accolade to be awarded to open, free Coventry or Rotterdam, not to Le Havre's *retardataire beton* Beaux Arts. The openness, informality, multiple levels and pedestrianized precincts of the Dutch and British reconstruction projects were celebrated, Le Havre's residual classicism and stiff, grid-planned severity were deeply unfashionable in the 1950s (though even in the 1950s it compared well to South-ampton). From the town hall onwards, that main street becomes Avenue Foch, and the axiality – terminating in twin towers, flanked symmetrically by squares of shops and cafés – can make you ask exactly what side of the Iron Curtain you're on, but for the very un-Soviet quality of the workmanship (the brothers Perret always signed their work 'Constructeurs', not 'Architectes').

On the spring day I first explored the city (as opposed to departing from there, to elsewhere), it was pissing with rain, and the concrete, organized into an articulated grid through courses and balustrades, looked impeccable, a lesson on its

properties as a material lost on most post-war Modernists
bar Perret students like Ernö Goldfinger. Seen in terms of
what is happening in architecture today, Perret's Le Havre is
fashionable as can be, an inadvertent precursor for contemporary architects such as Sergison Bates or Valerio Olgiati,
who favour a similar disciplinarian approach to materials
and proportions, a similar compromise between the classical and the modern. Appraised in the flesh, it is all a little
chilly, but in the most bracing, cold-water-in-the-face fashion. Yet step past those towers, and you realize they herald
a very ordinary, shabby little beach, while the grand axis is
diminished to one small part of a longer, more eclectic
promenade, as if it were all a dream. At least, unlike in
Southampton, you can get to the water easily enough.
Along here is the Résidence de France, the only major

Le Havre's Hôtel de Ville

housing scheme not under Perret's influence, designed along Brutalist lines by Georges Candilis. It's a series of asymmetrical, interlinked blocks sprawling along green space, a smaller cousin to Park Hill or Amsterdam's Bijlmer. It looks wealthy, with travertine entrance lobbies, amazingly open to the public, and it's ironic, given their usual liking for rough materials 'as found', that the Modernist hardcore used a smoother, machine-made aesthetic of marble cladding, steel and glass rather than the proudly displayed *beton* of the Perret school (or, indeed, the shuttered concrete of Wyndham Court, Southampton's far more vigorous Brutalist housing complex).

Just behind this is the symbol of the reconstruction, and of the abundant promotional literature and souvenirs for sale: Perret's church of St Joseph, organized around

Résidence de France, as seen from Brittany Ferries

one central, polygonal column lit by stained glass, looking from a distance like a hollowed-out interwar skyscraper. Inside, the first effect is elation and astonishment, as heavy concrete bracing hauls up the open tower, with its sparkling, abstract stained glass. That first impression might well inspire awe, but linger a little and you'll see how rational even this is, with the coloured glass precisely set as if according to an algorithm, and the concrete details hard and unrelenting. No Coventry Cathedral pathos here. Opposite is the bleakest part of the city centre: mean, hunched little concrete flats. Rather more warmth and passion is provided at the Perret disciple Henri Colboc's Saint-Michel, behind the town hall, which combines the teacher's mastery of concrete with a more expressive, Brutalist approach to form.

Inside the tower of St Joseph

Returning to Perret's axis, the points meet at the Bassin du Commerce. In one direction the generous concrete colonnades of Rue de Paris lead to the deeply surreal incongruity of the original Le Havre Cathedral, where the Perret school's high-windowed modules frame, but seem to look disapprovingly at, a proliferation of uncouth Baroque and Gothic details; and past that the sea and the Musée Malraux, a clear glass gallery with neat details by the engineer Jean Prouvé, and a good nineteenth- and twentieth-century art collection, albeit not as diverse as that of Southampton. Around the basin itself, a three-sided square opens out to the water, and leads down to Le Volcan, designed by Oscar Niemeyer, a social condenser with library, performance space and much else, properly used even in the dreadful weather. It is an unlikely meeting. Niemeyer's multi-level buildings consist of two intersecting curved, almost windowless shapes, coated in white render, organic yet abstract, evoking both cooling towers and the veteran lecher's favoured female body parts. It couldn't be more different in form and ethos from Perret – concrete as a textured grid with rigid laws, versus concrete as a plaster which the architect can cast into whatever mould they can imagine. Amazingly, it works, and they offset each other perfectly, a delightful union of opposites. In that juxtaposition, Le Havre's only British rival is the South Bank of the Thames, never mind Southampton.

On the other side of the basin is a large, uninteresting office block – red tile and glass, parody James Stirling – and beyond that the redeveloped docks. Here the bar is set low. Though both cities have redeveloped dockland

Le Volcan

and a working port, Southampton's Ocean Village is, as we've seen, a sad, car-centred effort. Le Havre just about manages to score this open goal – but compared to Rotterdam or Hamburg rather than Southampton or Liverpool, it's poor. After passing a subtopian arterial road, you get to the expanse of the Bassin Vauban; big, bland pseudomodern buildings on either side, and, converted to a mall, the incredibly long original dock structures. The continuous iron and glass space is converted inside quite intelligently into a rather daringly un-airconditioned shopping arcade, flanked by a crude car park and a lumpen multiplex not vastly better than those of Ocean Village, though admittedly nicer than West-Quay, Soton's disastrous late-1990s megamall. Opposite is the contribution from what *1001 Buildings to See before You*

Jean Nouvel, iconic architect

Die will describe as the 'iconic' architect Jean Nouvel's Bains des Docks. Inside, it is a fascinating Suprematist structure of overlapping cubic pools. Outside, however, it's a featureless shed, marked only by little square openings, through which you can see sudden flashes of pools and bodies: interesting architecture, disastrous urbanism, a mute slab whose blankness sucks life out of the barren post-industrial site before it even begins its planned repopulation.

Surface car parks, introverted planning and mostly indifferent new apartments give you little clue that just behind the Bains des Docks is a mostly complete nineteenth-century district. It's dilapidated and rough, reminding me more of Newport than of Southampton. It leads uneasily to the third and most interesting *bassin*, the Docks Dombasles. Here the landscaping and the architecture are deliberately unsentimental and industrial, from Hamonic + Masson's pitched-roofed, modular flats picking up the rhythm of the sheds, to the hard, ruin-chic landscaping, revealing views of the cranes, silos and chimneys of the working dock.

Given this is so close to Britain's sorry record of waterside regeneration – a few interesting structures by fancy architects badly linked to a working-class enclave and filled in with bland flats – the elegance of, and, crucially, the care and conservation lavished upon, the Perret-planned centre is all the more surprising. That reconstructed city is an exceptional achievement in its scope, its clarity, its ruthless logic and its utterly scrupulous attention to detail; but it is relentless. I find that constantly repeated concrete module really very elegant, but if you find it overbearing or staid, you'll find Le Havre hard work. Everything interlocks, with each balustrade calculated alongside that of the building behind it. You'll miss the wittier, friendlier aesthetic of a Coventry, with its mosaics, murals and changes in level and style. UNESCO ought to have space for both in its listings; I fear that one reason why 1950s Le Havre is so prized and the much more famous, in its time, 1950s Coventry is so abused and ruined is that the French city's recent past is much closer to current 'best practice', a logical set of streets, all at one level, with a middlebrow sense of order and decorum. Of all the aspects of avant-garde urbanism of the 1950s and 1960s, the one that has been criticized with best reason is zoning, where one area is for shopping, one for living, one for leisure, one for working, and so forth, and one aspect which makes the Perret plan work so well is that the zoning is so loose: unlike British post-war centres (before the rushed, somewhat desperate efforts of the post-1997 'Urban Renaissance'), it doesn't die at 6 p.m., and isn't so easily abused by the short-term interests of mall developers. It emerged out of very French circumstances, paid for by a Gaullist government and executed by a communist municipality – *dirigistes* both. What is unexpected, given how different the history of urban planning is in these two cities, is that their rather careless contemporary spaces resemble each other.

I took the ferry back home. It leaves from the Quai de Southampton, marked by two of the Perret school's Rationalist skyscrapers, and I felt more than a pinch of jealousy as I looked out from the deck. This working dock is all barbed wire, lorries, containers, the interchangeable, remorseless space of a twenty-first-century port. This, at any rate, is the same in the French's city's non-identical twin. The boat goes to Portsmouth.

More Boston Than Berlin: Dublin

Mary Harney, one-time enterprise minister of the Republic of Ireland, once claimed with an apparent air of
triumph that the Irish capital was 'closer to Boston than
to Berlin'. Culturally, if not geographically, this has a
considerable element of truth, but it was also a political
statement of intent. Although to a less violent extent
than its former imperial rulers on the other side of the
Irish Sea, Ireland has been a strongly neoliberal country
for the last few decades, and can fairly be considered an
'Anglo-Saxon' economy rather than a 'social market' one.
However, in terms of how it has reacted to the financial
crisis, of which it was an early centre, it has politically
cleaved much closer to Southern Europe, with a strong
anti-austerity vote and the near-collapse of its traditional
governing parties, Fianna Fáil and Fine Gael, and the traditional junior partner, Labour, with much of their vote
going to Sinn Féin and several far-left parties, as yet un-
united in a Syriza-style coalition. I visited Dublin for the
first time in 2010, when the crisis was still recent and raw,
and the streets were full of satirical stickers and flyers
for demonstrations. Unlike other places that were hit
heavily – especially in the Baltic – Ireland did not take
austerity quietly.

On immediate acquaintance, Dublin is familiar to a
British visitor, far more so than Le Havre. From the airport to the bus station, much of what you see is a suburban
sprawl of semis and bungalows from the 1930s to the
present, of the sort that would induce a warm glow of

depression to anyone who knows the West Midlands or south Hampshire. After a while, it all stiffens into a long, low Victorian street. It's not particularly promising, but then, when you get off the bus, you're in a Georgian city of impressive order and elegance. Street after street of square brick prospects, resembling most of all the aloofly affluent upper reaches of Marylebone. Unlike Edinburgh, where the local stone and the accidents of geology create a decidedly 'regional' spin of the classical pattern-book (no doubt also a partial consequence of the fact that Scotland was not, unlike Ireland, a colony), this architecture could be English. The level of rationality and severity closely links it to Bloomsbury and Toxteth; present someone with a picture of each, with the street signs cropped, and you'd get interesting results. Parnell Square, Mountjoy Square, Fitzwilliam Square – these are of such gentility that you become a little surprised to see Sinn Féin's bookshop occupying part of the first. Unlike the London squares they are modelled upon, their central green spaces are almost all now public.

This architecture is so likeable, and now so much a part of the city's branding, that it's hard to imagine it being the subject of hostility; but as recently as the 1960s prominent politicians celebrated the demolition of Georgian terraces on the grounds of rectifying historical grievances. These were, after all, the houses of the Anglo-Irish Protestant minority who governed city and country with the utmost ruthlessness, and on the northside in particular many were subdivivided into tenements, which were, by the early twentieth century, appalling housing. Some rhetorical redress of this came in the post-colonial

The terrible beauty of Parnell Square

renaming: Rutland Square into Parnell Square, Queen Square into Pearse Square. Some aspects of the Georgian legacy, though, aren't replicated in the imperial centre – Dublin boasts a few streets of that strange thing, Georgian one-storey terraces, the classical bungalow. Some of the better new buildings are slotted into the Georgian grid, such as the Scottish architects Benson + Forsyth's National Gallery, where a tense mesh of projecting granite grids are kept firmly within the order and roofline established in the eighteenth century.

Like Britain itself, Ireland in the 2000s shifted from sprawl towards inner-city redevelopment. Irish commentators sometimes present Dublin as a city without much experience in, or affinity for, inner-city high-density housing. On one level this is puzzling, given that Georgian Dublin is, whatever else it may be, a superb example of how to plan inner-urban housing, but there is little from the post-Georgian era to attest to serious continuity, bar some scattered industrial structures and the decent municipal housing of the interwar years. These blocks, with their long access decks and brick façades, are the product of the 'left' side of those consummate populists, Fianna Fáil, and they closely resemble the contemporary work of Red Vienna or the London County Council. During the 'Celtic Tiger' boom, during which Ireland overtook Britain on several measures of Human Development and Quality of Life, a new linear city took shape along the Liffey. After the liveliness of the (admittedly

Corporation housing

somewhat patrician) Georgian streetscape, one of the clearest contrasts is the relative desolation. It's a landscape punctuated with spaces which were nominally public, but are in fact spectacularly cold and inhospitable. Nothing seems to be occupied, and much of it appears halfway under construction, spaces somewhere between waste-land and plaza. These spaces might be a failure in any rational terms, but their quietness and eeriness felt, when I visited them in 2010 and 2012, like an emptiness you could fill in as you liked. The political stickers around everywhere provided some noise in that silence. Some of these were against the Lisbon Treaty, depicted as a seiz-ure of democratic power and an enshrining in law of corporate power; some against NAMA, the 'bad bank' into which Ireland's delinquent financial institutions were poured; others still against the Fianna Fáil and Labour politicians that are widely held to blame.

When I first visited, I took part in a guided walk, billed as 'Boom or Bust, an Alternative DIY Tour', organ-ized by the artist Aisling O'Beirn, through the spaces of banking and riverside regeneration. Some of these spaces were old, ageing institutions which had failed to provide the probity and self-regulation via which they had acquired their reputations. Architecturally, these range from the early-eighteenth-century classicism of the ori-ginal Bank of Ireland to the 1970s almost-Brutalism of Sam Stephenson's Central Bank of Ireland, which has a hint of Russian Constructivism about it, with its storeys suspended from the top, leaving a wide, open and usually gated space underneath. The walk ended at the new headquarters of the Bank of Ireland, much further upriver, an empty steel skeleton surrounded by dormant cranes.

Looking along the Liffey, the eye is drawn to the container port, in the foreground of which is a whole load of new housing and offices (in a vaguely Germanic, cold mock-modern style) built adjacent, as if this mechanical spectacle might be worth seeing, rather than being hidden away and ignored. It is surprisingly close to the port, but I suspect that the frantic land speculation that preceded the crash, rather than an unusual interest in the aesthetics of shipping, was the reason behind this proximity. Dublin builds anywhere and everywhere: a city the size of Berlin, with around a third of its population. The port is almost always visible, due to the Liffey's stiff, canal-like linearity, resembling a man-made waterway rather than a natural feature, thin and extremely straight. Even in the preserved, Georgian centre you can see the power station and the container cranes in the not-too-far distance; in Liverpool or London the extant ports are hidden away by the curves of the Mersey and the Thames (and in the latter case by extreme distance).

Architecturally, Dublin docklands is an example of the international phenomenon then usually described as 'regeneration', which can be defined easily enough as the redevelopment of former working-class spaces in post-industrial cities, usually accompanied by 'world-class', 'signature', 'iconic' architecture, designed explicitly to appeal to tourists. It's positively tasteful when compared to the mass architecture of the Tiger Economy, which is brash in the extreme, with none of the vogue for avant-garde shapemaking or fashionable fragmentation in

Custom House and International Financial Services Centre

Canary Dwarf

evidence: the International Financial Services Centre is especially gobsmacking in its crass, reconstituted stone and green glass bulk, something that's also true of the cluster of pyramids known as 'Canary Dwarf', which loom over the river. Although there was nothing subtle about the way finance capital proclaimed its presence and dominance in Dublin, what didn't happen here even during the boom was the building of skyscrapers. The crowding of the little towers of the 'Dwarf' is a case in point, a 'groundscraper' in the parlance. Dublin remains a low-rise city, with the main high-rise landmark being Liberty Hall, the fine, strip-windowed office block that houses the Irish T&G. A tall sculptural spike was placed on O'Connell Street, as if as a placeholder for towers which never arrived.

Liberty Hall is one of two buildings on the river that define the era between the Georgian colonial capital and that of the Celtic Tiger. Both were intelligently designed in an original, Modernist manner, without retro gesture or Expressionistic ego. Both replaced their transparent, ethereal glazing with hard mirrorglass after bomb attacks in the 1970s. The other, Busaras, the central bus station, has a claim, otherwise contested only by Ahrends Burton and Koralek's Berkeley Library at Trinity College, to be the finest twentieth-century building in Dublin. It was built between 1945 and 1953, the architect nominally Michael Scott, the Modern Movement's Irish emissary, but it's generally accepted that the main designers were Wilfrid Cantwell and Kevin Roche, the latter of whom would soon cross the Atlantic to work with Eero Saarinen, whose practice he would then inherit. We will encounter

Busaras

him again presently. What Cantwell did here is analogous to the work of Berthold Lubetkin in London, or the Royal Festival Hall – a public Modernism gone festive, full of mosaic patterns, lush materials, and an interplay of the wilful and joyous with the strict and rectilinear. It's a wonderful building, an example of what modern architecture can be, and, here, mostly isn't. The Berkeley Library, meanwhile, is a quite different beast – both Brutalist and classicist, with heavy granite blocks in a concrete frame, and bubble-like glass windows. Although one is an explosion of colour and whimsy and the other a compacted, aggressive and monochrome structure of considerable moodiness, both are buildings to admire for the quality and wit of their detailing.

What was five years ago the bare skeleton of the Bank of Ireland building (the huge public cash injection to the delinquent bank would eventually get it finished) defines the edge of 'Dublin Docklands'. These corporate spaces are still pockmarked by industry, which in the context resembles a series of scattered ornaments, accidental or otherwise, creating a landscape which gets ever stranger the closer you get to the centre of it, the piecemeal realization of the erasure creating, in a more tight, urban equivalent, the weirdness of the vague and dispersed expanse of the Royal Docks in London, a place where, unlike Canary Wharf, it hasn't all quite worked, it didn't all stick, and this sense of failure creates a sense of possibility. The surrealism only intensifies when you reach the bit of (in the offensive planning parlance) 'Public Realm' where the Dublin Docklands Development Agency has decided to be a bit ambitious – an intriguing square on Cardiff Lane, where it wasn't clear how much of the place was accidental. Its boundary is a poem of some description, inscribed on a snaking, low wooden fence, with lighting that has been torn apart at various points, which means that the promised 'butterflies in your tummy' may in fact be volts in your nervous system. They enclose a sandpit, climbing frames, palm trees and a Victorian factory chimney. All the office blocks around seem to be either empty or unfinished, or both.

This eccentricity is tucked away where nobody is looking. The shiny showpiece is further on, where a regeneration trinity of Santiago Calatrava, Martha Schwartz and Daniel Libeskind have created something much like the thing they have created everywhere else. With its tall sticks of light, Martha Schwartz's square is the most original. Libeskind continues a decline into self-parody. Here he designed two office blocks flanking a theatre. The offices are basic curtain walls given completely arbitrary slicing and dicing for no reason other than to remind you that *It's Danny*, and the theatre sits at the centre, its crushed polygons only as deep as the atrium. It's probably about war, independence and stuff, especially given that Éamon de Valera once hid in the silos over the river, or something. Then there's Manuel Aires Mateus's hotel, which faces a square full of palm trees, presumably to evoke the architect's native Portugal. This pan-European gesture is somewhat marred by lamentably poor detailing: as in the UK, contemporary Irish architecture is marked by a striking parsimony, a cheapness and carelessness in construction which is especially curious

Libeskind and Mateus at Docklands

given how these tend to be 'luxury flats' or 'stunning offices'. In the offices of the Dublin Docklands Development Authority, the models still show the U2 Tower, a shelved Norman Foster scheme where the Great Satan himself would rehearse, wear sunglasses indoors and not pay his taxes on the top floor. In a way, the sheer internationalism of Dublin Docklands is admirable, the fact that it could be built anywhere, up the road from Temple Bar's men dressed as leprechauns – a refusal to pander to tourist kitsch. They've gone for big names, and why not, it's a capital city after all. The problem is that said big names are clearly not especially interested in or attached to Dublin, and it shows especially in Calatrava and Libeskind's tossed-off efforts. But that would imply that (here, ex-) locals like Kevin Roche could do something better.

The other side of the river, reached by the Samuel Beckett Bridge (perhaps if he'd known, he'd have stayed in Dublin for longer?), is dominated by Roche's homecoming building, the Convention Centre. After emigration to the USA, Roche designed some fabulous Baroque Modernist buildings with and without Eero Saarinen – but this homecoming is sad indeed, a giant tilted barrel, the very kitsch that the rest of the place tries to avoid. Adjacent, the dead mall that was recycled out of the Custom House Quay Building is one of the quietest and airiest of these failed spaces. The advertisements that mark the empty spaces where retail 'units' could be or might once have been have a particular streak of desperation. And here even the CCTV cameras are 'contextual', designed to be in keeping with the industry that was once here. They look out over absolutely nothing.

The Meuse–Rhine Euroregion

European Union demographers like to define 'Euro-regions', conurbations which span two or more countries; a difficult concept for islanders. One such is the Meuse–Rhine Euroregion, which is focused on three nearly contiguous cities in three different countries, speaking three different languages. Aachen, in Germany; Maastricht, in the Netherlands; and the largest of the three, Francophone Liège, in Belgium. All three are on high-speed railway lines, so you can dash between each of them with more ease than crossing from south-west to south-east London, each city a distance of around twenty minutes from the other. As places to understand the affluent European heartland, they're essential, not least because of their pivotal geographical position – each city has changed hands a fair few times between different states and armies – and for an architectural distinctness that belies their proximity. Also, a rather important treaty was signed here.

Aachen has a claim to being the first pan-European capital, long before Brussels; tellingly, it's probably better known outside Germany by its French name, Aix-la-Chapelle. This was Charlemagne's capital, founded at the place where Latin civilization and its Germanic destroyers met, and where he commissioned the first major piece of architecture to have been built in North-Western Europe since the fall of the Roman Empire: the Palatine Chapel, constructed between 790 and 814: for centuries after his death, it was at Aachen that the Holy Roman

Emperor was crowned. Much as Charlemagne initiated the idea of Europe as we currently understand it, with France and Germany at its core (for the Romans, North Africa and West Asia were much more important than these northern borderlands), you could claim that the Palatine Chapel founded 'European' architecture, but that would be fanciful. Charlemagne's chapel is deeply Eastern, a Byzantine church that resembles the sort of thing you'd find in Thessaloniki or Kiev rather than Munich or Paris. Only the proportions of this octagonal, domed space and the openings that beam light into the murky interior survive from the original building, but its intense atmosphere is more Greek than German. The gilded mosaics are a Wilhelmine approximation of the originals, based on outlines uncovered after classical

The City of God

accretions were scraped away, as the German Empire
restored the cathedral in the late nineteenth century, as
part of its claim to becoming the central state of Europe.
The reconstituted mosaics are very pretty, if schematic:
one depicts the original Carolingian structure with the
words 'CIVITAS DEI': the Teutonic Rome.

If this is an ersatz Istanbul in the Rhineland, later additions are totally northern, so that Aachen Cathedral is a
building of two distinct parts. The fourteenth-century
choir is an extremely high, polychromatic glass hall,
thrusting and pulsating upwards, soaring while the Palatine Chapel glowers moodily. Because of this, the additive
nature of Aachen Cathedral is abrupt even by medieval
standards. The octagon of the Palatine Chapel, to which
was added, in the eighteenth century, a strange faceted,
stretched Baroque dome, is attached to the most Gothick
of choirs. Renaissance chapels are bolted on at random.
What coherence there is comes through the same
nineteenth-century restoration that returned Charlemagne's chapel to something like its original appearance;
its patronage is emphasized in the rose windows, remodelled into the eagle of the Prussian state. There is no space
that eases you from one to the other, each era is totally
distinct.

Tourists crowd around the cathedral and the Carolingian city hall near by, but they don't go much further, so
you can walk into the more straightforward, spired Gothic
of Saint-Follian and be the only person there. Presumably
all Aachen's firehoses were trained on the cathedral when
the city was largely destroyed in 1944, as the interior of
Saint-Follian was totally gutted. The restoration is an

attractively non-retro 1950s interpretation of the building's principles, membranes stretched across concrete ribs, and abstract glass inserted into the smashed frames.

Almost totally ruined at the end of the war, Aachen was rebuilt mostly with a warm Aalto-like brick vernacular, which extends into the peripheral estates. The suburbs also feature attractive, pompous villas pockmarked by Modernism and medievalism, and some excellent museums and galleries. One of these is housed in the Ludwig Forum, one of the city's major Weimar Republic buildings – a long, ship-like Expressionist umbrella factory, designed in 1928 by a local architect, Fritz Erler. More dominant is the 1930 Haus Grenzwacht, a mini-skyscraper, whose laconic steel-framed lines are Modernist, but whose tight, stern rhythms and neo-Biedermeier windows point towards the architecture of the Third Reich and to contemporary German classicists like Hans Kollhoff. It is impressively scaled for a city of this size, but was at the time a controversial boondoggle, whose frame stood unclad for years. Aside from the cathedral, there are two buildings in Aachen that are of major architectural note: an overdesigned bus station by the avant-garde American architect Peter Eisenman, whose splayed legs shelter drunks and passengers with adequacy, and the much more interesting University Clinic.

This gigantic building, built for the duration of the 1970s to the designs of the otherwise unsung Weber, Brand & Partners, is a long quasi-industrial structure housing blaringly colourful pop art interiors. The services are exposed, which can lead to easy comparisons to the roughly contemporary work of Richard Rogers, such

Aachen University Hospital

as the Pompidou Centre or Lloyd's of London. It's as crazed as the latter, and larger than the former, stamping its way across the flat countryside between Aachen and Maastricht. It's this spectacle, and not the Palatine Chapel, that nearly brought me to my knees. Like the harshest Gothic it acts as if it has a life of its own, an organism, hairy, sinewy and wiry, rather than a static monument – a classicist's nightmare. The pastoral landscaping outside and the generous social spaces inside make clear it's not all blare and power, but this is an overpowering architectural experience, and must be a memorable place in which to give birth or have your appendix out. It shows just how extreme Modernism had become in the early 1970s, a totally new and bracing conception of landscape, space and design.

The reaction to it can be seen at something close to its best a short bus ride away in Maastricht. The city was evidently chosen for the site of the Maastricht Treaty of 1992 – which created the EU as a more ambitious 'Union', carved out of the old European Economic Community – because of its position at the confluence of Germanic and Latin-speaking Europe, a mid point of the wealthy 'core'. Fans of Romanesque churches and over-restored historic cores will find much to enjoy in this geographically puzzling city, a Catholic yet Dutch enclave squeezed in between Francophones and Germans (it also has the most restrictive pot-smoking laws in the Netherlands, as a counter to stoners from said regions). But it also boasts an area called the Céramique, built on the site of a large ceramics factory complex, in connection with the treaty. It is EUtopia. The main square, Plein 1992, is in the tradition of ceremonial plazas far too large for any conceivable function. It features a neat, sober tower block by the near religiously venerated Portuguese classical-Modernist Álvaro Siza, in a style which recalls the stern lines of the Aachen Haus Grenzwacht, but most of the Céramique was designed and masterplanned by the workmanlike Dutch designer Jo Coenen. The architecture here is essentially conservative, without any of the aggression or ambition of, say, the Aachen University Clinic: the difference is encapsulated in the heavy, Roman symmetry of the Italian Neoclassicist Mario Botta's circus of offices. This is a showcase of European architecture after the era of experiments was cancelled – not just those of Fascism or Stalinism, but also any idea that social democracy could be radical rather than consensual and small-c conservative – a product of a centrist consensus which explicitly posits that Western Europe had by the 1980s reached the plausible peak of human equality and affluence. The result has everything but enthusiasm.

It is telling that the architecture which literally accompanied the founding of the EU is marked by a purging of Romanticism, but then boredom is sometimes better than vision. On the Meuse is a long housing complex designed by Luigi Snozzi, monumental and rhythmic. You could trace its stomping lines to a variety of sources: the Nazi holiday camp of Prora on the Baltic Sea, the 1970s ideal classical cities of the Italian writer, draughtsman and architect Aldo Rossi, or the perfect rationalized city of the Weimar-era German theorist Ludwig Hilberseimer. These all coalesce into an image of austere, sensible

Rational riverside

European collectivity. A shallow eye would find it authoritarian or dull, not noticing the sane, smart way it opens out towards a well-used riverside park. In fact, Snozzi appears to have been much better at being Aldo Rossi than the man himself, whose Bonnefanten Museum at the end of the enfilade is very puzzling. Rossi obviously decided at some point to take the weight of Europe on his architectural shoulders, to embody its history in all its complexity rather than simplify it, as does the EUtopia of the Plein 1992 – rather than an optimistic wiping the slate clean, a representation and montage with that which went before, which sometimes spills into coy jokiness. So here Rossi totally refuses the tasteful classicized Modernism of Siza, Snozzi and Coenen, has other games to play: assembling various odd little devices, toy flags, Mario Bros pipes running up the cupola, and an almost Portmeirion-like fantasy dome. It's big on ideas, low on 'good taste'.

Liège, further along the Meuse, is a different world to neat Maastricht and compact Aachen. It's a big, scary industrial city: bigger than the other two put together, the Sheffield or Birmingham powering Leopold II's genocidal turn-of-the-century empire. From the high-speed rail, you enter it at Calatrava's Liège-Guillemins station, completed in 2008. There are good reasons why people hate Calatrava, particularly his subordination of engineering, material and structure to contrived imagery, but his railway stations are among the great guilty pleasures of contemporary architecture: sentimental, thrilling, contrapuntal. The notorious expense and unfashionability of his buildings are only one reason why it's hard not

Aldo Rossi's Marioworld

to think 'We will never see the like again' while walking round an outrageously scaled shed like this. As of late December 2015, when these photographs were taken, it was being patrolled by the military with machine guns, as part of the near-martial law imposed against the threat of an ISIS attack on a Belgian city.

Liège is blessed with a thrilling hell of a setting, a basin ringed by mountains and blast furnaces, strung along a tightly built-up river, connected by grand Victorian bridges whose elegance is made illegible by 1960s highway engineering. In the centre is an acropolis, with nothing much on top but the remnants of Second World War bunkers, but leading to it is the Montagne de Bueren, a street of poky workers' terraces stepping, or rather leaping, up the hill at a ludicrous incline, Victorian vertigo. From here you can

Circulation at Liège-Guillemins

survey the city. If Maastricht and Aachen are flat, impeccable and conservative, Liège is a complex visual pile-up of towers, chimneys, hills and competing styles. On the ground, it is grimy, politically rancorous, with its streets plastered with posters connected to the recent General Strike, and much more visibly multicultural.

And, particularly, it's relatively unplanned: near the Meuse, the seemingly randomly developed streets are a controlled madness. Villa, mid-century high-rise, Art Nouveau tenement, Brutalist high-rise, villa, Art Deco high-rise, normal street rhythms pushed to the edge of chaos. Skyscrapers, like the evocatively named Tour Kennedy and Tour Simenon, are as thin as the 'pencil' towers of Hong Kong, remnants of a speculative boom that clearly bust some time ago. The monuments on the streetscape are extraordinarily odd: in one direction, two swelling domes, miniature copies of Brussels's famously bloated Koekelberg Basilica (one of them, Sacré-Coeur, left unfinished and half-derelict for over seventy years), a Moderne war memorial, and in the other direction, back towards Maastricht, the slabs of the peripheral housing estates. Beyond that, smouldering cooling towers, now owned by Lakshmi Mittal. Seedy, smoky, vigorous, it is quite the cityscape, and at ground level it is all hemmed in by grimy Victorian streets, making the monuments stick out all the more. There's even some forlorn fragments of boulevard planning, around a statue of Charlemagne, of course, on horseback.

Industrial city vertigo, Liège

It is European cities like this which are in the most trouble. University towns, tourist traps and bureaucratic centres can fend for themselves; it's places like Liège, lively and furious but stricken by industrialization, that are facing collapse. New development – a lonely shiny high-rise, and a standard shopping mall given some squiggly roofs by the eighties cult designer Ron Arad – is sticking-plaster stuff. There is much more hope for a Europe which will need to become more multicultural, rather than less, here in Liège. The city's great wish has been that its geographic position in the centre of the rich European heartland will rub off on it somehow, regeneration through transport network. Yet as the men with machine guns stalk nervously under Calatrava's overpriced steel ribcage, the future doesn't look encouraging.

Porto: The Vacation Rental Manifesto

There weren't many pictures on the walls of the flat we rented in Porto: just a photograph of the view from the river, of the city, framed; and a framed text – 'For just a short time,' it read in serif capitals, 'this is your vacation rental' (in big letters, emphasized). 'But, remember, you hold the key to someone's cherished home. Show you care' (last word again in big letters). Take the bins out, don't make too much noise, close the door properly – sound advice. But also 'shop in local stores, speak to local people, cook local recipes'. It then turns suddenly hectoring. 'Be curious and flexible. Don't compare your rental with your home. Instead learn how other people live.' Leave us a good review and 'praise all that you loved most', because we'll certainly be reviewing you. And don't forget – 'your vacation rental reflects YOU, so make it extraordinary'. On getting up in the morning (or afternoon) reading this message in the kitchen every day for five days was oddly infuriating. Not because it was one of the most passive-aggressive pieces of prose I'd ever had the misfortune to read, but because it was based on a fundamental fib – that is, that we were in somebody's home. We weren't. We were instead participating in a particularly novel form of commerce, in a city where, it seemed, everyone was intent on getting a good review from their many Northern European visitors.

The street we were staying in, the Rua das Flores, is at the absolute dead centre of Portugal's second city, and staying there in a 'vacation rental' (booked with the app, of course) was considerably cheaper than staying in a hotel a couple of miles out, and that is one reason why people do it.

The other is a touching belief in authenticity which a cursory exploration of the surrounding area could divest you of in a matter of minutes. Before we come to that, I should try to convey what sort of a street this is, and what the streets around are like. Architecturally, Porto is dominated by a distinctive, local eighteenth-century Baroque style, which has little correspondence outside Portugal, aside from in its once extremely extensive colonies around the globe. The streets are made up of tall tenements, with shops on the ground floor; the tenements are hewn from great blocks of granite, but their designers weren't much interested in showcasing this robust, occasionally beautiful material. Instead, distantly influenced by the Islamic architecture that once characterized the Iberian peninsula, with its tiles imprinted with colourful, abstract,

A room with a view

organic patterns, masons covered the granite with pulsing colour, or with narrative images, blue figures on white ceramic; washing is strung from the balconies between these. This, and the knobbly, irrational Baroque of the many churches, feels like nothing else I've seen in Europe, brighter, lusher and far less interested in the slightest conception of 'good taste' (although dilapidation has made many blocks more tasteful than they would have been when built). On first acquaintance with these gorgeous streets, their beauty and strangeness could make you gasp.

So too could the topography, which is demented. The 'upper town' of Porto is made up of a series of steep gradients, piled on top of one another. Nothing is ever entirely flat. In front of São Bento railway station, four different slopes clash into each other; standing in the middle of it is

Porto piles up

like being in a Cubist painting. An even steeper gradient charges at a lunatic angle down towards the river and the historic port which gave the city its name. It's a heady town-scape, and for me, as someone who feels most at home with northern climates and clear views, the effect is something between exhilaration and dizzy panic. Just one slip on some of these streets and I worry I would skid on my arse all the way into the Atlantic.

Northern (except in the context of Portugal itself) and rational and clear (or cold, even in the December week when we visited) Porto isn't, and that's why so many people from northern and cold and rational places are here, enjoying something that isn't much like home. And Portugal, like Spain, has long been adept at catering for the wishes of these people. As Franco's Spain developed the Costa Brava and the Costa del Sol on its long Mediter-ranean coastline, so Salazar's nearly equally brutally authoritarian right-wing dictatorship did the same in the Algarve. The world of the vacation rental threatens to turn places like Porto (or Lisbon, Barcelona, Valencia) into a peculiar new sort of Costa del Gentrification, where the physical fabric of the city actually remains, while, socially, it is transformed through catering to the needs of travel-lers from places with horrible weather. All around the Rua das Flores and its parallel streets, you can see tenements offering apartment rentals, and entire blocks being recon-structed in order to accommodate them. With that comes a particular tourist infrastructure, which does have some of the usual stuff (souvenir shops, places to buy port and chocolates) but also lots of craft beer and artisanal burgers and the most polite and eagerly informative service industry workers imaginable. Second-hand bookshops and hardware stores cling on from an earlier era, halfway between being relics and picturesque local colour.

Much as gentrification, when it took hold in London, New York, Barcelona, Berlin, represented a shift in middle-class taste, towards the layered resonances of the historic city rather than the open new start of the distant and low-density suburb or New Town, so too is this a shift in taste in holidaymaking: the intersection of the popularity of the European City Break (Porto has won various awards for being one of the 'top' European City Breaks) and the rise in alleged 'sharing economy' apps such as Uber and Airbnb. The myth of that stuff is that you're experiencing the real thing: rather than the non-place of hotel, airport, motorway, conference centre, you're staying in someone's flat. The owner of our vacation rental divested us of that idea quickly by pointing out he owned several flats in the same block. It had clearly just been renovated, with a new structure of minimal white walls and tasteful wood cabinets fitted into the tile-covered granite shell. And as with gentrification in the first instance, it probably has some appeal to people here, too; offered money for your dilapidated flat in the city centre which involves trudges up absurd hills every time you want to buy a pint of milk, you might well prefer to sod off to the suburbs. But what it does to the city's wider economy, and its social cohesion, may well prove to be unpredictable, as a historic city is not a holiday camp.

The highly conspicuous new tourism in Porto is a response to economic crisis as much as anything else. Like most of Europe, Portugal had a construction and speculation boom in the 1990s and 2000s, and, like most

of Southern Europe, its economy couldn't cope when it collapsed, and it received an early EU bailout. The angry
reaction to the austerity measures that resulted has given it
one of Europe's less-known leftist governments, with the
Socialist Party ruling with the support of the Communist
Party and the Syriza/Podemos-like Left Bloc (the Spanish
PSOE recently split in order to prevent its leader from
doing something similar); this government was briefly
blocked by the president, specifically because he argued it
would be unwilling to abide by EU rules, and austerity in
particular. So albeit less shockingly than Greece, this is
a country whose relationship with the richer North of
Europe has been somewhat tense of late. But this is perhaps
nothing new. The early colonial era made Portugal centre
of world capitalism, for a time. From here, ships went to
found colonies as distant as Brazil and Goa; some lasted
until very recently, with decolonization coming in the
1970s for Angola and Mozambique, the 1990s for Macau.
The rise of later slave-trading empires, like the Netherlands and, especially, England, put Portugal in check, and
a series of onerous free-trade deals were enforced by
England at the start of the eighteenth century.

This isn't ancient history, but something you can see
when you descend down the sharp hills towards the River
Douro from the centre of Porto. You can see large signs on
Gaia, the south side, with English and Scottish names:
Graham, Churchill, Cockburn, Taylor, Croft, Offley, in
white letters above long brick and stone vaults. These are still
extant wineries, the offspring of those trade deals, which
let British firms dominate the port trade; a global 'metropolis', in Andre Gunder Frank's words, 'turned into periphery'.

Revolution in the colonies in the 1960s and 1970s led to a revolution in Portugal itself, which was for a time very radical indeed, with the country featuring the professed aim of a classless society in its constitution until the 1990s. Little evidence of that revolution can be found in the streetscape beyond the chirpy Communist Party billboards protesting at the EU and the sell-off of São Bento station, or through the piles of faded copies of *Vida Sovietica* in the second-hand bookshops, but there are other, subtler legacies.

Porto's top-European-destination status owes as much to some highly intelligent modern architecture as to its historic beauty. While the latter is singular and exotic, marked by *horror vacui* and insane topography, the former is clear, pure and rational. A walk up the hills to the Italian-fascist-style Palace of Justice gives a good crash course in the city's historic face. Aside from the tile-covered tenements, the city's aesthetic was defined in the eighteenth century by the Italian architect Nicolau Nasoni. His church of the Misericordia, on Rua das Flores itself, was opposite our vacation rental, so we got a good look at it. To the street: a rash of decorative buboes, a façade engorged with crests, crusts and figures. The church can only be entered through the more sober, classical hospital which it was built to serve, now a very thoroughly renovated and extremely polite and friendly museum of itself; when you get inside, the overload of gilded statues and blue tiles is crushing or elating, depending on your view of the Mother Church. It is a showcase of just how rich Portugal had made itself through its exploring and slave trading, even while its economy was being made a vassal of England's. Nasoni also gave the city one of its symbols, the clocktower of the Clérigos Church, whose

Nasoni's Misericordia

combination of great height, elegant silhouette and trompe l'oeil visual effects, with curved excrescences which make the tower appear to vibrate, is among the headiest of the city's many heady experiences. Up here, you can get a view of the head-spinning engineering that makes this city possible. On foot, you get to the river through a series of steps that are fun to walk down and a back-breaking, panic-inducing horror to walk up. To cross that river from the higher level, you can choose from a series of bridges without rival in Europe with the possible exception of Newcastle upon Tyne – a victory parade of heroic engineering. Edgar Cardoso's 1960s Arrábida Bridge, concrete and clear; Gustave Eiffel's ethereal Maria Pia Bridge; the impossibly high, laconic, delicately curved white viaduct of the Ponte de São João, engineered by Edgar Cardoso in the 1990s; and, at the

Porto bridgescape

centre, the mindboggling Dom Luís I Bridge. Designed by
Eiffel's partner Théophile Seyrig in the 1880s, it is at two
levels, a simple crossing on the riverbank, and a tram and
pedestrian bridge on the high level, with trams in the middle and a thin, two at a time pedestrian path on either side,
and a drop of 150 feet. My companion on the journey crossed
it blithely, but I found even looking at it vertiginous enough.

The punishing steps upwards bring you to the blunt
medieval cathedral, given a heavy encrusting by Nasoni,
and then to São Bento station, with its lovely blue-tile
interior, and to the main contribution of mainstream,
conservative Beaux Arts urbanism to the city, the Avenida
dos Aliados, the Avenue of the Allies (those being the Allies
of the First World War, but not the Second, in which Portugal was in the curious position of being both fascist and

neutral). The avenue itself is certainly impressive, with great multistorey commercial palaces in an eclectic, commercial-Baroque style very unlike the crazier, fruitier Baroque of eighteenth-century Porto. Its edifices are now occupied by various banks and multinationals, around a relatively flat (i.e. a gently, rather than sharply, sloping) esplanade, with the city hall in the centre. It is very late indeed for this sort of pompous, conservative architecture, begun in 1916 and not entirely finished until the 1950s; a few buildings around it shift to something a little more contemporary for the time, with porthole windows, curved concrete balconies and streamlined trimmings. The avenue itself, though, is a showcase of conservative, authoritarian architecture for a conservative, authoritarian state. It is most obvious in the great metal eagle that stands at the glazed entrance to the Café Imperial, now a very busy McDonalds, one of the city's few (chain stores are still rare here, another reason why it's a 'top European destination'). The juxtaposition is startling: *Ein Reich, ein Volk, ein Burger.* The style of these buildings was known as 'Portuguese suave', though something must have been lost in the translation, as there isn't much delicacy in this architecture – it's impressive like the V&A, the Brussels Palace of Justice or a Stalinist Palace of Culture, as a showcase of someone else's power achieved with aplomb and maniacal intensity. It has been supplemented with some subtle landscaping and some attractively childish additions (swings!) by the city's (and the country's) two most respected architects – Álvaro Siza and Eduardo Souto de Moura.

These two, who came to prominence in the 1970s and found global fame in the 1990s for their minimal, white-walled, clear-eyed, classical-Modernist architecture, have

Ein Reich, Ein Burger

taken on much of the design of the city's recently opened
and extensive Metro, and in design terms it is excellent.
There is nothing fancy, either in terms of the spacey grey-
concrete vaults of the Bilbao Metro or London's Jubilee
Line, or in terms of Moscow or Kiev's underground
palaces – just simple, clean, airy architecture, fading into
the background but never feeling mean or cheap, though it
is all quite ad hoc, slotted into nineteenth-century cuttings
in many parts, and working more as tram than Metro in
others. Often trains have only three carriages, causing
much overcrowding when we visited, and there have been
complaints that the city can't afford infrastructure this
attractive and well-designed; a good reason, maybe, for
the city fathers of far bigger and richer cities such as Manchester or Birmingham to excuse themselves for never

bothering to build their own systems. A few of the Porto Metro's stations achieve something better than simple functionality. Souto de Moura's Casa da Música station is one of them, an exceptionally elegant work of architecture, its underground halls capped by a low concrete roof which spreads out unfussily to encompass a bus station.

It is a different conception of modern architecture to that of the Casa da Música itself, a concert hall built in the mid-2000s on the site of a former tram depot, as a new house for the city's philharmonic and as an iconic building, an all-important great cultural project to put the city On the Map, something which Nasoni, Eiffel and Airbnb couldn't quite do on their own. The designers were Rem Koolhaas's Office for Metropolitan Architecture (OMA), the Dutch firm known first for the excitable (and exciting) dystopian theorizing of books like *Delirious New York*, *Content* and *Great Leap Forward*, and later for knowingly ironic, allegedly 'critical' icons like the China Central Television building in Beijing or the Rothschilds HQ in London. It is not to endorse these to say that the Casa da Música is a building to reckon with. As an 'icon' apparently must, it commands an entire square to itself, its pavements raised in billowing layers like in Niemeyer's Party HQ in Paris (ironically, the PCP's own offices are near by, with their hammer and sickle relief along the street), and its shape is instantly memorable, fit to be doodled on a napkin or used as a logo, which it is. It is without doubt an immensely powerful building, a tensed muscle of concrete, improbably engineered into a Cubist, non-Euclidean, tortured cube. The interior, on the other hand, is typical of OMA's work in that it tries to make an expensive, bourgeois structure look impoverished and thrown together, all wire

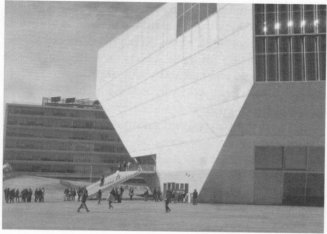

Casa da Música

mesh and neon (and, as for the concert we saw, I was reliably told that the acoustics were good but the conductor mediocre and the pianist ridiculous, but that's not my department). It's the outside that really makes it, as intended. What makes its exterior so successful isn't just its 'Gosh, how does that not fall over' form (courtesy of the engineer, Cecil Balmond) but something much harder to achieve – superb concrete work. Everything I saw in Porto was exceptionally well made, which was hard to account for. How had they managed it? Strong trade unions, craft traditions, historical backwardness are all candidates for explaining a puzzling fact: everything newly built here looks far more *rich* than work of similar vintage in much more wealthy cities like London, Dublin or Melbourne. Maybe that's why all us Brits, Irish and Australians are here on holiday.

Not far from here is another essay in concrete Expressionism, the Vodafone headquarters by Barbosa and Guimarães Architects. Here, although the concrete shuttering was equally enjoyable for *beton brut* enthusiasts, the tension between architectural wilfulness and wilful shape-making was more unbalanced than at the Casa da Música: all the things it holds in tension allowed to spill out, the compacted crush turned into a tectonic scrunch of collapsing forms, held in photogenic suspended animation mid-collapse. Nearby is a new skyscraper by Souto de Moura, one of Porto's very few, showing the tasteful, mannered alternative, a precisely proportioned grid. This tasteful tradition in Porto's architecture is showcased abundantly at another 'icon' of a very different sort, the Serralves Museum of Contemporary Art. Famous as it is – one of the museum's promotional leaflets was placed discreetly on a desk at the entrance to our 'vacation rental' – it is tricky to get to, involving buses from Casa da Música station, to Porto's nob hill of pretentious nineteenth-century villas. The museum is in two parts, across the extensive grounds of a textile magnate's estate. The earlier part is a piquant Art Deco villa, curvaceous and painted pink, slightly asymmetrical to a Rationalist park, with pools, fountains and Modernist sculpted topiary. In the 1980s, this was opened up to the public – although you still have to pay a fair fee to get in – and supplemented by another, later and more 'contemporary' vision of luxury, an art museum designed by Álvaro Siza. It is a very clever design, with intersecting levels both inside and out, working as a sort of platform to view the park as much as a means of looking at art, but the aesthetic is tasteful to a

Tasteful Serralves

rather infuriating degree, white-cube purism at its most obsessive-compulsive.

An earlier work by Siza in the inner city for quite different clients shows this aesthetic put to better use. The Bouca housing scheme was part of a widespread effort to build public housing, instituted in the immediate aftermath of the Portuguese revolution in 1974 – like most of Southern Europe under its right-wing military dictatorships – Spain, Greece, Turkey similarly – Portugal did not have the sort of mass state house-building programme that was common in North-Western Europe and in the Eastern Bloc. One result, aside from the speculative development which dominates Porto's suburbs – concrete tenements of differing heights and styles crammed into tight plots – was shanty towns. The new housing schemes of the 1970s were meant to provide an alternative to both, with a significant amount of community participation (squatters' movements had been heavily involved) compared to most state-sponsored housing. Some of the new districts built as a result were very ambitious, but Bouca, the most famous of them, was always small – a few short terraces by a railway line. It says something about Portugal in the 1970s that even this was never fully finished, until 2007, when the planned community facilities were finally built – a completion surely caused by the buildings' global fame as an exemplar of an intelligent compromise between history, locality and modernity. The complex had been left unfinished in 1977, as the revolution's 'excesses' were curbed and Portugal opted to become a 'normal' social democracy rather than an experiment in participatory Socialism.

Architecturally, these maisonettes, laid out in a series of multi-level low-rise terraces, display Siza's minimalism and obsessive-compulsive preoccupation with light and shade more impressively than the tighter, blander Serralves Museum. Simple concrete blocks with walkways, sheltered from the railway's noise by a concrete wall, open straightforwardly to the speculative streets on the other side. The terraces are rhythmic and geometric, and the passageways around enclose and create atmospheric views. They were often photographed, even before their belated completion, and they helped contribute to Siza's reputation as a designer wedded to the Modernist break with nineteenth-century pomposity and decorative display, but favouring also a new emphasis on civic decorum, order and rational urban values.

Bouca

This makes more sense on the page than in their actual context in Porto. Conventionally, these buildings are praised as being in the local 'vernacular', but they resemble neither the tall developers' tenements of the 1960s, thin and stylistically diverse, nor the obsessively decorative, polychrome tile-clad blocks of the 1760s. Rather, they were a new start, the white light of a new aesthetic, owing more to a general Mediterranean manner of white walls and public spaces than to anything built here before in this specific place. This is one reason why, although it is easily walked to from the streets around, and right next to a Metro station, Bouca feels a place apart, a piece of a different kind of city. One of these chic little Modernist houses would be quite the success as a vacation rental, but for the fact that the poor people still live next door.

2 Mediterranean

Conservative Communism in Bologna

The use of Italy as exemplar has a long history in British architecture. Inigo Jones's importation of piazzas and colonnades, Ruskin's decorative and devout Venice, the post-war use of 'Italian hill towns' as models for the West Riding of Yorkshire, and, most recently, Richard Rogers and the Urban Task Forces of the New Labour era, for whom every depressed post-industrial town was a potential Siena, given a square and a coffee bar or two. One of the lesser-known moments in this passionate, if rather one-way, affair came a few decades ago, when a minor stir was caused by an anthology about the policies of a medium-sized, communist-ruled Italian city. The book, called *Red Bologna*, was read by every London leftist, from Scritti Politti's Green Gartside to Ken Livingstone, a young radical about to seize control of the London Labour Party. It was published in 1977. The same year, Bologna erupted with student protests, the height of a short-lived movement called 'Autonomia', aimed, among other things, at the apparent conservatism and conformism of the official communist movement.

There's little obvious trace of this movement on the

streets of Bologna in 2015, aside from some graffiti around the university and some good radical bookshops, but there's subtle evidence of the city that so enthused Red Ken. Autonomia lives on in the writing careers of 1970s Autonomists like Antonio Negri, 'Bifo' Berardi and the Wu Ming collective, but we never got the chance to see what its architecture might have looked like – at least, until the inevitable *Negri for Architects* volume gets published. But then, similarly, the communist reign in the city – unbroken until the Party dissolved itself in 1990, although its various fractious successors still hold power here – was, according to *Red Bologna*, less a matter of what it did build, and more of what it didn't. You can read almost every current received idea into its 1970s programme, albeit in somewhat more strident form. The 'Urban Renaissance' begins with Italian Communism in the 1970s.

That's partly political happenstance. Italy's 'Red Quadrilateral', where communists dominated local politics from the war until the 1990s – Tuscany, Umbria, Emilia-Romagna – just happened to contain many of the country's most famous, and most compact, medieval and Renaissance cities. Accordingly, they were already considered an urban model for the rest of the world centuries before late-twentieth-century municipal communism got hold of them. Bologna was an early advocate of total historical preservation. Like the radical architects of the GLC spot-listing everything in Covent Garden to stop development, in the 1970s Bologna council slapped a preservation order on everything within the historic city walls, giving it the biggest single heritage site in Italy, which is no mean feat. Conservation extended to preserving as much of the communities that lived in the Old Town as possible. 'Buildings must be preserved in their original form, with their original tenants, and at the original rent,' asserts one of the contributors to *Red Bologna*. 'In Bologna, pensioners and workers – and not architects, artists and intellectuals – live in carefully restored Old-Town flats.' Public housing was kept at 10 per cent of market rents. Property speculation was banned in the city as much as it was legally possible to do so. The city's planner, Pier Luigi Cervellati, described these policies as a response to 'the catastrophic results of growth-oriented planning', exemplified by that New Left fixation, the 'mistakes of the 1960s'.

Surprisingly, perhaps, given that the city was ruled by an avowedly Leninist party, local democracy was considered key to the project. Neighbourhood assemblies were not just consulted, but their decisions were legally binding – 'without their approval, no street or school is built, no bus-line extended, no shop opened, no nursery set up and no house demolished'. Meanwhile, the 'compactness' and manageability of Bologna was hugely important for its success; free from the massive urbanization of Milan in the north or Naples in the south, Bologna's (and Emilia-Romagna's) economy was – and, to an extent, still is – based on small firms, co-ops and cottage industries, rather than mass production. So here we have, in the mid-1970s, such recent fixations as the 'compact city', walkable and coherent; the historic city, where all new developments must respect context; a co-operative, diversified economy, organic farming and neighbourhood committees. So how is this apparent model city – described as 'the best-governed state in Europe' by *Newsweek* in 1974! – faring forty years later?

You wouldn't notice anything particularly specially 'communist', let alone modern or futuristic, about most of Bologna, and that was the point of the policies of the Red municipality. Unlike, say, Milan, Rome, Turin or Venice, it did not have a distinctive school of twentieth-century architecture, either before or after the war. What it does have is one of the most distinctive and unusual urban structures of any historic city, one which has been scrupulously maintained since the late Middle Ages: that is, the system of porticoes which extend below almost every building in the historic centre, providing informal social spaces and shelter from the (in July 2015, at any rate) furnace-like heat. They're in every style and idiom, from early-medieval columns in wood to elaborate Baroque arcades, to the simple arches of every side street in the city centre. Though the porticoes began life as landlords' attempts to annex public space by extending their buildings out into the street, the effect is the opposite, an extension rather than a limiting of the pedestrian's experience. Then there's the colour. Bologna was 'red' long before it became the showcase of Italian Communism. The wonky medieval 'two towers', the town halls and palaces of Piazza Maggiore and Piazza Nettuno, the maze of streets around the university – all are red as in red brick, a hot, bright southern form of brick Gothic, castellated, square and harsh. Subtler, lighter reds are used in the Baroque gateways preserved after the city walls were

The arcades project

Via Antonio Gramsci

removed in the nineteenth century; occasionally a bit of ochre or mild yellow comes into the palette, but, overall, Bologna is a strange example of colour determining politics.

As an urban experience, it is rich and exciting, both open, in the sense that all the porticoes are kept free for public access, and enclosed, in that you can stride in and out of them, making getting from A to B unusually dramatic. In Piazza Maggiore, a large open-air cinema is showing an Orson Welles film every night, and you wonder what he'd have done with a city so full of spaces both strongly defined and decidedly shady. Reading *Red Bologna*, you might assume that all the city really needed to (or intended to) do was preserve this remarkable urban structure and block any attempts by developers to mess it up. That's accurate insofar as little has happened here since the 1970s. However, the book does allude to two post-war projects of which it is exceptionally critical, examples of the inhumane bombast of the 1960s, to be replaced with the historic, contextual, consulted community of the 1970s. Both of these districts are a great deal more interesting than they let on.

The first is the immediately post-war Marconi district, noted for its 'unattractive façades, grim office buildings and barrack-like blocks of flats. This district is a blemish on the *Centro Storico*.' It extends down Via Marconi, a north–south route on the west side of the historic centre, and it is the sort of architecture that is now achingly fashionable in the big European cities. Six- to eight-storey blocks of flats and offices are vigorously modelled with clear concrete frames and detailed brickwork, and with rectilinear concrete

117

colonnades to the ground floors; a few old neon signs still cling on to the façades. A couple of buildings are pre-war, such as the Palazzo de Gas, with its concave façade and sculptural reliefs, evidence of how little difference there could be between fascist and post-war era architecture here – although if you see a relief of a heroic worker in Bologna, most likely it's *pre*-communist. In both eras, local architects favoured a classicized, precisely proportioned modern architecture, but it isn't 'contextual' – too big, too square, too aesthetically distinct from the rest of the city, even while continuing its typologies rather closely. In fact, with their mix of uses and 'active frontages', the buildings of the Marconi district anticipate current Design Guide rules rather closely. If you look at later buildings, those of the 1970s and 1980s, such as the infill around Bologna

Colonnades and rationalism

University, you realize what the difference was. These later buildings are small-scale, neo-medieval, with design gestures explicitly mimicking their neighbours. Architects had not been literal enough.

The other large-scale plan in post-war Bologna is much more easily described in *Red Bologna* as an 'embarrassing testimony to the megalomania of the sixties'. Kenzo Tange was commissioned at the turn of the 1970s to produce a plan for 'Bologna 1984'. It was rejected, but not before the Japanese architect got to build a huge chunk of the Bologna of the future – the Fiera, or fair district. It does have porticoes, but in every other respect breaks totally with all Bologna's traditions. It's Tange in his Brutalist, rather than Metabolist mood – heavy, monumental, its towers displaying a raw physical heft like skyscraper-sized grain elevators, forming an asymmetric composition around a wide, raised public square. You reach Fiera north of the city centre, along Stalingrad street, past the junction with Labour street, past normal Bologna housing (straightforward, brightly painted tenements, with the odd, usually well-designed tower thrown in). A grand arch in attenuated, pseudomodern style is the gateway to the area, and then at the entrance there is, puzzlingly, a reconstruction (built in 1977, while the barricades were being put up at the university and the students revolted against the 'planner state') of Le Corbusier's 1925 Esprit Nouveau pavilion, seemingly disused, a contextless bauble. Tange's clustered skyline is much more impressive than either. It's hard to imagine there was much neighbourhood planning here, but there's still a mix of uses. Aside from the trade fairs in the main building, the towers

Bolognese Brutalism

house municipal and regional offices, as well as flats, and have cafés in their ground floors, rather than the pejorative post-war dead space. Either way, this is still Brutalism at its most hardcore, a fearsome instant city, thrilling in its sculptural drama and placid in its scale and emptiness.

Having had its experiments with Modernism, Brutalism, radical communist traditionalism and Autonomist occupations of disused buildings, and with a recent history marked by partisan warfare and urban insurrection, it is impressive how calm and coherent Bologna feels – like a well-managed Northern European city, only with richer architecture and the useful knowledge of when to let go (nothing in Bologna is over-restored, there's still just enough graffiti and grime).

The contemporary city is showcased in the small

Pavilion of the New Spirit

Urban Center Bologna, which takes up the top floor of a very pleasant, relatively new (opened in 2001) library and mediatheque in the Palazzo d'Accursio, flanked by the rum Mannerism of the Neptune fountain and the moving partisan memorial, made up of hundreds of photographs of local resistance members.

Reached at the top level of an elegant, arcaded, open hall, it contains much the same thing you would find in any building centre in any European city, right down to the obligatory big model of the city, with flashing lights showing you the new things on the way. The future city, it tells us, will be green, 'resilient', will involve lots of new housing projects on former industrial land, and will be embarked upon with close consultation with local residents. None of it looks terribly exciting – sensible

121

The Partisans of Bologna

modern architecture in green squares. Soon there'll be a Metro, some towers surrounded by car parking, and some cubic blocks of flats, suggesting that the extreme Rationalism of Ludwig Hilberseimer and Aldo Rossi is still a big influence in Italian architecture schools. It may have been radical, all of this, in the 1970s, as an alternative to 'comprehensive redevelopment', boondoggles and slum clearance. It has been the norm for so long that we ought to hope that the 'laboratory of Italy' has some surprises in store sometime soon. When the next change comes, though, the last city whose architecture will be affected by it will probably be Bologna itself.

Arborea: The Fascist Garden Village

There are a few associations that might be brought up by the phrase 'fascist New Town'. You might imagine ruthlessly centralized Neoclassical buildings, formal axes, some haranguing statues and eagles, lots and lots of marble. You wouldn't necessarily imagine palm trees, cottages, canals, a Gothic church, bustling cafés on a piazza and the nearby smell of manure. That is, you wouldn't imagine Arborea, a New Town founded in Sardinia in 1928, and possibly better known – if known at all – by its original name, Mussolinia.

This was the first of several New Towns set up on drained marshland in Mussolini's Italy, a project that once spurred widespread admiration. For instance, in his popular Pelican book *Town Planning*, published at the start of the Second World War, Thomas Sharp draws attention to the 'half-dozen boldly planned New Towns' of fascist Italy, and suggests that they might be a possible model for post-war Britain – in a democratic way, of course. One of these towns, Sabaudia, in Lazio, was on the cover of the first edition of the book, before Penguin Books opted for a less-tainted exemplar. More recently, Jonathan Meades's TV show *Benbuilding* praised the eclecticism and experimentation of interwar Italian architecture; the sharp contrast with the officially prescribed classicism of Nazi Germany was so pronounced, he argued, that it supported the questionable view that the Third Reich was so different from fascist Italy that it didn't even merit the term 'fascist'. Certainly, the Nazis never got round to

123

New Towns, though they planned a few – folksy places, designed to colonize the newly acquired territories of Poland and the Soviet Union. Arborea, Mussolinia, reveals itself to be something rather similar.

The most famous fascist New Town is not in Italy at all, but in Eritrea, then part of newly conquered Abyssinia. This is the much-photographed Asmara, designed in the late 1930s by designers from the Rationalist school of Italian architects, inspired compromisers between a futuristic Modernism and the classical heritage. Mussolinia was part of an earlier, less violent but similarly clear process of colonization, this time within the Kingdom of Italy itself, where Sardinia was always somewhat apart, linguistically and culturally. The project, begun in the 1920s, of draining the malarial marshes in the south-west of the island was undertaken by settlers from north-east Italy, rather than Sardinians. Most people in Arborea can trace themselves back to these arrivals from the Veneto or, after the war, to migrants from the formerly Italian-speaking coast of Yugoslavia – an unusual case of northern Italians moving south, rather than vice versa. In theory, settling these pestilent lands and making them productive would help Mussolini achieve his much-vaunted goal of Autarchy, economic self-sufficiency. You notice something is different when you drive from the nearest railway station, at Marrubiu, to the New Town. Suddenly, the roads are all rigid straight, running alongside canals, in rich arable land, in the shadow of harsh, bare mountain ranges. On that level, the project worked.

The architect of Arborea, between 1928 and 1939, was Giovanni Battista Ceas, a critic and historian as well

Canal-side Mussolinia

as designer. Accordingly, in the first clutch of buildings there's very little trace of the more modernizing trends in fascist Italy, whether the monumental dreams of Futurist architects like Sant'Elia or the cold Rationalism of Giuseppe Terragni. The buildings are of a piece, so you can easily see they were planned at once. A town hall, hospital, school and police station are in an invented vernacular which bears very little resemblance to any historical Sardinian architecture. Rough, rusticated stone takes up most of the ground floors, with warm, yellowish render on the upper levels; roofs are pitched, and ornamentation is limited to little gestures, like growling faces above the windows of the small shopping parade. But most of Arborea is cottages, one or two of them Rationalist but mostly like little Roman villas, with sgraffito cherubs and rural-Neoclassical details. The main north–south street runs alongside a canal in concrete cuttings, which eventually leads to a much more modern pumping station out of town, also to Ceas's design. Aside from the usual rural Italian shrines to the Virgin Mary, the only statue is a bust to the engineer of the drainage project, Giulio Dolcetta, his bespectacled, square-jawed face aligned perfectly with a cypress tree. Cross a pretty little concrete bridge over the canal, and you're at the main piazza.

The piazza is symmetrical, but subtly so, with the buildings on either side evenly spaced, but not identical. In the middle is a Gothic church, with a tower in a free style somewhere between a very mild Art Nouveau and Venetian, bearing the legend 'RESURGO'. Inside is one of the only clues to the date of the town's founding, in the very interwar, muscular, realistic scene of Jesus and the Disciples painted behind the Altar. Next to this is what turns out to be a disused cinema, in a similar eclectic style – though you wouldn't necessarily guess that's what it was, as it looks more like an unusually architecturally ambitious barn. On the other side of the main north–south road – now Via Roma, but originally the streets all had numbers rather than names, as the grid of country roads around it still do – is a grain silo complex. One part is in Ceas's neo-Roman manner and the other in a much more dramatic industrial concrete.

This towering silo is one of three buildings that make up Arborea's skyline, the others being the church and the Casa del Fascio, the (former) House of the Fascist Party. Leave the square and walk towards the edge of

Concrete grain silos of Ancient Rome

town – not hard to do, as you can cross Arborea east to west in ten minutes – and you'll find a suddenly much more confident architecture, as Ceas suddenly switched towards Rationalism. The Casa del Fascio, of 1934, is a laconic assemblage of cubic volumes in concrete and brick, stepping upwards to a gallery and a tall concrete belltower. Alongside this is a long, low sports hall in a similarly confident style. Those three punctuations on the skyline sum up the values the New Town was meant to embody – Fascism, Catholicism, Autarchy.

After Mussolinia became Arborea, it ceased to be an architectural showcase, with the same suburban buildings of any small Italian town. The only exception is the Hotel Le Tolli, which is in a strange, monumental neo-Rationalist style, with looming, square, pink towers.

Casa del Fascio

Inside the lobby is a bound collection of the local paper from the 1930s, *Brigada Mussolinia*. Here, you can see what sort of a place it once was, and not just from the articles on the colonization of Abyssinia and Libya, on royal weddings, or the praise of Autarchy and Italy's German ally. 'The Story of Mussolinia' shows the main square devoid of the palm trees and benches that give it life today, open and imposing. The Casa del Fascio is opened, and Il Duce speaks from that gallery beneath the elegant Modernist campanile. Without this – and that strange, un-Sardinian landscape, and the gridiron imposed upon it – you might never guess that Arborea was once Mussolinia.

Red Madrid

It is quite hard to locate the centre of the Spanish capital. The guidebooks will tell you that it's the Puerta del Sol, or as it is known on the Madrid Metro, 'Vodafone Sol', a little crescent draped in giant canvas adverts, but it doesn't feel like the heart of the third-largest city in the EU. Madrid isn't built around a river or an acropolis, and the most famous monuments of the Spanish monarchy are just outside the city, at El Escorial. So my guess is the Plaza de España, which is after all called the Square of Spain. This is a classic bit of imperial urbanism, a grand square at the end of a grand road: fountains and an Art Deco monument to Cervantes, and two skyscrapers – the tallest, the Torre de Madrid, is an unremarkable late-1950s high-rise that you could imagine on the Costa del Sol were it faced with concrete rather than marble. But it's the slightly smaller Edificio España that you notice, aligned as the square's dark heart.

Edificio España was designed by Julián Otamendi in 1948, at the height of twentieth-century Spain's longrunning experiment in Fascism. A friend who has lived here all his life tells me 'to understand Madrid you have to understand the legacy of Franco', and so this seemed like a good place to begin understanding it – stamping itself across an entire city block, it's a stepped, stone-clad ziggurat, with restrained classical detail in the local tradition and extraneous little obelisks on the top of each tier. Built as a hotel, it currently stands derelict and empty: a Chinese developer, promising to turn it into flats, has sat on it

The Edifice of Spain

for years. Another friend who moved here from London ten years ago tells me of 'two Spains', living here side by side since the Civil War. The newly elected mayor, Manuela Carmena, a leftist lawyer backed by Podemos, clearly represents the other Spain to that which produced this square. Spain was once a centrist, post-dictatorship EU success story, but the sheer extent of the crash since 2008 here – a housing crisis, massive evictions – has pushed many to the left.

Ignore the weather, and the history of Spanish modern architecture, at least in the capital, resembles that of countries east of Germany. A brief flowering of 'heroic' era functionalism in the 1930s, cut off by neo-Baroque authoritarianism for two decades and then from the late 1950s followed by a thoughtful, regionalist form of Modernism.

The difference is that here, unlike in post-Soviet Europe, these trends were allowed to flower after the fall of the dictatorship, rather than being sidelined by developers' banalities. Edificio España may prove the 'theory' of extremes meeting, with its combination of Albert Speer detail and Lev Rudnev profile, but after it Madrid architecture is anything but extreme, seeming to have passed the whole twentieth century without ever having an avant-garde. Unlike Barcelona or Bilbao, it shows no interest in appearing in the starchitect map of Europe. The only recent buildings that might appear in any '1,000 Amazing Buildings to See on Easyjet' list are Herzog & de Meuron's Caixa Forum, a perverse contextual bricolage built on top of (and suspending in mid-air) a red-brick substation, and the Dutch spectacle-Modernists MVRDV's Mirador apartments, which we will come to later. In fact, Madrid seems a rather unknowable city, keeping its secrets, quite happy about the fact the tourists prefer Barcelona.

The main drag is Gran Vía, a fabulous transatlantic Broadway of wedding cake apartments, a couple of pre-Civil War skyscrapers like the flamboyantly spired Telefonica building, and the streamline Moderne Capitol building, swooping into view like a bullet train. Clotted streets of opulent blocks march down long, wide, straight streets; going east, past the fruity Gothic-Moorish Las Ventas bull ring, one of the symbols of the city, you pass over the network of urban motorways that come surprisingly close to the centre. In this mostly late-nineteenth- and twentieth-century city, it's hard to find much trace of the historic architecture you'd expect in the capital of the country that dominated the early modern world, but there are exceptions, most of all the majestic Plaza Mayor. This rectangle of red-rendered Neoclassical flats, demarcated by spindly spires, is a great illusion. Only inside it can you imagine yourself in the capital of a vast colonial empire. It was laid out in the seventeenth century, yet the arches that pass through into it lead to late-nineteenth-century tenements and underground car parks. Madrid vernacular veers from a flamboyant neo-Baroque that lasts well into the twentieth century to huge quantities of sober red brick. I'm taken to the top of the Circle of Fine Arts, where you can pay for a view of the skyline; close by, the fussy pinnacles of Belle Époque boom architecture, like City Hall (currently decorated with a 'REFUGEES WELCOME' banner); to the north, a tightly drawn cluster

Headless on the Plaza Mayor

of skyscrapers; and in a ring around everything, just in front of the mountains, sheer cliffs of red-brick blocks of flats, as if speculative development has become a geological feature.

The nearest thing Madrid has to a common aesthetic, the red-brick fixation may have emerged with the first, tentative Modernist buildings when Francoist architectural traditionalism loosened. The earliest of these is the stepped tower of the 1950 Ministry of Work and Social Affairs, designed by Francisco de Asís Cabrero and Rafael Aburto, and built initially as the headquarters for the Falange's state-run trade unions. It stands just opposite the Prado, and has a strict classical discipline, yet it doesn't pay lip service to Spanish heritage like the Edificio España does, resembling Italian rather than German fascist-era architecture, balancing Modernist precision and authoritarian hauteur: blank, scowling and impeccably made; it's a short step from here to our contemporary classical Modernists. The red style could develop into something much looser, as seen at the 1966 Girasol apartments by the Barcelona architect Josep Antoni Coderch, whose curving red-tile walls and delicate louvres swing casually around the corner of a street of pompous luxury buildings of various styles and eras. The strict version of the same can be seen at its peak in Rafael Moneo's Bankinter offices, begun in 1972, with its tripartite structure and its mechanistically perfected, unromantic brick detailing. In these buildings, late-Francoist Madrid can be seen as being as influential on current European urban orthodoxy as Schinkel's Berlin or Berlage's Amsterdam, an urbane, street-oriented architecture without sentiment.

Red-brick banking minimalism

These, though, are the city centre versions of the Madrid vernacular. The Madrid Metro – fast, cheap, bright, a less smelly version of the Paris Métro with good street furniture and the odd bit of enlivening mosaic and sculpture – will take you to the suburban equivalent. Around Buenos Aires station is Palomeras, a district of the strongly leftist working-class suburb of Vallecas. By the 1970s this was a sprawling shanty town, slated for a slum clearance that was fiercely resisted by residents. From 1979 until 1992, Palomeras was gradually redeveloped as council housing by a huge team of local architects. It's a red-brick grid, mostly of no more than five storeys, with three linear towers on the main Pablo Neruda Street, shops on the ground floors, pedestrian streets and squares and impressive, if shabby, internal courtyards. The style is actually interwar retro, the social architecture that the Spanish Republic never got the chance to build in the 1930s, with obvious references to the giant courtyards built by the 'Red' Vienna council in the interbellum, but on a much smaller scale. Everything is clad in a lower-budget version of the precise, hewn-from-one-rock red brick used by Rafael Moneo for bank HQs. The complex interpenetration of public and private space recalls both 1920s Red Vienna and 1980s IBA Berlin, but, unlike those, it's kept in less than perfect condition, with grass and weeds growing from the stairs leading down the hilly streets. Nonetheless, for its time, Palomeras is a triumph, and a welcome reminder that in Southern Europe the social-democratic welfare state and its architecture come from the 1980s, not the 1940s.

Red Palomeras

Vallecas is on a hill, and here you can get a better sense of Madrid's metropolitan sprawl than you can in the centre itself, where the Torre Madrid is as tall as it gets. Around eight miles down the bottom of that hill, as if a symbol of unattainable wealth, are the city's two adjacent clusters of skyscrapers. Most of the high-rises, which were developed from the 1960s on as a result of the late-Franco-era economic boom, run along Paseo de la Castellana, originally Avenida del Generalísimo. They're on a straight line, and the earliest and closest to the centre are the most interesting – the sharp, tense Brutalist angles of the Torre de Valencia and the bizarre, semi-Postmodernist Torres de Colón, with its green plastic condom pulled onto a red-tinted curved glass shaft. They get duller closer in, like Minoru Yamasaki's preciously named Torre Picasso. Then, Madrid is demarcated from its satellites by a very late Philip Johnson and John Burgee project, the Puerta de Europa. There were few people more apt to design the 'Gates of Europe' along a street once named after Franco than Johnson, who had been an enthusiastic fascist in the 1930s. These two tilting mirrorglass towers, both pompous and cheap, serve almost as well as Johnson's political record to caution against recent attempts to restore his reputation.

But at least they try to carve out some sort of urban drama from their tawdry means, unlike the more recent Four Towers. These four skyscrapers, built in the 2000s, sit on the edge of the city by the equivalent of the M25. They're most notable for their extreme height, although Foster's Torre Cepsa, with its cubic offices held in a vast steel vice, has a certain cold elegance, and the splayed legs of Pei Cobb Freed's Torre Espacio look impressive from a distance. But their lack of urbanist ambition is striking. Compared to La Défense or even Canary Wharf there is no attempt to pull these skyscrapers into a coherent continuous space with (even pseudo-)public squares and reasons to visit if not an office worker. It's aptly named: Four Towers, that's all you get. Madrid's most interesting high-rise is an outlier, on the other side of town – the Torres Blancas, an early-1970s luxury apartment block, designed by Francisco Javier Sáenz de Oiza. Bizarrely, Moneo was on the team, but it's the reverse of his sensible, considered architecture. Given the city's lack of an architectural avant-garde, this experiment in extremist organic Brutalism is a one-building manifesto, a writhing, contorted wail against all that overpowering order.

Virulent Brutalism, Torres Blancas

In that, it isn't that different from the city's most famous recent building, MVRDV's Mirador, in the recent exurb of Sanchinarro. To get there and back, your bus or tram loops around seemingly endless five-storey speculative blocks, the ground zero of Spain's housing disaster. Unlike in Palomeras, it's clear what's public (the strips of greenery between the streets, with playgrounds) and what's private (everything else), with little relief from the relentless humidity. MVRDV's two social-housing blocks, the monumental Mirador and the lower, longer Celosia, try to provide an outward-looking, public alternative to the endless streets of orange tenements, but they can only do this via formal melodrama, and, in the case of the Mirador, through an ingratiating game with colours and cladding (each colour denoting flat

Mirador

types). The vertiginous open spaces the architects have created in both buildings are strictly residents-only. The image of this would-be enigmatic iconic edifice with its hole in the middle has been widely published, an emblem of post-OMA 'Supermodernist' eclecticism, but unless you've visited you wouldn't know that it holds the space at one end of an oversized roundabout, a lonely sentinel in the suburbs. Ending the deals the city has cut with developers that created places like this is one of the leftist mayor's goals. Sadiq Khan – and Jeremy Corbyn – may be watching her intently.

The Walled City of Nicosia

As the minibus makes its way across a long, wide, clean motorway to the capital of the Republic of Cyprus, two unexpected things become apparent. One of them is the fact that, just as if you were on the M1, everyone is driving on the left-hand side. The other suddenly flashes up at you, as its lights twinkle on and off – an enormous illuminated Turkish flag, on a mountain. These two contributions by occupying powers, encountered as you glide along a very smooth and modern piece of infrastructure, are a good introduction to Nicosia. 'The last divided capital city in Europe', only if you don't count Belfast as a capital city (which it is, of Northern Ireland), it has been sliced in two by the UN-monitored 'Green Line' since 1974. Accordingly, it is one of the places where the EU ends and something else begins. Geographically, it's debatable whether the island of Cyprus is even in Europe, lying closer to Damascus and Beirut than Athens and Istanbul. However, the Republic of Cyprus – not including the Turkish Republic of North Cyprus, recognized only by Turkey – is not just in the EU but in the Eurozone, and was one of the first countries to be bailed out in the financial crisis. Only in Nicosia can you cross the EU border within one city.

Even by twentieth-century standards, recent history in Nicosia (Lefkosia to Greeks, Lefkoşa to Turks) is complex. Occupied by, respectively, French Crusaders, Venetians, Ottomans and the British Empire, mostly Greek-speaking with a large Turkish minority, it was heavily repressed by the British, especially after an uprising in 1931. In the 1950s this came to a head, with an armed campaign to join with Greece, following an unrecognized referendum; reluctantly, the UK pulled out, keeping two very large bases, but left its car-driving habits, electric three-pin plugs, and a toxic legacy of imperial divide-and-rule. A Non-Aligned government under the Orthodox Archbishop Makarios III dealt not altogether impartially with both Greek and Turkish paramilitaries (both of which had a tendency to assassinate members of the only non-confessional political organization, the communists of AKEL, Cyprus's largest party since the war), until in 1974 Greek far-rightists mounted a coup with at least tacit support from the United States. This was swiftly followed by a Turkish invasion and mutual ethnic cleansing. Makarios returned to power when the coup collapsed, but Turkish troops never withdrew, a stalemate which was reinforced when Greek Cypriots rejected a referendum on power sharing in 2004. There is talk of another referendum soon, but everyone I spoke to expects the division to be final. Since the 1950s, one of the main dividing lines has been within the capital itself, a line that became fully militarized in 1974.

This is a bloody post-imperial history similar to that of nearby Lebanon or Syria, which makes it perhaps surprising that Nicosia comes across very much as an affluent, relaxed, 'normal' city, in both halves, but for the scar that runs right across it. Although local architects inform me that the port of Limassol is where the money and the new building are mostly to be found, Nicosia, handsome, small-scale, modern, is as pleasant a city as has ever been crossed by a line of barbed wire and machine guns. The nearest thing to a centre is Eleftheria Square, which is currently undergoing heavy engineering in order to remould it to a design by Zaha Hadid. The resultant building site stood as a symbol of the financial crisis here, a crash so sudden and sharp the AKEL government was forced to raid private bank accounts. It marks roughly the start of the perfectly round, planned, walled city built by the Venetians, of which mostly only the walls and a few churches survive. The Zaha scheme, for a landscaped, multi-level sunken square with much parametric billowing and swooping, is actually now being carried out, albeit slowly; you can peek into it from a temporary bridge, alongside the Neoclassical town hall.

Two recent towers look over the square, both of them expensive and high-quality. One of them, the AG Leventis Apartments and Art Gallery by Feilden Clegg Bradley, is a less controversial British contribution to the city than, for instance, the interwar Anglo-Levantine style of the Government House, designed by Maurice Webb, architect of Kingston Guildhall, which still has the imperial coat of arms on the façade. FCB's tower is clad in the local limestone, which you soon notice is one of the best things about the city's architecture. The tower is heavily rectilinear and angular, and, after you become familiar with the city around, is essentially, you realize, the local interwar Modernist vernacular extruded upwards, simple and confident. The function – luxury flats and an oligarch art gallery – is given a very swish finish. Jean Nouvel's Tower 25 is similarly 'inspired' by the city's texture, with the idea for the perforated, thick concrete curved side-walls taken from the bulging buttressing of the Venetian walls; these enclose

Leventis Gallery (and apartments),
Feilden Clegg Bradley

seventeen storeys of luxury flats and offices, in the city's
tallest building. It has been criticized for the gleaming white
paint job, when concrete would actually fit better with the
local stone, but is sensitive by the standards of Nouvel's
recent work (as Londoners familiar with One New Change,
Nouvel's hideous mall opposite St Paul's, could attest). Both
buildings were finished just before the bubble inflated by
Cyprus's 'relaxed' financial services industry burst, and as
monuments to avarice go, they're of a good standard.

Morality and architecture part company elsewhere.
The most interesting architecture in central Nicosia is
actually from the colonial interwar years, when Cyprus
wasn't even allowed a university by the British occupiers,
lest it sow sedition. There are streets upon streets of small

Nicosia Moderne

houses and apartment buildings, with delicate Moderne details in honeyed limestone, metal screens and decorative doors, sometimes sleek and streamlined, sometimes 1920s Neoclassical, sometimes Ottoman vernacular with cantilevered wooden bays, but all of it is bright, imaginative and mostly in good repair. Walking these streets is a great pleasure: cafés, junk shops and repair stores with only one central strip of international chains. Neoclassical civic structures and religious buildings from various denominations – Greek Orthodox, Armenian Apostolic, Catholic, Sunni Muslim – are scattered around the squares, with small gardens around them. The Renaissance gateways of the Venetian walls lead to what ought to be a continuous public space but is more often a series of sunken car parks, although you can suddenly find your-self on a raised park, with oranges falling and rotting from the trees around you, and a view of mid-rise apart-ment blocks stepping off towards the mountains, and offices and low-rise factories along the ring road. Further in, away from the walls, you find as you go deeper into the city that increasingly the houses are boarded up, and that just beyond them is piled-up rubble and barbed wire.

On the main shopping zone along Ledra Street, you can find an explanation for the sudden dereliction. Amid the parade of fine classical, Moderne and post-war Mod-ernist department stores is, of all things, a multistorey Debenhams, leading upwards to a public viewing plat-form. This is the Shacolas Tower, a simple high-rise which was opened in the mid-1990s but looks a few dec-ades older. For a long time, going up to the tenth storey was the only way to see over the other side to North

Nicosia skyline

Nicosia, survey the minarets and towers of the capital of the Turkish Republic of North Cyprus, and see where that flashing Turkish flag comes from (it's draped across the Kyrenia mountains that overlook the city, and also features the words 'How fortunate is the person who can say, "I'm a Turk"'). It officially commemorates Turkish Cypriots massacred in a nearby village in 1974, but nobody in South Nicosia thinks it's anything other than a daily provocation. In fact, it feels a great deal more aggressive than the actual main border crossing in Ledra Street – at least, for the EU citizens and Turkish Cypriots who are allowed to cross it, which excludes many people in North Cyprus.

There are few transitions quite so sharp as the way this ordinary and very attractive street suddenly becomes a militarized border. Sandbags, armed guards, barbed wire, concrete and steel walls can all be found around it, making sure you don't wander off the main drag, but the Ledra Street crossing itself looks almost flimsy, booths with passport control staff and small fences – though one suspects that someone trying to run through it would be dealt with quickly. When past that and into North Nicosia, the first thing you notice is the much more aggressive commerce: lots and lots of shops selling tax-free goods to wealthier tourists coming from the other side, which immediately makes you realize how signage and advertisements in South Nicosia have an almost Dutch level of order and politeness. Beyond that, it soon becomes obvious that you're in exactly the same city. The Art Deco limestone blocks of the 1930s, with their sweeping curves, the Ottoman houses painted white with their wooden

Friendly neighbourhood checkpoint

Wall from the North Nicosia side

projections, they're all there, just a fair bit more dilapidated, and the population is visibly poorer; but around the
cafés, and in the central Atatürk Square, around a Venetian column, men and women sit around and chat and
smoke exactly as they do on the other side of the wall.

Some wag of a kebab shop owner on the south side of
the border has called his stall by the Green Line 'Berlin
Wall'. Much as poorer East Berlin included the actual
city centre of Berlin around Unter den Linden and
Museumsinsel, the obvious civic and historic heart of the
city lies in North Nicosia, around the Selimiye Mosque,
the municipal market and the Büyük Han, the largest
and most impressive buildings within the city walls.
The mosque's limestone minarets are a monumental

Büyük Han

presence in most of the city, especially in the view from the Shacolas Tower, but on the ground you realize that they're additions to a French Gothic cathedral, built by the French Lusignan kings in the thirteenth century – and it's recognizable as such, with its delicate tracery and tall arches. Inside, the structure is still visible, but has been made clear and bright through whitewash. After the Ottoman conquest in the fifteenth century, minarets were added in the same stone as the bulk of the cathedral, in the place reserved for unbuilt Gothic towers.

The disjunction between the two styles is obvious. They really do look like two very different forms of architecture bolted together, whereas Byzantine and Ottoman buildings tend to complement each other. The tapering cylinders of the minarets and the filed-flat skyline of the mosque are a strange fit, and stranger too at the smaller Haydar Pasha Mosque, where typically Gothic figures of dragons stand over the entrance to a high-windowed flamboyant church/mosque with a single minaret. The Büyük Han and the municipal market are much less uneasy structures: the former is a delightful two-level inn, with delicate arched galleries around a central dome, designed by Ottoman architects in the late sixteenth century, close in style to a Renaissance square, only enclosed. The market, meanwhile, is British iron and glass, an Edwardian arcade on the Med. It stands right next to the Green Line, so that if you take the wrong entrance out you're at a dead end of barbed wire and signs reminding you that men with machine guns are watching.

Nicosia Airport has been disused since 1974, lost in the demarcation zone of the Green Line. Cyprus's main airport is instead at coastal Larnaca. In its main hall is a Modernist ceramic relief, which was taken from the derelict airport and remounted in Larnaca as a marker, until the Republic of Cyprus gets its airport back. On the day I left Larnaca Airport, the headline 'WHO WILL SPEAK FOR BRITAIN?' was yelling at passengers from the cover of the *Daily Mail*. It referred to the apparently poor deal Britain was receiving from the European Union, and recalled language used in Parliament in 1940, when Britain apparently *stood alone* against the hordes. Leaving an EU country, in the company of a very large quantity of British families on their way back not only from holiday but also from visiting expat relatives, this outrage seemed particularly peculiar. I wondered what elegant, pleasant, but inescapably depressing divided Nicosia might say if it got to speak for Britain.

3 Central

Munich: The Sugary Sweet Smell of Success

Only yesterday, Germany was considered by elite opinion to be a fiscally conservative industrial dinosaur with an oversized public sector and lamentably unsexy architecture. Its capital was a chaotic squatland, and its big cities made stuff, as if it were the nineteenth century. Yet since the financial crash of 2008, Germany has assumed an unquestioned role as European hegemon. Its policies towards Southern Europe expressly stop those countries from building the powerful industries, stable economies and large welfare state which makes German cities so 'liveable' and faintly dull. There are less pleasant secrets to German industry's success, like stagnant wages and workfare, but neither is on a British scale. Within Germany itself, it works. As the sublimely sleek ICE train approaches Munich Hauptbahnhof, you pass a line of sensible, classical-modern apartment buildings, connected to smooth infrastructure via exceptionally well-made and elegant vehicles. It's what us frustrated aesthetes condemned to Stratford, Leeds or Bristol all dream of, our path not taken.

The machine of German dominance is much better

seen outside the capital. Sprawling, depopulated, post-industrial Berlin, deep in East Germany, is much poorer than, say, Düsseldorf, Stuttgart, Frankfurt, Hamburg – and Munich, which fairly drips with wealth. It's a Social Democratic island in conservative Bavaria, but given the SPD and the Christian Democrats are two wings of the same governing coalition, the difference is barely relevant any more. So Munich, regularly at or near the top of all those 'liveable city' polls, should be a good place to see what power and success look like.

One unexpected aspect of Germany's apparently retro economy is the continued seediness around most of its railway stations, long expelled from King's Cross, Piccadilly or indeed Berlin's epically shiny new *Hauptbahnhof.* Munich's station is a post-war box gone shabby by German standards, or compared with the iron cathedrals of Hamburg and Cologne; there's some neat 1950s details in bronze and travertine underneath the adverts. Around this are the hotels and hostels, and at night neon signs, kebab shops and gambling dens give the area a Fassbinderian unease. By day, walk round the corner and you're at the Theresienwiese, the big park where the Oktoberfest takes place, looked over by Wilhelmine neo-Baroque villas and the distended dome-spire hybrid of St Paul's Church. In the other direction from the *Hauptbahnhof* is the historic city centre. While you might still feel permanently hustled on the street, it'll be more because of the sprawling Christmas markets that last seemingly from October till March rather than the more cloak-and-dagger stuff around the station.

Towards the historic centre, a *Ringstrasse* is lined with

hulks like the Palace of Justice, resembling a more grace-less Vienna. Nearby is the best part of the post-Royal Air Force rebuilding, the New Maxburg, designed by Sep Ruf and Theo Pabst in 1954. Curtain-walled offices, with shops on the ground floor, form a square, and are enlivened with bright, semi-abstract mosaics. As a particularly neat gesture, the ruined corner of a Renaissance palace is used as a stair tower. Pretty, unfussy and relaxed, it's a great model for rebuilding, but then Munich avoided both the multi-level experiments of Cologne or Coventry, and Dresden- or Warsaw-like historicist reconstruction. Tenements and offices were rebuilt where they stood in the style of the day, often with applied medieval-cum-mid-century modern decorative details. The larger, more important buildings had their spires and domes pieced back together, with nothing new allowed to steal their prominence on the skyline, so from a distance the centre looks as it would have in 1939, dominated by the flamboyantly prickly neo-Gothic city hall, the two bulbs of the Dom and the tall plane of the Peterskirche. At the Christmas market that spreads interminably across the Marienplatz, people wait until the bells of the churches and the city hall belfry all chime in together, and get their phones out to record the moment.

The relaxed nature of post-war Munich was praised by Ian Nairn as a counter to the era's grand plans. I found it smug and cloying, but the streets leading out from the centre have more than enough stern authoritarianism. The eclectic 1850s Gothic Rationalism of the Maximilian-strasse looks like a possible model for Berlin's Stalinallee, a meticulously calculated axis ending over the River

Toy Dom

Isar at the Bavarian Parliament, encrusted with a whole V&A's worth of imperial murals and statuary. Past one corner of the enormous Englischer Garten you can find a contrast in Gasteig, a large House of Culture cramming a library, cafés, concert halls and much else into a structure on the early 1980s cusp between sensible red-brick Aalto and mirrorglass Postmodernism. It's on the site of the beer hall where Hitler attempted his first, famously abortive *Putsch* in 1923. The eventual result of that can be seen at the end of the other axial street: the stark brick march of Ludwigstrasse, which leads out to a half-destroyed Victory Arch. The side leading into the city is battered, but that facing the centre is half-bare but for the inscription: 'Dedicated to victory, destroyed by war, urging peace'.

'Dedicated to victory, destroyed by war, urging peace'

After forming the capital of a brief, violently suppressed Bavarian Soviet Republic in 1919, headed by a motley succession of anarchists, communists and Expressionist playwrights, Munich became the unquestioned centre of the German right in the Weimar Republic. Accordingly there's very little of the Expressionism of Hamburg, the 'New Objectivity' of Frankfurt or the streamlines of Berlin, but for two or three minor efforts in the suburbs. The dominant inter-war architecture of Munich comes not from Weimar, but from the Third Reich. There is more prominent Nazi architecture in Munich than in any other big German city, and it is a useful refutation of the popular myth that the architecture of German Fascism was awesome, powerful and seductive. Paul Ludwig Troost's House of German Art is a stripped classical temple on the ring road; the cars divert through an underpass in front, as if to stop them looking at it. It sounds too facetious to say this about a building constructed for such patently evil purposes – to showcase German rather than Degenerate Art, and to make the same distinction in architecture – and of a building which Hitler liked to claim a role in designing, but nonetheless – it's quite boring. It's nothing special. You will not be awed. You might admire the detailing, the red granite floors and Art Deco trimmings. It is like a Swedish classical building of ten years earlier without the wit or imagination. The current management quite rightly draw attention to its true purpose with integral artworks – Mel Bochner has draped a canvas of Yiddish words in Latin script across the frieze, while Christian Boltanski pasted paper prints of the eyes of members of the Red Orchestra, the largely communist resistance network, all the way across the limestone colonnade.

The culmination of the Nazis' attempt to redesign Munich as the 'capital of the movement' came in the redesign of Königsplatz, also at the hands of the talentless Troost, before his early death in 1934. This was already the monumental showcase of the Kingdom of Bavaria, as the large square flanked by the Glypothek and the Antikensammlungen culminate in the heavy twin towers of Klenze's glowering Propylaea, which has far more real power and presence than Troost's tasteful neo-Georgian contributions: the Führerbau and the Nazi Party headquarters, both of them cap-doffing, tight-arsed and basically forgettable, notable mainly for their sternly fluted columns. Ironically enough, the Propylaea was designed as a monument to Greek–German friendship.

The Führerbau

Both of these have long since been converted to civilized purposes. Adjacent, the white walls and slit windows of the Nazi Documentation Centre, a museum opened in 2015 to the designs of Georg Scheel Wetzel, take a minimal approach to tackling the Nazi legacy, far from the neo-Expressionist *Sturm und Drang* of works like Daniel Libeskind's Jewish Museum in Berlin. There are plenty of other new monuments on the fringes of Königsplatz. The Pinakothek der Moderne, by the Bundestag's architect, Stephan Braunfels, displays delicate, polite modernity; Sauerbruch Hutton's Museum Brandhorst does the same but with a colour scheme resembling hundreds and thousands sprinkled over the façade; and at the Academy of Fine Arts extension, the veteran 'Deconstructivist' architects Coop Himmelb(l)au cram in as many angles and devices as they can while maintaining the scale and colour appropriate to its context next to a historic building. It's an instructive selection of recent mainstream German architecture; Modernist but not too disruptive.

To see what is really special in twentieth-century Munich, you need to head out on the U-Bahn – eight lines, regular trains, beautiful stations, in a city smaller than Greater Manchester – to Olympiazentrum, a Brutalist station leading to the ensemble laid out for the 1972 Olympics, which just happens to be right next to the BMW factory complex, and the car manufacturer's world headquarters. Its reputation precedes it, but Frei Otto's work at the Olympic Park does not disappoint. Photographs don't usually capture the almost casual way these sheets of steel and glass are thrown around the site, over and

Frei Otto's lost future

across the stadium and the smaller sports halls, and around the telecommunications tower. The combination of the organic sweep of these roofs – a glass cloth that has been suddenly frozen in the act of being draped over a strategically scattered series of poles – is combined with hard, brittle, totally modern materials. The imitations of this in teflon, like London's Millennium Dome, are more functionally sensible, as it gets hot under these glass canopies even in December, but they lose that tension entirely, feeling more like modernized tents. This is not from the same planet, the same dimension, as the Millennium Dome. To imagine this all ended in grimy teflon is to insult one of the most beautiful structures of the twentieth century.

Opposite there is the less sui generis, but also outstandingly impressive Olympic Village, most of which is now a social-housing co-op, but the first part you come to from the park is low-rise student housing, concrete terraces in a De Stijl manner, often painted up attractively by their short-term residents. Above this, connected via walkways, is a series of monumental stepped-section housing blocks, with a shopping centre and public facilities on the upper level. It is indisputably successful, and an entirely ordinary – not poor, not rich – street life goes on underneath these enormous structures. Councils and housing associations everywhere should be compulsorily taken here to ascertain just how Munich managed to get it so right. One answer, conceivably, is the working car factory just down the steps of the walkways, its long titanium-clad machine halls cleverly integrated with the linked circular towers of Karl Schwanzer's BMW

How to design an Olympic village

headquarters, one of the most futuristic of European sky-scrapers.

It is here, not in the over-sweetened centre, where you can see just how much, by contrast, Britain managed to screw up. If the equivalent to the Munich U-Bahn, the Olympic Village and the Olympic Park is the Manchester Metrolink, grimy, half-destroyed Thamesmead and the Queen Elizabeth Olympic Park, the UK should just give up and apply to join the Bundesrepublik so they can sort our cities out for us. However, this impression of awe and shame is shaken a little when you look at the additions to the 1972 ensemble, and you realize Germany couldn't maintain this level either. The *Autobahn* that cuts between the Park and Village points in a perfectly straight line at Ingenhoven Overdiek's O2 headquarters, but in the other direction, underneath the BMW tower, is Coop Himmelb(l)au's BMW-Welt (BMW-World): a ridiculous, pompous piece of overdesigned nonsense, a clumsy, fumbling, self-important Deconstructivist car showroom, a building approximately as infuriating as the Olympic Park is uplifting.

Of course it's cruel to compare anything to the Olympic Park. Yet near the end of the most recent U-Bahn extension is Herzog & de Meuron's Allianz Arena, built for the Bayern Munich football team, which rather begs for the comparison with Frei Otto's stadium. Whereas the 1972 buildings are a landscape, this is an object, a monument, a balloon of ethylene tetrafluoroethylene, atop a walkway with car parks underneath. Unlike Coop Himmelb(l)au's effort, it does not embarrass itself, but it is isolated, aloof. An image of power and modernity surrounded by emptiness.

Not match day at Bayern Munich

Leipzig: Anglo-Saxony

Sometimes, the happenstance that comes with visiting a city you don't know can lead you to interesting and unexpected conclusions. So it was when I went to Leipzig in late autumn 2016, for an academic conference on the 'post-socialist city'. My first impression was determined by the sheer wonder that is Deutsche Bahn. It is a silly view in many respects, and often receives short shrift from Germans, who will point to persistent delays and endless station upgrades, but it is hard for anyone used to Virgin Trains not to feel that they are in the presence of a higher civilization when on a DB train. Partly this is a question of absences – for one, of the tinnitus-inducing noise and persistent smell of faeces piped around the carriages by Virgin's dubious air-conditioning and Tannoy systems, but it is also one of clarity and elegance. Rather than cheesy Madchester colour schemes and stiff seats, even second class is a world of plush chairs and dark colours – restful blacks and greys, and the unmistakeable feeling that you are being treated like an adult. The station buildings can't be accounted for in this way – and Britain has little to be ashamed of here, once you take away the pigeon spikes and the Upper Crusts – and Leipzig station would be magnificent even if it were run by Network Rail and Govia Thameslink. Soon after arriving, however, I found myself in a zone of inner-city decay, overbearing commerce and characterless exurbia, a place which compares rather easily to Leeds, Birmingham or Southampton, more than it does to Munich or Hamburg.

Leipzig Hauptbahnhof

Like many of the best things in the city, Leipzig Haupt-bahnhof is the product of the immediately pre-First World War era, when this was one of the five largest cities in the country, a major trading and industrial centre, something which ended, for better or worse, when it found itself in the Soviet zone of Occupation after 1945. The outside is staid sandstone-stripped classicism, but the interior is the point. A heavy steel train shed leads through huge stone arches to a concrete hall, lit with glass bricks, clear, monumental and open; there is a banal shopping mall tucked in here just underground, but if you go into the station shops, you can admire the comfort and luxury of late, bourgeois Wilhelmine Germany just before it made the mistake of invading its neighbours, something which in addition means that Leipzig has perhaps Europe's most glamorous Starbucks. From this amazing concourse steps lead down to the exits, which are anterooms for some sort of cult ceremony, half-domed Pantheons with coffered ceilings and grand staircases. So what is all this in aid of? Leipzig was the *Messestadt* (trade fair city), known for hundreds of years largely for these fairs, which saw people from all around Western, Central and Eastern Europe come to the city to sell their wares; when combined with intense industrial development in the nineteenth century, this made the city a major capitalist centre in what was becoming Europe's second most powerful economy. Some of the warehouses where travellers could inspect products are clustered around the station, in a similar big-boned style to the Hauptbahnhof, such as the Industriepalast. But in front of them you'll find a much less romantic image of contemporary commerce – a great big retail park. This is the first time I've ever found an exurban retail park, with its surface parking, nondescript sheds and totem poles of logos, in the city centre of a historic city outside Britain; even there, only a few places – Southampton, Bradford – have disfigured themselves in this way. How did this happen?

The answer was eventually granted to me at the conference venue, the Leibniz Institute for Regional Geography, out in the suburban site of Engelsdorf. A one-an-hour regional train took me there in less than ten minutes from the city centre, but you could be in the direct middle of nowhere. Passing derelict yellow-brick factories, I came to a stop shrouded in mist, surrounded by several little houses, a massive MediaMart, a big PC warehouse, some outlet malls, and incongruously, for this classic product of the private car, a tram stop. The institute stands, along with some local-government offices and the police headquarters, in a street of sober, urban and very 1990s German buildings, modern, but with a classical sense of order and rectitude. They look like they might be in the newspaper district of Berlin, but here they are, surrounded by what looks like a slightly less ritzy version of the Lakeside Centre, Thurrock. After asking pretty much everybody I could what on earth this place was doing here, a professor at the institute explained it to me. The city centre of Leipzig was beset with competing restitution claims when former property owners had their pre-1945 rights restored, meaning that public institutions like these – in a country, East Germany, where all

From the window of the School of Geography

land had been public for forty-four years – decided to get out of the way, and get themselves virgin sites on the outskirts. In order to recharge the stricken economy of the area, as its industries were greedily dismantled by their new West German owners, the government basically let developers do what they liked. Here's the result – Surrey Quays, Saxony. It is the reversal of how British architectural enthusiasts conventionally understand Germany, as a holdout of planning and order.

The only other insight I had into this strange city by the end of the conference was via the district where I was staying, Sellerhausen, at the end of the long Eisenbahnstrasse ('Railway Street') that forks off from the Hauptbahnhof. Arriving late into Leipzig I took a cab rather than wait for a night bus, and the driver was most surprised by my destination. 'Not a nice place.' A little googling later, and I discovered that Eisenbahnstrasse is, apparently, the 'most dangerous street in Germany' due to the amount of gang- and drug-related turf wars and murders it apparently plays host to. I can't say that any of this danger seemed apparent to me, though the street was indisputably seedy; I shall merely note that the man who got off the tram at Annenstrasse and pissed in the middle of the road, before hopping back on, was most definitely white, German and bald. Walking along it the next morning, in daylight, it seemed rather attractive, especially compared with the dispiriting exurban sludge of Engelsdorf. Unusually for an East German city, it is a multicultural area, with Vietnamese and Middle Eastern shops, cafés and restaurants. The street itself is Wilhelmine: tall ornamented tenements, with shops on the ground floors and, on the side streets, cobbles angled to hook your ankle. Streetlights barely operate on the eastern end of the street. Some blocks are derelict, some, amazingly, still have bullet holes from 1945, some are squatted, and individual tenements have been gentrified, with the plaster cornices, pilasters and caryatids that had long since melted off the brick structures being reapplied and remade. It has the exciting, Interzone air that Berlin once had, something which has attracted quite a few young exiles from the nearby capital city. Parallel, midway along, a *Plattenbau* (a compound meaning 'concrete-panel-build') estate from the late years of the German Democratic Republic shows what the alternative to this sort of nineteenth-century speculation once was – ordered, rectangular blocks of flats, with much more

Railway Street

manageable balconies and real public spaces rather than courtyards to throw your rubbish into. Ideological opposites though they may be, these two areas fit together much more neatly than the retail park and the Industriepalast.

The city centre itself is a similar beast to Munich – a medieval tangle with almost entirely non-medieval buildings, bound by a partly parkland *Ringstrasse*, with a chocolate box collection of Renaissance (the town hall), neo-Renaissance (the new town hall) and Gothic church towers, but the subtle differences come from the city having been less heavily bombed by the RAF than its Bavarian cousin, and from the presence amid the spires of two DDR-era high-rises. There is the tower of Leipzig University, a design by the prolific East German designer Hermann Henselmann, who was behind more than half the interesting buildings of post-war Berlin, and there is the Messeturm (trade fair tower), an angular shaft topped by a revolving logo for the Trade Fair. Both of these were renovated after 1990 with slightly duller and more expensive materials, but along with the towers of the churches and the town halls they give the city a great skyline, keeping its historic and Modernist sides in a hard-to-achieve balance.

The University Tower is best seen when walking around Augustusplatz – from the 1940s till the 1980s Karl-Marx-Platz – a rare renaming in a city that still has central streets named after Rosa Luxemburg and Karl Lieb-knecht. Augustusplatz is the heart of the city, a tram interchange in-between the Opera House, a stiff, prissy but beautifully detailed piece of Stalinist classicism, and the Gewandhaus. Designed by Rudolf Skoda in the late 1960s, this is a flamboyantly Brutalist concert hall, a heavy volume containing the hall cantilevered out over a glass foyer jutting out towards the square (these two, facing each other, are part of the extensive classical-music provision considered necessary in the city of J. S. Bach). This is just at the base of the University Tower, and the two are obviously conceived as a unity: one of them a matter of tight, compacted volumes, the other a broad, sweeping structure overlooking the city. The tower's sail-like profile may seem pat at first glance, but, after walking around it for a while, you might note its grace and subtlety, and the way it is never quite the same tower twice, no two views identical. Around it are some much more boring, and smaller, towers of the Weimar Republic, both in a style somewhere between classicism and Modernism but not really convincing as either, and with the taller of the two, the 1929 Europahaus, in need of renovation, with its rain-streaked travertine looking rather sad. In old photographs of the square from the DDR, it's just a car park, so the Christmas market there at the time I visited is probably an improvement, though it is as overbearing as in Munich. Practically no space in the city centre has been spared men in costumes doing 'traditional' versions of 'Jingle Bells', sugary treats and mulled wine and fifty stalls selling hand-made Santas, but it all congregates here: this is what all the coaches parked outside the Hauptbahnhof are here for. It's all less offensive than the new university buildings by the Dutch architect Erick van Egeraat. Like the 'Walkie-Talkie' designer Rafael Viñoly, Van Egeraat is one of those bafflingly popular 'signature architects' whose work is instantly recognizable, facile and sentimental, and here his attempt to replicate Gothic principles via a splintered barcode façade and a transplanted rose window (from a demolished church that was once on the site) is acutely embarrassing, one-dimensional and ingratiating.

Within the centre, most of the buildings are roughly from the 1870–1914 *Belle Époque*, replacing the Baroque or Gothic structures that would have been there before, but nearly equally tourist-pleasing, with mosaics, integrated statuary, gilded gables and all the sorts of things that apparently go well with being drunk in a city at night wearing winter clothing. The best of these places is the terrific Madler Passage, very akin to the Hauptbahnhof in its soaring, top-lit concrete spaces, integrated with a residual classicism. East Germany's lack of property development saved most of these buildings from the replacement they might have faced elsewhere, so clutches of Leipzig are as close as you can get in a big city to imagining yourself in a 'Germany before the collapse', and before all those things start to happen that Germans might feel ashamed of – though the colonial imagery in the Riquet café, or the exaggerated black faces set into pediments, are reminders that German imperialism and *Lebensraum* was about Africa before it was about Poland and Russia (as ever, best not to enquire where the cotton in those mills came from). There are a surprisingly large amount of holes in the city centre, gap sites and unexpected dereliction, which jars with all the cutesiness. So too does a clutch of modern buildings, a few examples of DDR Futurism, with prefabricated abstract patterns in

The non-capitalist department store

concrete set among the office blocks and housing complexes, and especially the fabulous Sputnik style of the Karstadt store, a windowless curve with shimmering, concave metal panels, deliberately eye-catching as much as the pre-war commercial buildings. More recently, there are some dull hotels, and the Museum of Fine Arts. Designed by Karl Hufnagel, Peter Pütz and Michael Rafaelian and opened in 2004, it is heroically oversized, with at least half of its cubic volume, glazed to the outside and smooth slabs of concrete in the interior, made up of double- or triple-height circulation spaces rather than galleries. These huge square spaces are concussive, thuggish, with even the lifts the size of an entire exhibition space. This alignment with the DDR's blocky, pugnacious architecture rather than all the Wilhelmine fol-de-rol is very daring by the standards of contemporary German architecture.

Moving southwards out of the centre, you come to a fragment of Stalinist boulevard planning, the Ringbebauung, designed by 'Rudolf Rohrer and Collective' at the start of the 1950s. Commanding the green space of Rossplatz, it is a smooth, aloof castle of flats for those more equal than others, topped with dynastic obelisks. With several other streets or bits of streets in a similar style around, you can see that the idea was to surround Leipzig with a circular version of Berlin's Stalinallee, a showcase of heavy Socialist Realist splendour to counterbalance the bourgeois trading city within. This never took place, of course, but you can get a fix of the peculiar values of 'proletarian classicism' and socialist luxury within, as at the Ring Café, with its chandeliers, murals and inexplicable opening hours.

The trade fairs continued under East German state Socialism, this time being an opportunity for the socialist camp to display its wares to itself and to make tentative contact with the other camp. Visiting the Messe today is dispiriting. The buildings are slightly neo-Egyptian stripped classical pavilions of the 1920s, big, square pylons and columns with a couple of DDR experiments in the colour orange; but since the Messe moved out into the suburbs (more of which later), it has become little more than a scrubby retail park. Its main monument is the Soviet pavilion, with its unmistakeable red star on a gold spike, derelict and part-dismantled. In the near distance, as another vision of people from all over Europe coming together, is the preposterous Battle of the

Stalinist trade-fair city

Nations Memorial, designed by Bruno Schmitz as a Wagnerian *Gesamtkunstwerk* – art, architecture and landscape, all in one definitive statement.

Again, this is the Wilhelm II style, reliant on advanced engineering and then lumbering it with a J. R. R. Tolkien aesthetic. Commemorating the Battle of Leipzig at the end of the Napoleonic Wars, when the anti-French coalition had a definitive victory against the Emperor's armies, it was opened on the battle's 100th anniversary in 1913 – and then another Battle of the Nations happened. It does look like the expression of a place bursting for war. Its gargantuan bulk, placed on a mound overlooking the city, is decorated with relief sculptures of huge warriors, who are all hard to imagine on an early-nineteenth-century battlefield, but which could fit much more neatly

The Battle of the Nations

into the medieval fantasies common to most European countries circa 1900 – the longing, of people bored with civilization, for knightly virtues, rippling muscles and suits of armour. The modernity of the sculptures, which anticipate the reduced, abstracted bodies of Art Deco advertising, is used to express blood and soil malevolence. The local SS chose the memorial, with an eye to symbolism, as their last stand against the US Army in 1945. But it got retained in the DDR, partly because it commemorated Russians and Germans fighting on the same side (and, even better, against an enemy from the west). A more effective image of the city as a meeting point between German and Slavic Europe is attractively commemorated in the Russian Orthodox Memorial Church built at the same time nearby, a little Kremlin whose scaly, fairytale spire is a piquant addition to the skyline.

There is, happily, an antidote to the demented militarism of the Battle of the Nations Memorial, about a mile away: the Rundling, a social-housing estate built during the Weimar Republic. The street names of this 'Ring', designed by Hubert Ritter in 1929, are taken directly from Wagner's *Ring* cycle, but enthusiasts for the anti-Semitic composer are unlikely to have been pleased with the architecture. This Ring is interwar Modernism at its purest and least ingratiating; sometimes, as in Frankfurt, Weimar Modernism – the New Building (*Neues Bauen*), the New Objectivity (*Neue Sachlichkeit*), as they called it at the time – can be unromantic to the point of bluntness, and you'll find yourself presented with a row of flat-roofed

The minimum dwelling

terraces or concrete bungalows, which don't seem quite so impressive as an alternative to the nineteenth-century city as they may have done in 1925. The Rundling, though, still convinces. A series of concentric circles with spokes on plan, and terraces of excellent flats with big balconies and lots of trees on the ground, it is light and spacious, coherent and collective. Munich, governed in the Weimar era already by the far right, has nothing like this – a *Neues Bauen* as a proposal for a new city which would abandon all the rhetoric, bombast and cutesiness that have otherwise defined so much of German architecture. The big round space in the middle is a little empty, though – maybe a Christmas market would liven it up.

The new Messe, where the trade fairs happen today, is best reached via the Leipzig S-Bahn, which has recently been expanded with several lofty, atmospheric underground stations. The need to get on a train that takes you to the edge of the city to go somewhere that was once in the city centre confirms Leipzig's peculiar encouraging of suburbanization, and then trying to chase after it with elegantly designed public transport. The Messe site is around the same size as the old, although it is much more organized and controlled as an architectural ensemble – two glass curtain-walled wings, redolent of Milton Keynes railway station, flanking a vast centralized hall, like one of those massive Wilhelmine *Bahnhofs* realized with a much bigger budget and better technologies. It seems senseless that it wasn't simply built on top of the straggling emptiness of the original Messe site, but it is much better connected to the *Autobahn* and the airport, and this, more than the tricksy politics of post-communist restitution,

New Messe

must be the pretext for its siting. A looping journey on a bus from here will take you to a twin of Munich's BMW-World, a factory complex also with the input of a computer-aided design team that was once big in the 1980s and 1990s. You're taken through a sprawling retail park – 'Saxon Park', presumably in the 'Anglo' sense – through lots of little houses (some of them rather big little houses), each with a locally made BMW in its driveway, out to open fields, and then, eventually, to the BMW-Werk, noticeable only by the greenwash of its wind turbines. The days when you could build a car factory and then connect it to the U-Bahn, as in 1970s Munich, are long gone; suburbs and cars do have a natural affinity after all.

Once you've actually got there, the BMW-Werk is considerably more rewarding than Coop Himmelb(l)au's

atrocious showroom in much richer, much more cohe-
sive, much more chic Munich. The factory buildings are
mostly corrugated-metal sheds, where robots and a couple
of thousand workers piece together and customize the
cars, but bringing them together is the Central Building,
designed – as a plaque set into the concrete tells you – by
Zaha Hadid Architects, London, in 2003. Hadid's architecture was always beset with the problem of reconciling the
image – frequently painted – that she would produce, of
kinetic, shuddering speed and movement, with her firm's
frequent inability to get the materials to manage to convey that in real physical space. But the BMW Central
Building is one of the places where it came close to achieving that aim. A long, lozenge-like corrugated-metal-clad
volume (here, the cheap material works with the context,
rather than seeming an unfortunate accident in amid all
the CGI bling), raised on four thick, inclined concrete columns, contains part of the car factory's assembly line, on
an elevated conveyor above the staff canteen and a BMW
gift shop. The partially assembled cars move slowly above
visitors (of which there are a few, despite the distance) and
factory workers alike.

The conveyor itself is the organizing principle for the
entire space, and it swoops around corners at whip-crack
angles, making for an incredibly exciting space if you are
a new visitor, and perhaps a tiring spectacle if you have to
deal with it every day. The bumf that you are handed
here as a non-worker will tell you that this space is actually all about working practices and encouraging the
different sections of the plant to congregate, but it seems
equally plausible that it is as much a front as Himmel-

Zaha Hadid's post-Fordist spectacle

b(l)au's showroom, a fireworks display for fans of architecture and motoring. Maybe. But, for a moment, it is a glimpse of an architecture of endless movement, achieving that impossible thing in an intrinsically static object. That it is here at all is the result of the schizophrenic politics of reunified Germany; first destroying East German industry, then coming back with some belated replacements, building arguably the world's best public transport systems and then extending them out to blank, aimless suburbs, pioneering green energy while maintaining and covetously protecting one of the world's premier auto industries. It clearly wasn't Hadid's intention, but to capture all this engineering skill, historical drama and utter hypocrisy in one building is some kind of feat.

Łódź, the Polish Manchester/Polish Hollywood/ Polish Detroit

The main street of Łódź, Piotrkowska, is the longest, flattest, straightest main street of any major city in Europe, and certainly of the European Union. Beginning with a complex of factories and lined on each side by tall, opulent (when restored) and *jolie-laide* (when not) commercial palaces, it points relentlessly onward, with the vanishing point uninterrupted by any turnings, any hills, any points on the vista, as if it could go on for ever. Beginning at the circus of Freedom Square, around a statue of the revolutionary Tadeusz Kościuszko, it drives on through some of the most encrusted, ornament-festooned buildings you'll

Morning in Piotrkowska

find anywhere – no turning is complete without a dome, no entrance without caryatids, few corners not supported by gnomes. It is quiet in the daytime but kicks off at night, its courtyards hiding dubious bars such as Łódź Kaliska, a hangout organized by the conceptual artists of the same name, decked out with 'ironic' photographs of the artists surrounded by large breasted women, in tableaux inspired by the great European paintings, its mirrored dancefloor with buzzcutted men and tall women dancing to dubious pop. Many of these palaces have neon signs from the 1970s, stuck there for so long they've since become fashionable. The mammoth Hotel Grand radiates a level of seediness seldom seen in the urban European Union; underfoot, you'll find a Hollywood hall of fame, with the likes of Roman Polanski immortalized by stars set into the pavement. Step off into a side street, and the caryatids have limbs falling off and the domes trees growing out of them – this sort of detail, when mocked up in plaster, falls apart quickly if not frequently cleaned and repaired. Continue a couple of miles down Piotrkowska, and you'll find a half-dozen stepped high-rise blocks looming just behind the courtyards. Even then, after ten or so visits to the city, I've never quite managed to find where the street ends.

Piotrkowska was planned in the second half of the nineteenth century in the far west of the Russian Empire, on the site of a conveniently placed village. It was laid out essentially as a New Town, an industrial city at the crossroads – for once that cliché is necessary – of the German and Russian worlds, stamped upon Poland, a country which the two empires had helped wipe from

the map at the end of the previous century. This was its
commercial centre, the shopping street, largely aimed
at the bourgeoisie who were, uniquely for nineteenth-
century Poland, created and dominant here. The street
has been spruced up of late with European Union money:
pedestrianized, some of its more monumental edifices
cleaned up, and bronze sculptures of its famous sons and
fictional characters dotted along the promenade. Trams
have been rerouted to the parallel Kościuszko Street, a
comparatively chaotic thoroughfare, one side of which
was demolished in the 1960s for an uncompleted modernization project, surviving mainly in the cement shoebox
of the Hotel Światowit, with its marvellous 1970s
neon signs. The brick gable ends of tenements are bare,
unrelieved except for adverts, street art and the odd
communist-era mural promoting the local wares. A photograph of Piotrkowska, empty – which seldom happens
unless you get up exceptionally early in the morning –
was printed in the habitually factually deficient British
tabloid the *Sun* a few years ago, to illustrate a story about
'the town that moved to Britain'. Łódź has not moved
to Britain, but its population has haemorrhaged in the
twenty-seven years since Poland achieved 'freedom'. For
most of the last hundred years it was the second-largest
city proper in Poland, but it has been overtaken by the
rather more conventionally attractive, more 'Polish' and
much more 'historic' Kraków, something more to do
with population collapse in Łódź than growth in Kraków.
It has become a classic shrinking city, evocative of all
manner of things people would rather forget – industry
and revolution, Stalinism and Fascism. Situated in the

most monolithically monoethnic country in Europe, it is a city that was multicultural from day one.

What was missed in the *Sun* story, somewhat unsurprisingly, was the fact that Łódź was modelled very precisely on the British cities to which its inhabitants have been moving since 2004. Of the cities in this book, the only examples to be more obviously influenced by British practice are Dublin and Nicosia, both capitals of former British colonies. Łódź was deliberately planned as a 'Manchester', at a time when the 'Little Parises' and 'Little Viennas' that dot Central, Southern and Eastern Europe came to be supplemented by 'Little Manchesters', built around red-brick Molochs of cotton mills, in which an industrial proletariat would labour at their machines and produce at a rate previously unimaginable. 'Manchester' was widely considered to be what had made Britain so rich and powerful, and if you wanted to follow suit, you built one. The Russian Empire alone had a few – Ivanovo, Narva and the suburbs of St Petersburg – but Łódź was always the largest.

In the 1970s, Andrzej Wajda made a film about the way in which this happened, and how it related to the tense multicultural politics of partitioned Poland. *The Promised Land* focuses on the efforts of a Pole, played by the charismatic Daniel Olbrychski, to go into a textile business dominated by factory owners of different nationalities: Germans (a character based on Karl Scheibler) and Yiddish-speaking Polish Jews (a character based on Izrael Poznański), under the administration of a Russian government; the proletariat driven into the mills was equally multicultural. The buildings, and the planning, of

Scheibler, Poznański and their contemporaries still dominate the city, and are central to its quixotic attempt to remake itself into a tourist draw. What sticks in the mind in Wajda's film, more than the machinations of his capitalists, is the depiction of industrial labour, something that makes you realize that nobody has ever really attempted to film an industrial revolution and what one did to people. The thudding, whirring cacophony of the lines of looms, which slice arms off careless members of the largely female workforce, is depicted through the fast, darting tracking shots of a slasher film. The reason Wajda could do this so convincingly is that few of the mills had significantly changed since the 1905 events the film depicts. By that time, the mills were largely devoted to churning out unspectacular product to markets to the east, easily done with the landscape from here flat all the way to the Urals. When the Comecon trade bloc collapsed, so too did Łódź, utterly unable to compete in the world market. The result: a city with a population of 850,000 in 1990 and 715,000 today, and with emigration the main solution to endemic unemployment.

As well as being Poland's Manchester, and, today, its Detroit, Łódź is also its Hollywood, the centre of the film industry that for a few decades between the 1950s and the 1980s made Poland, briefly, one of the great film-producing countries in the world. With directors like Wajda, Jerzy Skolimowski, Krzysztof Kieślowski, Roman Polanski, Agnieszka Holland and Andrzej Munk being trained there, and with many of the small production companies of the era working out of Łódź rather than Warsaw, the city became, unusually, both a cultural and an industrial centre. A perambulation of Łódź would once have begun at Łódź Fabryczna railway station, close to Piotrkowska, which has been closed for around six years at the time of writing in mid-2017, so that it can be transformed into the sort of mall and transport experience currently considered essential in European railway stations. When I was first taken to Łódź, in 2010 by my partner at the time – she thought I'd like it, and she was most definitely right – the area around the station, dominated by a large chemical works, was about to be transformed by none other than David Lynch into a combined cinema, arts and transcendental meditation centre – with the help of a local property developer, of course. That fell through, but Lynch did manage to film *Inland Empire* in the city, still able to provide the *Eraserhead*-like dilapidated steampunk landscapes that are no longer on offer in the cities of the United States. In front of the chemical works is a snarling statue of inter-war dictator and national hero Jozef Piłsudski and an ensemble of 1950s and 1970s towers, where the dark, sooty, vaguely Socialist Realist high-rise of the TV headquarters is more notable than the taller but blanker cut-price glass skyscrapers. This is a deceptive view of Łódź, as the city centre is otherwise very much visually untouched by 'Communism', something that oddly doesn't mean Łódź much resembles Lviv. Industrial aesthetics predate state Socialism. Flat, harsh, straight, this is the nineteenth-century city as practised in the north of England, not along the Danube; more Huddersfield than Budapest.

Much more typical, though, of the sort of city this is, is the Alexander Nevsky Cathedral, on Kilińskiego next

The Polish media is imposing

to Fabryczna station. Built in 1884, and funded by the city's industrial dignitaries such as Poznański and Scheibler to service Russian bureaucrats and Belarusian and Ukrainian workers with Orthodox ritual, it was designed by the city's main architect, Hilary Majewski, one of those typical nineteenth-century designers who could design in Gothic in the morning, Baroque in the afternoon and Byzantine in the evening. It has a wonderfully tasteless splendour, polychrome – blue, gold, green, orange – with an onion-topped tower and a spreading Byzantine dome. It doesn't look like a Pole's attempt to 'do' Russian architecture, but is one of many efforts in a pan-imperial neo-Russian style, which would distribute onion domes, and with them Russian power, across the

Alexander Nevsky Cathedral

skylines of cities that had never been part of Orthodox Europe – Warsaw, Tallinn, Vilnius, Riga. Yet the stylistic promiscuity of Łódź is such that the styles sometimes bleed between each other: the spindly red-brick towers of the St John Lutheran Church, built for the German industrialists and Silesian weavers, are Kremlin-like, and the dome of the Catholic Holy Trinity Church could be in Kiev as much as in Rome.

The missing dome on the nineteenth-century skyline is that of the Great Synagogue, once one of the world's largest, destroyed by the Nazis, who occupied and renamed the city Litzmannstadt after a Nazi general, and built a walled ghetto in one of Europe's most successfully multicultural cities. The defining event in twentieth-century

Łódź before 1939 was the 1905 revolution, a socialist rising centred on the textile mills, and where workers of all nationalities fought against the Tsarist government, before being brutally repressed; the city was celebrated for its heroism by such disparate figures as Lenin, Rosa Luxemburg and Jozef Piłsudski, a one-time socialist leader before he became a patriotic military dictator. There are few monuments to the revolutionaries in the centre – though there is at the time of writing still a '1905 Revolution Street'. There's a concrete monument in the Jozef Piłsudski Park, a couple of miles out of the centre, but mostly the revolutionary history of the city is something you find by chance, in murals and plaques hidden in public buildings.

The largest of the three huge factories that dominate Łódź to this day is the Izrael Poznański Factory, built in the early 1870s to Hilary Majewski's designs – it's here that *The Promised Land* was filmed. It is at the far north of Piotrkowska, and was built as a city within a city, including mills, power stations, workers' housing and the factory owner's palace. Remarkably, all of it is still intact as a complete ensemble, and the red brick has been so polished and sandblasted that it glows. If you've ever set foot in any major mill complex in the north-west of England you'll find it instantly familiar: the same scale – utterly monumental, the size of several street blocks, blunt and thuggish – but with some of the monumental motifs, half-Florentine, half-Russian, locating it geographically. The Poznański Factory has been comprehensively transformed and rebranded as 'Manufaktura', through an injection of EU capital to attract mall and leisure developers, and many of the new functions have been accommodated in

A hidden red mural

the old building. You can eat vegan food in part of the generating station, you can stay in a hotel (with a glass penthouse) in the main multistorey mill, and you can visit a branch of the Museum of Art, more of which later. In the middle, there is a large and windswept square, and a totally generic shopping mall. It's state of the art in the 'regeneration' of an industrial area, and it does all the sorts of things a development like this is meant to do: it generates jobs in retail, it brings businesses to set up shop there, it re-centres the city by putting all the stuff you can usually get in an out-of-town mall into the middle of town, and it brings tourists (me, several times). Poland itself hasn't actually deindustrialized, as the smoking chimneys of the country's far west make clear, but when

The back end of Manufaktura

it does, few old factories will find themselves as perfectly located as this, right in the centre of a big city. The centrality of Łódź's industry must have been unusual even at the time. Just right next to the ornate factory gates, Poznański's own palace is a lumbering composite of about ten different historic styles.

On the other side of the factory are the workers' tenements, all still there – grim, blackened little hovels, currently being gradually upgraded to be fit for human habitation. North of the factory is the 'Old Town', a diminutive Stalinist attempt to re-create the historic market town that the city never was, leading to streets of heavier Stalin-era tenements to a never-finished axial plan, with wide-open spaces between them and the post-1956 high-rises. Here, these are quite attractive, the Modernist contrast with

Victorian pollution and crowdedness a lot more apparent than it would be in a more rigorously 'zoned' city (the huge estates on the outskirts do not have this contrast, and are a lot less interesting as a result). These spaced-out towers and Moscow-style monumental tenements are on the site of the only part of the city to have been destroyed in the war – the Litzmannstadt ghetto, today demarcated, as in Warsaw, by a line set into the street. The ghetto here survived for longer than most, the city's industrial importance meaning that its inmates provided manual labour in atrocious conditions in the city's factories, rather than in one of the many nearby concentration camps. There are several memorials to the victims left there since the 1960s, and there is anti-Semitic graffiti, somewhat astonishingly – the extermination of nearly all Poland's Jews by the Nazis didn't manage to end Polish anti-Semitism. Like many of the nastier things in Poland, this is football-related – one of the local teams, Widzew, are considered 'Jewish', and the graffiti is actually aimed at them, though since the ghetto the graffiti is scribbled on was 'liquidated' in 1944, extremely few, if any, of their supporters could possibly be Jewish. The ignorance is head-spinning.

The menace easily found in residential Łódź is absent in the centre, and each of the major factory complexes has become a tourist site, of a sort. The archaeologist of nineteenth-century capitalism will find a similar sense of concentration in each of them, each one a microcosm. There are several, but the two largest and most restored are the White Factory, owned by the Saxon industrialist Ludwig Geyer, and the Księży Młyn ('Priest's Factory'),

The White Factory in the white snow

owned by Karl Scheibler. The White Factory is the earliest surviving, dating in parts from the 1830s, and has been home to the Central Textile Museum since the 1960s (though production continued in parts of it until the 1990s). This makes it a very good place to track where the components, particularly the spinning mills, came from. The factory is laconic, classical, white plaster over the local red brick, and relatively low-rise. Inside, you can admire the innovative construction techniques imported here from Manchester – an iron frame, enabling flowing spaces into which the engineers could lay out the complex production process. You can also note how the machinery – initially from Hattersley's of Keighley, Platt's of Oldham – was, by the 1930s, being imported from the United States, as the United Kingdom ceased to be the innovator in textile production. After 1945, any new machines there were made locally. There's also a very diverting display of textiles, both in terms of the variety of styles Łódź catered for in its 150 years of mass production, and in terms of 'art' textiles, commemorating and later satirizing historical events. The small park behind the factory has been turned into what they'd call here, using the Swedish term, a *Skansen* – an open-air museum of wooden buildings, something which bears next to no relation to this city here, but which is a delightful vision of the sort of place Poles feel they're supposed to like, wooden Art Nouveau villas, wooden farmhouses, wooden churches, deep in the trees, snow outside.

Housing in Łódź has always been about flats, whether nineteenth-century walk-ups or 1970s tower blocks, but outside the Scheibler factory are a couple of squares of terraces, modelled on the 'English style'. And they are indeed red-brick terraced houses, although there's no chance of it being mistaken for Oldham or Keighley, largely because they've been so obviously planned as a showcase, more an essay in the 'industrial philanthropic village' genre than in the long, speculative rows of streets that most workers inhabited in industrial England. There are neither front nor back gardens, just dark-red little houses in front of a tree-lined central park; at the end of it is the clocktower of the factory, imposing the carefully managed time of capitalist production upon these recently uprooted rural Poles, shtetl Jews and Silesian weavers. The factory buildings have, unlike in the other two big complexes, become *lofts*, for *loft living* in. Next to a plaque

Workers' housing, factory, clock

commemorating the visit of John Paul II to the workers in
1987 is another commemorating the more recent benedic-
tion of an Australian property developer. That is, they've
become luxury flats, rather optimistically, possibly to lure
students at the many educational facilities here to stay
here after their degrees. On the other hand, here, in Scheibler's palace adjacent to his mill, is the Museum of
Cinematography, and it's enough for a day's sightseeing
on its own. Not just because it 'tells the story' of the great
post-war Polish film school, which is what one might
expect, but because it's one cabinet of curiosities – full of
brilliant avant-garde film posters, fragments from sets
and, best of all, puppets from Surrealist children's
animation – overlaid onto another, the tasteless world
of the parvenu bourgeois, more complete here than just

about anywhere. Scheibler's taste runs from stoves encrusted with blue ceramic oculi (no central heating here) to several 'naked nymphs frolicking in the sky'-type frescoes on the ceiling, to chairs held up by terrifying half-woman, half-dog creatures. It's the interior-design equivalent of eating ten cream cakes at once. It explains a few things about Łódź – one, the violence and fervour with which it exploded in 1905 (the contrast between this house, and those built so close by for the workers – and these were the best of them! – is grotesque) and two, the imagination of many of the film directors, many of them specialists in strident moral assertion.

Another response to this can be found in the Museum of Art, which was placed in one of the Poznański dynasty's palaces, in 1930, by members of the a.r. group

Interior design, factory-baron style

of Łódź-based Constructivists – Katarzyna Kobro, Władysław Strzemiński and Henryk Stażewski. Even in the Piłsudski era the city was dominated by the Polish Socialist Party and its close allies, the Jewish Labour Bund, and the museum can be seen as part of their attempt to modernize this extremely Victorian and anti-egalitarian city. Although not as wild as the Scheibler House, these rooms, in a Romanesque villa with armadillo-like rustication, are still showcases of High Victorian bad taste and the mysterious creatures it creates. Into this, the Constructivists placed, pointedly, their design for the new everyday life. Strzemiński, a painter, and Kobro, a highly original abstract sculptor, had worked in Soviet Russia in its early years – Strzemiński in UNOVIS, the Suprematist abstract workshop presided over in Vitebsk, Belarus, by Kazimir Malevich, himself of Polish-Ukrainian background. When at UNOVIS, Strzemiński designed abstract agitprop posters. Returning to Poland in the early 1920s, the pair brought these ideas with them. Their collection still forms the basis of the museum, and much of it is arranged in the 'Neo-Plastic Room', aligning works by a.r. members themselves with those by Dutch De Stijl, German Bauhaus and Soviet Constructivist artists, through an all-embracing architectural design by Strzemiński himself, of primary colours, clearly defined volumes, and a grid of patterned roof-lights. The room was destroyed during the Nazi occupation, and Strzemiński reconstructed it after 1945. The dialogue of eclectic-modern is now supplemented by works 'commenting' on the Neo-Plastic Room, in the manner common to much contemporary art of thesis–antithesis–commentary.

Constructivism inside

The Museum of Art keeps its post-1945 collection – every bit as good as its interwar stock, especially good for Pop and Conceptualism, and able to hold exhibitions on a par with the Tate or MOMA, on figures from Pauline Boty to Ewa Partum – in several floors of Manufaktura, making it the most complete, and most interesting, modern-art museum between Berlin and Moscow. But to find its influence in urban space, the place to go is not to the Postmodern industrial-heritage consumer utopia of Manufaktura, but a small housing estate, Osiedle im. Józefa Montwiłła-Mireckiego. Planned at the turn of the 1930s, the estate was designed according to the same precepts as the Neo-Plastic Room. The point of Constructivism was never the creation of nice things in galleries, but the revolution of everyday life. Constructivism's clear-eyed approach to the modern,

Constructivism outside

mass-production world and all its incredible possibilities –
previously blocked by the fantasies of the industrialists'
palaces – marched out of the ateliers of Dessau, Vitebsk or
Łódź and into working-class everyday life, which artists
touchingly imagined was unaffected by bourgeois bad
taste. Their utopia can be found literally on the other side
of the railway tracks: go past the grandiose Orthodox,
Catholic, Jewish, Lutheran mausolea in the cemetery, past
the allotment gardens, and you'll find it. Like most of Łódź
outside the narrow strip of Piotrkowska, the estate looks
like it needs some help.

The plan is still there, obvious enough in its break
with the closed, claustrophobic blocks of the nineteenth
century. No front or back, no enclosed courtyards, just
blocks in space, sometimes throwing themselves out into

geometrical arrangements so that the balconies could catch the sun. It was named after a socialist activist, killed by Tsarist troops in 1905, and the streets were and are still named after revolutionaries. Typically for interwar 'workers' housing estates' from Wythenshawe to Brussels to Leipzig, they were too expensive for the unskilled factory hands who made up most of the population – but Strzemiński and Kobro moved in, immortalized now by a plaque.

Łódź today has banked a lot on regeneration through culture and heritage, as if unsure what else could possibly work in a city whose purpose has been evacuated. Unlike many cities to resort to this out of desperation, it has more than enough culture in the first place. That this won't be enough to sustain the city, especially if post-Brexit UK starts deporting its citizens back, is clear enough. There's another Poland suggested in this place, though. A country beset by a government obsessed with ethnic purity, paranoia, a conspiracy theory of history and a gross martyrological sentimentality, and a combination of thuggish statism and flat-tax neoliberal cargo cultism, has within it a city like this. It was an industrial dystopia, cruel, hypocritical and kitsch. But what it longed to become was a totally modern city, a multinational experiment, a socialist city-state, where artists and activists helped design housing estates and where some of the best films of the twentieth century were made round the corner from workers making things. Łódź is a living repository of that hope.

Lviv, a Hapsburg Capital

In the aftermath of the overthrow of the Ukrainian president, Viktor Yanukovych, when protests against the new
government in Crimea and eastern Ukraine blurred into
the machinations of Russian Special Forces, journalists
liked to make a little comparison in their travelogues. On
the one side, there were places like Kharkiv or Donetsk,
which were *Soviet*. They had statues of and streets named
after Lenin, they had heavy industry: ugly relics of a dead
empire. These would be contrasted with a visit to Lviv,
with its beautiful, Western, European architecture and
culture of proud patriotism – and it had completed its
'decommunization' of street names and monuments
already in the early 1990s. In these stories, Lviv is the
most European, least Soviet, and also, linguistically and
culturally, the most Ukrainian city in Ukraine, and the
implication is that everywhere is now following its lead.
Judged on a straightforward architectural and aesthetic
level, it's all true. You really can walk around Lviv, with
its Baroque domes, Neoclassical squares and fin-de-siècle
gardens, and imagine you're in an Austria that has
become suddenly impoverished and adopted the Cyrillic
alphabet. But what does that easy judgement reveal, and
what does it obscure?

Beautiful as it may be, Lviv's twentieth-century
history is as ugly as anywhere else in Europe, probably
more than most. Lviv – Lwów, Lemberg, Lvov – began
the century as one of the biggest cities in the Hapsburg
Empire: German-ruled, but Polish-, Yiddish- and

Lovely Lviv

Ukrainian-speaking, in that order. After 1918 it was one
of the main urban centres of the revived Poland, where
local politics were tense. Polonization measures led to
Ukrainian resistance, first from the left, and increasingly,
in the 1930s, as the famine next door made Communism
somewhat less appealing to western Ukrainians, the far
right, in the form of the Organization of Ukrainian
Nationalists (OUN). In 1939, Lviv was annexed to Soviet
Ukraine as part of the Molotov–Ribbentrop pact, and
thousands of people (in all of the city's ethnic groups)
were deported to Siberia. As the Nazis approached in
1941, the NKVD massacred anyone left in Lviv's prisons.
When the Wehrmacht arrived, the OUN – conflating
Jews and communists, as fascists did then and do now –
orchestrated the ferocious Lviv Pogrom, and attempted

to set up a Nazi-backed independent state, only to be rejected by the Germans, who wanted Ukraine as a colony, not an ally or even a puppet state. Even so, the two factions of the OUN collaborated with the Nazis – and the Holocaust – to varying degrees over the next few years. The OUN's more radical Bandera faction (OUN(B)) set up the Ukrainian Insurgent Army (UPA), whose main action in the war consisted of ethnically cleansing western Ukraine of Poles. After Lviv, and the other formerly Polish-controlled parts of Ukraine, were re-annexed into the Ukrainian SSR, Poles were expelled to formerly German Pomerania and Lower Silesia, and the Insurgent Army led a brutally fought rural insurgency against the Soviets and newly Sovietized Poland, suppressed with great ruthlessness by the 1950s.

Now, it would be asinine to suggest that this horrific history overdetermines Lviv today – though similar generalizations are routinely made about eastern Ukraine. If nothing else, Lviv in the 1940s and 1950s was another reminder that being European and being barbaric are in no way mutually exclusive. But, ethnic cleansing aside, what is it that makes a place 'European'? And what is it that makes Lviv 'non-Soviet'?

Lviv was founded as part of the medieval kingdom of Ruthenia, but its architectural form comes from the Polish–Lithuanian Commonwealth, a vast, peculiar state which existed from the sixteenth until the eighteenth century. An anarchic Polish aristocracy commanded an enormous multi-ethnic territory that, at its height, stretched from the borders of Denmark to Smolensk. Fiercely Catholic, the Commonwealth's rulers were enthusiasts for the Counter-Reformation, the reason why its major cities – Kraków, Vilnius, Lviv – took Baroque and Rococo design to florid, picturesque extremes. A Vilnius native, Czesław Miłosz, compared its architecture to that of colonial Latin America, and both politically and aesthetically there's much in that comparison. Central Lviv is full of the sort of architecture tourists love, and there is nothing wrong with that in principle. Any city would love to have something like the encrusted high Baroque of the Bernardine church, or the later, more serene Dominican church and monastery; the architects were Dutch and Italian, respectively. Similarly, anywhere would be proud of the Rynok, with its gabled townhouses, full of sgraffito and reliefs, around the Renaissance tower of the town hall. A lot of Lviv Baroque is of the most fruity, obsessive sort, like the organic figures and motifs crowded onto the façade of the Boyim Chapel.

Rather than being kept as a relic, fit only for snapshots, souvenir shops and stag parties (as it would surely have become in a few years had war not led to the cheap airlines cancelling their budget flights), there's an actual living city occupying all of this. On an informal little square, between the two Baroque beauties of the Dominican church and the Dormition Church, beneath a colossal statue of the sixteenth-century printer Ivan Fedorov, there's the best book market I've found anywhere in Ukraine. The streets around the Rynok are full of interesting cafés and bars, used by the city's large student population. Here, judging by the youth of the residents and the anti-homophobic graffiti ('LGBT RIGHTS = HUMAN RIGHTS', stencilled, in

Florence on the Carpathians

English – quite a sight in Ukraine), Lviv appears precisely the progressive European cultural capital its admirers claim it to be.

If there's one architectural era as popular as the Renaissance and the Baroque, it's the fin-de-siècle, particularly courtesy of the Hapsburg Empire. Lviv was the largest city in Galicia, the morsel of the Polish–Lithuanian Commonwealth taken by Austria when Poland was carved up between the imperial powers at the end of the eighteenth century. Galicia itself was notoriously poor (as it still is – in 2013, before the revolution and the war, income and GDP in the region were far lower in Galicia than in Donbas), but in terms of cultural and national policy the Hapsburgs were rather more enlightened than the brutally nation-building Prussians and Russians. A large degree of linguistic and educational autonomy was permitted for Poles and Ukrainians. In the 1870s, Lviv was made the capital of a semi-autonomous Galician province, and its parliament was built in the city, along with the obligatory *Ringstrasse*, a green circular boulevard boasting the usual opulent, overripe neo-Baroque opera houses, theatres, museums, universities and bourgeois apartment blocks.

The Hapsburgs had an International Style, deliberately creating a familiar environment whether you were in Trieste, Zagreb, Budapest, Cluj, Vienna, Prague or Lviv. Full of clichés and mannerisms though it may be, the style resulted in some of the easiest, most elegant townscapes of the late nineteenth century, something which often lulls observers into assuming the empire to have been richer and more developed than it was. Even so, in 1914 Lviv was a growing, powerful city, and the streets of tenements that wind around the centre are exceptionally attractive, with plenty of iron and majolica Vienna *Secession* experiments around the balconies and gables. The city's grim history has left some scars, but they're hard to find – the great Rococo bulb of St George's Cathedral, for instance, conceals a shoddy restoration with a supermarket-style wipeclean floor, the result of its transformation into an Orthodox church in the 1940s, and its re-Catholicization in the 1990s. Mostly, it's complete. Interwar Lviv added little to the picture, aside from some chic Moderne buildings, and a few interesting experiments like the ship-style municipal power plant, just outside the centre, now used as offices by the security services, of all people. Lviv is hilly, so the bosky, winding streets – with just the right measure of tasteful decay – often have views of towers and domes. How wonderful to see a city left alone by bombers and communist town planners . . .

Soviet Lviv, from 1945 to 1991, did indeed leave the historic centre alone, as Soviet planners usually did, hence all the stag parties to Vilnius, Prague, Budapest *et al*. The odd bit of heavy, spiky Socialist Realism lurks in the inner suburbs, but the place to survey Soviet power in Lviv is the Hotel Dnister, a glass and concrete slab instantly recognizable as a product of Intourist, inserted subtly into a corner street next to the lovely Ivan Franko Park, so you can't actually see it unless you're looking for it. Look at Linda Alexeyeva and Grigory Ostrovsky's 1987 *Lvov: A Guide*, and they recommend starting here, from the panorama on the ninth floor, where you can survey that Florentine skyline. You can also see just beyond it the exact same prefabricated slabs and points that surround every other Soviet city, and the authors are proud of them. 'Whereas before Soviet power was established in Lvov there were well-built residential and public buildings only in the centre and certain privileged districts, they are now to be found all over the town, and of course, in the industrial areas, where tens of thousands of workers live. As far as the housing standards go, there is now no difference between the centre and the outlying suburbs.' In standards, perhaps. In aesthetics, not. Lviv got the same stuff here as Donetsk did.

However, even within the pre-Soviet borders of the city, there are plenty of remnants to find, even after Lviv's precocious Leninoclasm in the 1990s. For one, there's the

1964 red-granite statue of the poet and journalist Ivan Franko, chisel-cheeked and fierce, surrounded by insurgent workers, opposite the old Galician parliament. Franko was one of the founders of Ukrainian nationalism, but very much a figure of the left, and the first translator of *Das Kapital* into the Ukrainian language – so, along with the ubiquitous Taras Shevchenko and the socialist poetess Lesya Ukrainka, he has the rare honour of being honoured by both Soviet and post-Soviet Ukraine. Just outside the centre, the Bogdan Khmelnitsky Park of Culture and Leisure is a typical mini-Gorky Park, with a Stalinist-classical porte cochère leading to a path which rises up, step by step, to culminate in the Memorial to the Valour of the Soviet Armed Forces, winner of the Taras Shevchenko State Prize of the Ukrainian SSR for 1972. The otherwise so totalizing, blanket de-communization laws have a clause leaving Red Army memorials alone. Alexeyeva and Ostrovsky tell us that 'the combination of dominating vertical and horizontal lines, massive forms and stark, concise contours create a complex and yet harmonious whole and give the monument heroic stature'. It is undeniably impressive, and like many late-Soviet memorials has a powerful and uneasy combination of macho figuration – the detailed narratives of fighting and mourning, in realistic bronzes – and abstraction, in the hard polygons into which the stories are fixed. The hammer and sickle and the words 'VICTORY OVER FASCISM' remain in place and, presumably, will remain so. Just opposite is the local HQ of the Ukrainian Army, with a screen in front of it blasting out recruitment videos; militarism in both eras, side by side.

That continuity is much more in evidence along the nearby Stepan Bandera Street. Unveiled in 2007, the monument to the OUN(B)'s leader is ironically and comically Soviet in its architectural expression. A tall curved colonnade that looks not unlike a gallows is made of the same polished red granite boasted by almost every Lenin memorial; and in front of that the bronze figure of Bandera strides purposefully, his trenchcoat's billowing captured for ever in stone. Give him a goatee and then tell me who he looks like. Yet while Lenin's ideas were hardly reducible to Stalinism, Bandera's legacy of ethnic cleansing and senseless violence is purely a politics of hatred and racism. The 'decommunization' laws – drafted, after all, by Yuriy Shukhevych, loyal son of Bandera's OUN/UPA colleague Roman Shukhevych – legally

'Victory Over Fascism'

mandate the construction of monuments to the OUN, so there'll be more in this vein to come. Yet the statue is used in the same casual way as any other authoritarian monument, with the same lunchtime loiterers, drunks and skateboarders.

There is one Soviet thing in Lviv that is genuinely surprising, and its deft avoidance of political symbolism means that the only threat to it would be developers, not ideology. Lviv Circus, built in 1968, is a big, jolly piece of pop Modernism whose lightness and levity are deeply incongruous in Lviv. Next to it is a playground made up of sculptures – little men, monsters, creatures, animals, covered in mosaic, shaped into slides, swings and climbing frames. It's a beautiful place, surreal, cute and unmistakeably Soviet and Modernist, and it contrasts as

'Victory of Fascism'

The Circus

See-saw

sharply with the pompous Socialist Realist blocks on one side of the street as it does with the fading Hapsburg grandeur on the other. A year after I visited the city, most of these delightful sculptures were destroyed. A short walk away in Ivan Franko Park is another playground, which, kindly, the French processed-cheese company Laughing Cow have sponsored for Lviv City Council. Their brand is stamped on its every swing and round-about. Europe, after all.

4 Balkan

Split, Numbers 1, 2 and 3

Within the Schengen zone, you can traverse the once-bloodsoaked distance between Tallinn and Lisbon on high-speed trains without needing a passport, shunting between pedestrianized historic cities, full of marvellous new buildings, galleries – Kraftwerk's 'Europe Endless'. But, even within it, there's another EU, where barely functioning rail systems can't connect up individual countries, let alone link to neighbours. Nationalism is on the rise, those lovely historic cities are choked to death by tourism, a retail park exurbia as grim as anything in the USA spreads at the edge of every city. That's the Europe you arrive at when you disembark at the railway station in Split, the second city of Croatia – the Union's third-poorest, most recent, and probably last, member. If you manage to get your train – on returning, mine was cancelled ten minutes before arrival and replaced with a coach – you'll find a tiny, rotting, semi-derelict station. The rail connections between Croatian cities mostly go through non-EU territory in Bosnia-Herzegovina, so have been barely reliable since the wars of the 1990s. No gliding between Schengen states here. Croatia is now in the club, the one Bosnia, Serbia, Montenegro, Macedonia, Kosovo, Albania, Turkey may never get to join – but its neglected historic infrastructure disobeys its new categorization, enmeshing it into a Balkans it would prefer to ignore – something so much easier in, say, Slovenia, whose Alpine location makes it easier to act as if the sole historic link is with Austria.

Just outside Split's residual railway station, you'll find a rookery of stalls selling Chinese-made Split-related tat, looked over by a looming statue of Franjo Tudjman, the founding president of Croatia, who, in terms of post-Yugoslav leaders, presided over war crimes and ethnic cleansing on a scale exceeded only by Serbia's Slobodan Milošević. It's an ugly scene, suggesting somewhere cheap, nasty and nationalistic; and Croatia's current regime is very right-wing indeed. However, Split is, historically, anything but insular. This port on a peninsula jutting into the Adriatic has been claimed by a dizzying number of European states. Among others, the Roman Empire, the Byzantine Empire, the Kingdom of Bosnia, the Venetian Republic, the French Empire, Austria–Hungary, Yugoslavia (in both monarchist and socialist variants), Mussolini's Italy, the fascist Independent State of Croatia, and, since 1991, an independent liberal-ish democracy. However, the two states which have had the most effect on its built environment – and certainly produced the most interesting architecture – are the first and the second to last: the Roman Empire and the post-war Socialist Federal Republic of Yugoslavia.

Split emerged within the shell of the Palace of

Diocletian's peristyle

Diocletian, completed in AD 305, close to the large Roman–Illyrian city of Salona. It is an imposing, subtle design, fortifications enclosing a sequence of grand spaces, around a haunting central peristyle, many of its features familiar from the borrowings of eighteenth-century Neoclassicists such as Robert Adam, who published a book on it. The palace is the most convincing example in Aldo Rossi's *The Architecture of the City* of the 'locus', the architectural structure so strong that it can define an entire city within itself. In Diocletian's palace, this happened in a very literal way. When Salona was besieged during the barbarian invasions that ended the Western Roman Empire, its inhabitants sheltered in the abandoned palace, and over the centuries bent it to their needs. Hundreds of tenements were built in the spaces of, and with materials plundered from, the grand corridors and boudoirs, and the elaborate basements became a rudimentary sanitation system. The result has a certain historical justice, as a complex intended for the comfort (and worship) of an absolute emperor became a shelter for thousands of refugees. The possible fate for a post-apocalyptic One Hyde Park, perhaps.

Although the Roman architecture was treated roughly – the joins are obvious, where chaotic masonry is piled on top of the cleanly cut Roman limestone – the shanty town the refugees and their descendants built still, as Rossi makes clear, bears the clear outlines of the original palace's structure, and the peristyle remains the central feature. Walking around it is an elaborate guessing game. The route through the peristyle leads to a roofless rotunda with an open oculus, or, below, to a brick crypt; fragments from Diocletian's mausoleum were piled up into the tiered Romanesque tower of Split Cathedral, but the mausoleum's outline is still clear round the back; tightly packed tenements give way to traces of the palace's hydraulic engineering, and washing is hung out over lonely Corinthian columns, visible through cyclopean archways. It's extraordinary, though it would all be a lot more so were it not also the home of sundry crap tourist restaurants and barrier-like rows of souvenir stalls.

Around the palace is a long, recently renovated quayside corso and the Venetian city, with its instantly recognizable triangular belltowers and pointed-arched palaces, mostly in extremely narrow streets. The only pre-twentieth-century civic gesture, aside from the accidental one of the peristyle,

Diocletian's washing line

is the Venetian architect Giovanni Battista Meduna's Prokurative, a colonnaded square in scarlet overlooking the Adriatic, begun in the 1860s and completed half a century later. There's a scattering of interesting things immediately around that – the typically Hapsburg National Theatre, a yellow stucco and glass *Secession* façade which could be anywhere in the Austro-Hungarian Empire, packed streets of limestone tenements with tiny, shuttered windows, and a few worthwhile villas and apartment blocks in nautical streamline Moderne style – but the 'other' Split is that built between 1945 and 1991.

In the 1960s, Yugoslav planners divided the city into 'Split 1', the palace; 'Split 2', the unplanned city that had grown up around it; and 'Split 3', a planned extension that would run eastwards along the Adriatic coast. 'Split 2' was infilled with a variety of strong Modernist structures, such as the laconic, classically proportioned Prima department store opposite the National Theatre, or Dobri Square, a once-sleek ensemble just north of the historic centre. A series of stepped-section apartment blocks rises up the cliffs above the port. These all share the gleaming whiteness of the local limestone tenements, but the jumbled arrangements are smoothed out into more conscious compositions. This is all elegant modern architecture, more redolent of affluent, Alpine countries than the quickly built prefab blocks notorious in 'communist' Europe. That's partly because Yugoslavia was an odd geopolitical exception between the 1940s and 1980s. Internationally part of the Non-Aligned Movement, which it formed with ex-colonial countries like India, Indonesia and Egypt,

Dobri Square

internally its system was 'Self-Management Socialism', where workers legally and practically controlled their own industries. Housing was owned and allocated by the self-managed workplaces, not by the state.

Accordingly, Yugoslavia was able to traverse the binaries of 'West' and 'East', and was markedly outgoing and internationalist in its outlook. So Split 3, this tripling of the city's size, was not going to be a numbers game, but an experiment. Modernist in conception, made up of towers and slabs raised above car parking, it would nonetheless attempt to factor in streets, in an attempt to create an attractive communal life rather than empty spaces. The pan-Yugoslav designers – a Slovenian planning team headed by Vladimir Munić, with Croatian architects, Ivo Radić and Dinko Kovačić – contacted Jane Jacobs herself to assess the completed estate. Apparently, she approved. You reach Split 3 walking east from the city centre, past some more 'normal' 1960s housing estates. The difference is obvious, as you go from vague in-between spaces turned into car parks, into a series of wide, stoneclad walkways. Split 3's central 'street' projects outward as steps lead down towards the sea, flanked by polygonal, low-rise offices, shops, and about a dozen bars and cafés. Were it not for the melodramatic Brutalist cruisers above them, with their cantilevered balconies and turret-like service towers, these small blocks processing their way to the Adriatic might recall Louis Kahn's Salk Institute in San Diego and its alignment with the Pacific. It is both an awe-inspiring vista and a clearly very successful, ordinary pedestrian space. A plaque with an inscription reads 'Tehnogradnja 1976': Techno City, 1976.

Walkways of Split 3

Walk along the street – it cleverly dips below the main service road, to form an arcade – and you assume it will lead, as it appears to, straight to the sea. It doesn't. Split 3 was left unfinished in the 1980s, and the main street reaches instead an overgrown ravine, marked by allotments, abandoned hotels with rotting reinforcement jutting out of the concrete balconies, an incongruous and careless new Radisson, and wasteland. Get past this, and you find more stepped-section blocks and a beach, evidently part of the same composition as the Brutalist streets above, but unconnected to them.

Nothing much has happened since Split 3 was left unfinished over thirty years ago. A small extension has been built in recent years for the University of Split, some of which is decent, such as Jasmin Semović's 2008 University Library, a multistorey glass block on pilotis, happily connected to the walkways of Split 3 rather than aloof from them. Then there's some grim exurbia a couple of miles beyond that, best passed over in silence. Within the city limits, Split has conserved what it does have, and has refrained from (or hasn't had money for) adding anything meretricious to the skyline, but the ruined railway station makes clear just how steep the decline has been since 1991. There's an odd symmetry between the Roman palace turned into a chaotic bazaar first by early-medieval emergency and then by neoliberal tourism, and the way that Split 3 was left as an unfinished grand blueprint ending in weeds, ruins and speculation. Both also happen to share a street life that is not common to their typology. However, Split's roots are so deep, and so strange, that it is hard to imagine this stasis will be permanent.

A mile or so north of Diocletian's palace are the estate of Split–Poljud – striking, almost medieval towers leading to the city's northward terminus – and the Hajduk Split football stadium, an unusual design by Boris Magaš, its seats formed into a half-opened oyster crouching in the shadow of the craggy limestone peaks of the Dinaric Alps. Nearby is the Archaeology Museum, built in 1914 to the designs of the Austrian architects Friedrich Ohmann and August Kirstein, at the end of Split's tenure in the Hapsburg Empire. Curiously for a country and city that often define themselves as a Catholic bastion against the nearby Orthodox Christians of Serbia and, even closer, the Muslims of Bosnia–Herzegovina, it is a very 'Eastern' design, its chunky rusticated stonework and red-tiled

Hajduk and the Dinaric Alps

A Roman tomb

roof more Byzantine than classical Roman. Inside, there isn't much from Diocletian's palace – so many people live there that it will probably never be possible to make a full excavation – but in an open-air exhibit in the courtyard is an almost complete necropolis, taken from abandoned Salona. Every variant of Roman tomb, devoted to every cult, with monuments to patricians and plebeians, freemen and slaves, men and women, but all in a recognizable, realistic Roman style. It is a museum of monumental sculpture, a showcase of ancient typography and an act of creative grave robbing. The world it presents is fascinating, but of the three cities that have existed here, give me Split 3.

No, No, No, No: Thessaloniki

One potential criticism of the European Union is that, for all its pretensions to be universal and post-ideological, a model for the world, it's really a rebranding of something much older and much more exclusive: Christendom. Accordingly, the EU excludes, for the most part, the large chunk of South-Eastern Europe that spent hundreds of years as part of the Ottoman Empire. The only exceptions are Greece, Cyprus, Bulgaria and, partly, Romania. From 1453 until 1912, Thessaloniki was the second city of that empire, as it had been for the Byzantine Empire before it. A hundred years ago, Thessaloniki (Salonika, Salonik, Solun) was the home to a majority population of Spanish-speaking Sephardic Jews, with the rest divided nearly equally between Greeks, Turks and Bulgarians. It was famed for a picturesque skyline of domes and minarets. In 2015, it is an almost entirely Greek city, and has one of the bluntest, flattest skylines of any European metropolis.

As the second city of the Hellenic Republic, it's a declining industrial centre, a university town and a strongly left-wing city. Syriza won the city comfortably at both elections in 2015, and during the September elections, when I visited, the city was dominated by posters and graffiti for groups further left, like Anatarsya and the Communist Party of Greece. Syriza's manifesto, on which they were elected in January, was and is known as the 'Thessaloniki Programme'. It promised a decisive break with austerity, in favour of public ownership and public works. There's little doubt that it had much support here, as did the 'No' vote on the bailout referendum – some streets are still lined by a repeated, spray-painted 'NO NO NO NO'. The current bail-out terms make it legally impossible for Syriza to actually implement the Thessalonki Programme.

Thessaloniki was liberated from the Ottomans in 1912, and – entirely coincidentally – suffered a severe fire in 1917. The city's new authorities got in the Beaux Arts planners to provide a replacement for the chaotic, unplanned streets. According to the historian Mark Mazower, in his book on the city, this provided a decisive 'Europeanizing' change, but he notes that the city had already undergone modernization – wider streets, trams, sewers – under the Ottomans for some decades. The French architect Ernest Hébrard placed a grid over the city's (Jewish and Greek) 'lower town' and largely left the (then largely Turkish) 'upper town' alone. The main thoroughfare of the city

After the referendum

since the Roman era, Via Egnatia, was widened, with the curious consequence that the Roman triumphal arch that once straddled the street became a relic at the foot of a pedestrianized square instead. Hébrard's project also entailed de-Ottomanizing the city, removing minarets at such a rate that, eventually, only two survived, and orienting the new streets around the city's Roman and, more interestingly, Byzantine monuments. Its mosques and synagogues were neglected, and the latter were almost entirely destroyed during the Nazi occupation. So it's not too strong to suggest that Hébrard's plan assisted, albeit passively, the eventual homogenization of the city. However, something happened in the 1960s that meant all his efforts to create an elegant Beaux Arts metropolis came to little.

Greece's transformation between the 1950s and 1970s into an urban and industrial country had fairly drastic effects on Thessaloniki. Hébrard's planned lower town, originally filled with Art Nouveau and streamline Moderne blocks of four storeys, was suddenly taken over by a rash of speculative blocks, almost all of 8–10 storeys, in concrete with glazed balconies. It is an interesting contrast to other parts of the Balkans. Here developers, rather than communist bureaucracies, were the drivers of urbanization; instead of the largely preserved Old Towns and slabs in green space on the outskirts you'd find in the same era in nearby Bulgaria, the historic city centre became the space for riotous speculation, with cramped tenements to the street, shops and cafés to the ground floor and shabby courtyards behind, where nobody's looking. It's what would have happened everywhere else had they read the advice of Jane Jacobs about what makes a city 'vibrant'. It

also has the unintended effect that Hébrard's axial planning only makes sense in a tiny handful of places, because
the Byzantine domes the streets are meant to lead to are
dwarfed by the cliffs of flats everywhere.

Although they look a lot more diminutive than they
ought to, the Byzantine churches of the city are genuinely
extraordinary – the city is on the UNESCO list as having the
best-preserved Byzantine legacy of any city anywhere.
Hébrard's plan was actually quite enlightened for its time in
valuing Byzantine work as much as Roman or ancient
Greek (it's unfortunate maybe that he didn't get round to
making a similarly revisionist judgement on Ottoman
architecture). The central church is another Hagia Sophia,
considerably smaller than its Istanbul namesake and built
much later, in the eighth century. Approached from the
west, it's a Greek cross plan with a dome, with a flat front,

Byzantium and speculation

painted a worn yellow; from the east, its apse is in the bare local red brick. It is given lots of space, with a big square around it, which makes it even less dominant, rather than more, in the tall streets around, but the interior is staggering. Lit by strategic shafts of light from windows just below the dome, its structure marked out by green and red patterns, it is rich, dark. Gold mosaics, in the severe Byzantine manner – staring straight and clear at the worshippers – cover the apse and the dome, which is much more impressive inside than it looks from the street.

You can track the development of Byzantine architecture across the city, if you want to – from the long, double-height arcades and clear open spaces of the early-seventh-century Hagios Demetrios, to the cluster of multiple domes and decorative brick patterns in the remarkable St Panteleimon, from 500 years later – united mainly by their intricate red brick and the Orthodox mosaics and wall paintings. All of these were converted into mosques after the conquest, and reconsecrated as Christian churches only after 1912. Given the polarization of the politics – Muslim residents of Thessaloniki were 'exchanged' with Christians from Smyrna/İzmir in the 1920s, in an act of mutual ethnic cleansing – it is worth noting that the two major surviving Muslim monuments are architecturally clearly of the same family as the Byzantine churches. Although they're both much less well-restored. These are the Bey Hamam, a bathhouse, and the Hamza Bey Mosque, both built soon after conquest in the fifteenth century. They're both on Egnatia, and their multiple domes and raw, unpretentious red brick are clearly derived from the city's architectural traditions, which you can date as early as the fourth-century Rotunda of Galerius, a massive structure which has been mausoleum, church, mosque and now occasional concert hall. Outside it is the city centre's only surviving minaret. As for the Jews who were the largest group in the city right up to the eve of the Holocaust, they're remembered only in a small museum and the Monastir synagogue, a surprising presence in an unassuming side street.

Twentieth-century planning meant a stripping from Thessaloniki of any shred of exotica, the slightest whiff of the 'Orient'. Because it also lacks, say, the quiet, brightly painted Neoclassical streets you can find in the centre of Athens, it's never going to be a tourist draw, something which may explain why it has quite so many exceptionally pleasant and cheap cafés. It also has one great moment, to give Hébrard his due – Aristotelous Square, planned in

Monastir synagogue

1918 and completed after the Second World War. It leads from a statue of Greece's unifier, the liberal politician Eleftherios Venizelos, to the sea, and is planned on an axis with Mount Olympus. Arcaded blocks lead down towards the water, with (very welcome, in Greek weather) colonnades, before spreading out to form a ceremonial open space. It's the obvious icon, if you will, of the city, a showcase of what aggressive planning makes possible.

The major Ottoman survival is actually the city's fortifications, which begin by the sea with the isolated 'White Tower'. From here you can survey that flat skyline, a single, unbroken file of ten-storey blocks, or you can explore some public buildings which say a great deal about Thessaloniki's self-presentation. There are two major, purpose-built museums in the city, both of the narratives that are considered most important. The classical heritage

Opening to the sea and Mount Olympus

is dealt with in the Archaeological Museum, completed in 1962 to designs by Patroklos Karantinos. It's post-war and Modernist – light, elegant, without any kitschy references to Ancient Greece. Its slim columns lead to a series of gardens, some of them with sarcophagi and sculptures left around, others with cafés. Its brightness and openness contrast with the nearby Museum of Byzantine Culture, which is, fittingly, a much more murky affair, in concrete and, of course, red brick. The 1977 design by the 'critical regionalist' Kyriakos Krokos – finished in 1993, by which time it must have been incredibly unfashionable – is best described as Byzantine Brutalism, though it is careful to avoid any obvious monumentality, consisting instead of shadowy pathways across overlaying levels.

These two excellent Modernist museums show the city's twentieth-century self-confidence better than the Hébrard

Byzantium and Brutalism

plan. The recent City Hall, designed in 2006 by Tassos Biris, continues the museums' interest in fragmentation, informality and the always useful shading. It's one of the few buildings from the more recent boom: Thessaloniki does not, from its architecture, appear to be a city that was in any way spendthrift before the Greek economy's immolation in the Eurozone crisis. Like the Byzantine Museum, Thessaloniki City Hall verges on Brutalism, with two hard-edged concrete structures linked around a square. It's Brutalism of a more imaginative kind than the 1960s buildings of the Thessaloniki trade fair, where the usual Corbusian bullhorn profiles and grids do their thing around what must be the world's shortest telecommunications tower, a fun proto-high-tech design which only slightly exceeds the seemingly mandatory ten storeys inflicted on the city. When you make it up to the upper town for a panorama around the city, you can barely even see it.

The upper town is something of a ghost. Any route uphill will get you there. You could detour via the State Museum of Contemporary Art, housed in Moni Lazariston, a former late-Ottoman hospital; it boasts a terrific Soviet Constructivist collection, courtesy of the Moscow-born Greek diplomat and art collector George Costakis. From Hagia Sophia, it's easy to know when you're reaching the upper town, as you pass one of the few Ottoman houses – preserved by the Turkish government (whose embassy is next door) because it's where Kemal Atatürk grew up. The majority of the houses in the Old Town have been rebuilt in 1980s approximations of the Ottoman designs, rebuilding in painted concrete their cantilevered balconies and irregular skylines, though there are a few

The upper town

'authentic' survivals too. The fortress itself gives spectacular views of mountains, sea, and endless flat tenements. Looking at this, you could admire the way that Thessaloniki's architects and planners have avoided either monumentality or sentimentality. The lack of tourism, and the common sentiment that the city is 'ugly', is Europe looking at itself in the mirror and recoiling. However, Thessaloniki is, like the rest of Greece, in profound crisis – its economy strangled by the debt repayments insisted upon by the European Central Bank, and geographically the first port of call for migrants – from those nearby places that are not Europe – on their way elsewhere. Even that Thessaloniki Programme, which the ruling party was elected on, is officially blocked by European officials. Thessaloniki has staked a lot on being European, and residents might well have the right to ask whether it was worth it.

Instant History in Skopje

'Changes like this usually happen through wars and natural disasters.' Iskra Geshoska is describing to me something called 'Skopje 2014', a comprehensive plan to 'beautify' the city centre of the capital of Macedonia. It is seen at its most extreme along the River Vardar, where the construction work is intense on an instant nineteenth-century city centre, replete with more heroic statues than you'd find in most cities ten times its size. With astonishing speed, in around five years, a Modernist city has been transformed into a mini-Vegas. Along the river you'll find two very approximate reconstructions of historic buildings, and several oversized government headquarters in an idiom of Corinthian columns and mirrorglass that has been absent from most European cities since the late 1980s; these are linked by bridges lined by golden candelabras and yet more statues. Just behind these, you can see a 1960s city of Brutalist high-rises and office blocks, but many of these are undergoing an extraordinary redesign, as hollow Doric columns are affixed to slender concrete pillars.

For the government of the ex-Yugoslav Republic, this project will make their capital truly *European*, and link it, through a process of 'antiquitization', to the glorious past of Alexander the Great, which the Greeks would deny them (Greece has, absurdly, regularly blocked Macedonia's accession to NATO or the EU for its use of the name). For its opponents like Geshoska, of the Skopje NGO Kontrapunkt, who have campaigned against the new plan, it is a catastrophe, not least because the Skopje 2014 plan aims at

Art, Skopje 2014

erasing another plan altogether, one which was as futuristic as the present plan is deliberately retrograde – the 1965 Skopje City Centre Plan, by the Japanese architect Kenzo Tange. The two plans are totally opposed in their ideas about what a city is and what it is for: two incredibly extreme examples of Modernism and Postmodernism violently forced into the same space.

The 1965 plan was the result of a genuine natural disaster, the Skopje earthquake of 1963, which destroyed around 70 per cent of the city and buried tens of thousands of people under the rubble. As reflecting the Socialist Federal Republic of Yugoslavia's 'Non-Aligned' geopolitical status – communist, but outside the Soviet Bloc – the relief and reconstruction effort crossed the borders of the Cold War. Temporary, prefabricated housing estates were designed and donated by the USA, Denmark, Britain, Bulgaria; Polish planners applied their expertise in reconstructing destroyed cities; Switzerland contributed schools, Poland the Museum of Modern Art; the USSR contributed a concrete panel factory; American Universities offered scholarships to Macedonian architects; and a plan by the Greek firm Doxiadis Associates plotted the city's infrastructure and future growth. But the competition for the city centre was won by the Tokyo office of Kenzo Tange, who was then much feted for his Hiroshima Peace Museum and for a wildly ambitious plan for Tokyo Bay. Tange's planning was influenced by Metabolism, a Japanese movement for an architecture that would be adaptable, fast, ultra-modern

Art, Skopje 1965

and ultra-urban. In the 1960s Japan had the highest growth rates in the world, but the second-highest were in Yugoslavia: it wasn't so extravagant to imagine that the future of Tokyo and the future of Skopje might not to be too far apart.

Looking at the remnants of the plan from the Polish-designed Museum of Modern Art, a concrete and marble gallery placed at the top of the fifteenth-century Ottoman fortress, an architect, Vladimir Deskov (who worked on the Macedonian entry to the 2014 Venice Biennale, celebrating the Tange plan), tells me: 'The plan was a hundred years in advance of the city.' Historic Skopje is centred on the Old Bazaar, a series of winding, cobbled streets with a skyline of domes and minarets; by

Cyril and Methodius University, by Skopje Old Bazaar

the 1960s, a modern city had grown up around this, mostly on the other side of the Vardar, which marked an informal divide between the Christian and Muslim parts of the city. Recognizing this, Tange intended to bridge the two parts of the city through a 'City Wall', modelled partly on the curved walls of the fortress. Surrounding the centre like a modernized *Ringstrasse*, the wall consists of interlinked blocks that provide a strong, defining, monumental presence. The UN's seismic experts warned that the area around the river was the most vulnerable to another earthquake, so Tange planned the embankment as a green, open space, for cultural centres, concert halls and the like, which would help bring the two halves together. The City Wall was largely completed, although executed by Croatian architects rather than by Tange himself, but it never actually crossed the river. Various of the planned central buildings were realized on both sides: the clustered, sculptural forms of the SS Cyril and Methodius University and the extraordinary Opera and Ballet Theatre, both designed by Slovenian architects; and from Macedonian designers, the Telecommunications Centre, a strange, individualistic example of organic Brutalism, and the Trade Centre, a long, low shopping centre of overlapping terraces stepping subtly down to the river, its combination of enclosure and openness inspired by the structure of the bazaar. The result was a city where the monumental 'Wall', which had gardens and squares behind, enclosed a loose, green centre. It had no historical reminiscences in its details or imagery, but modelled its spaces on particular historical structures it found nearby: the bazaar, the fortress. Tall buildings were planned at strategic points, arranged like castles, as with the dramatically Brutalist Halls of Residence, a rough image of medieval futurism.

If this part of the plan was largely executed, the more ambitious City Gate was a failure from the start. A railway station designed by Tange was opened in 1980, a long, sleek steel and concrete tube on a high viaduct – but the complex system of towers and walkways which was supposed to lead from here, through the Trade Centre, to the river was never realized. Today this area consists of wasteland, informal housing, big box malls and new/old churches under reconstruction. In the 1980s, just as the reconstructed city had been mostly completed, the Yugoslav 'economic miracle' faltered, with mass unemployment and a huge national debt, which was exacerbated massively in the 1990s as the pan-Yugoslav economy collapsed into war. Macedonia stayed out of the war, but hundreds of thousands of workers, mostly recent incomers from the countryside, lost their jobs. Yet this alone doesn't explain the extreme nature of Skopje 2014.

The contrast between the two plans is best seen from the small park between the Trade Centre and the 1930s National Assembly, a rare survivor of the earthquake. A diarrhoea of statuary has flowed at random into the space between the two, variously celebrating Ancient Macedonia, the early twentieth-century anti-Ottoman nationalist insurgents of the Internal Macedonian Revolutionary Organization (the current ruling party considers itself their successor), sundry medieval kings and folk heroes, a rotunda decorated with Third Reich-esque golden statues, a monument to wartime partisans at a table on a

Halls of residence walkways

Welcome to Skopje

plinth, and of course a triumphal arch, which the government immediately listed as a 'national treasure' as soon as it was constructed – all crammed into a space the size of one city square, and all of them enormous.

There is no classical or Baroque symmetry in any of this: the sculptures have been scattered utterly randomly. They're the result of one of the central parts of Skopje 2014, an 'open call' for amateur sculptors. Populism is one of the most important parts of the plan, deliberately bypassing any notion of professionalism and expertise in favour of a heavily mediated 'people's choice' – though the prime minister, Nikolai Gruevski, has proudly proclaimed himself the author of the plan. Almost all the buildings surrounding these have been 'antiquitized' to cement the connection to Ancient Macedonia, with thin

Come and see the sights

classical dressings affixed to the concrete, glass and tile underneath. There is nothing like this in any other country that has democratic elections – the sort of demently authoritarian, wildly kitsch assemblage usually seen in autocracies and despotisms. The effect is North Korea without the planning, its 200-million-Euro (or more, depending on who you talk to) cost borne by the state, albeit via massive borrowing. Everything about Skopje 2014 is about façades, where the actual historic legacy is covered with a new narrative which concentrates on Greek-speaking warlords of the fourth century BC or Bulgarian revolutionaries of the 1900s. The minarets of the Old Bazaar are screened off by ludicrously tall monuments, the international modern buildings of the socialist era are given mock-classical dressings. The Opera and Ballet Theatre, a staggering work of architecture, its irregular, angled forms flowing down to the river, could have been built yesterday, but today it is screened off from view by structures that try (albeit with impressive ineptitude) to look like they were built a hundred or 2,000 years ago, with mock-nineteenth-century candelabras and a Roman portico with allegorical figures in what looks like gold lamé. I asked a member of staff at the theatre who was paying for all this, in one of the poorest countries of Europe. He replied: 'Well, I've not been paid in nine months, so I guess I am.'

How did the international project of 1965, in which the UN and the world's finest planners and architects reconstructed a city on the most advanced lines, fail to leave a legacy? Goran Janev, an anthropologist at SS Cyril and Methodius University, puts it down to the way that the links created in the 1960s were forcibly closed off, as former Yugoslav citizens, who could travel without visas to both sides of divided Europe before 1989, were suddenly pushed into isolation, their new passports worthless – 'I had five passports at one point in the 1990s.' Skopje 2014 has not passed without protest. The former head of the Macedonian Architects' Association, Cigi Danica Pavlovska, who trained with Alfred Roth, a Swiss designer who is one of the many major international figures to have work in the reconstructed city, tells me with some pride how a referendum managed to stop the Trade Centre being 'antiquitized'. However, it has all happened with breathtaking speed. While Tange's plan took twenty years to be (partially) completed, Skopje 2014 has transformed the city's look beyond recognition within just four years. Janev points out that this speed is part of the point, creating facts on the ground before municipalities or locals have the chance to react, a sort of urban shock doctrine (and shock is very much the effect). Yet, according to him, all this spectacle has a real purpose, cementing the networks of clientelism that keep Gruevski's party in power: 'All the nationalism and symbolism is just dust in our eyes, the point is profit.'

It is easy to laugh, and some will surely travel to the city just to see these hilariously clumsy statues of painters wielding paintbrushes, large-breasted maidens and the seemingly dozens of rugged warriors on horseback; as my Wizzair flight touched down, I overheard a middle-class English voice quip: 'Here we are, lads, Alexander the Great airport.' Many residents do not find it quite so amusing – a wave of protests in 2016 saw the statues, arches and 'marble' cladding regularly spattered with paint, in acts of justified vandalism. Nonetheless, a city which appears as if redesigned by the furnishers of *MTV Cribs* will appeal to those with a cruel sense of humour.

The differences between Skopje's two great plans are a stark vision of contemporary priorities. Equality replaced with populism, futurism with 'antiquitization', spaces by façades, the sublime by the 'pretty', internationalism by provincialism, architecture as function by architecture as language. Eccentric as it may look, the ideas behind Skopje 2014 are mainstream today, and those of Skopje 1965 usually summarized as 'the mistakes of the 1960s'. The city centre today is the terrifying end result. A city which was designed and built by experts and enthusiasts from across the entire world has become a stage set for petty thugs to realize their fantasies. Everyone who thinks they'd like a city where the traditionalists get to win over the Modernists should visit Skopje, to find out if they like what they see.

Sofia, Open City

The cities in this book fall into a few obvious categories.
The Year Zero open spaces of Le Havre or Narva, the
total preservation of Bologna and Lviv, and the pruning
of the past in Thessaloniki. The area around Serdika, the
central Metro station of Sofia, presents a much looser,
much more all-encompassing kind of city, where the past
is neither erased nor obsessively maintained. The station
entrance, in a clipped, Modernist style, gives out to a
sunken square, littered with tablets and foundations
from Sofia's Roman incarnation, after which the station
is named; a tiny, peasant-like Byzantine church is just
outside the entrance. Walk up the steps and look around,
and everything is happening at once. Around you are
two mosques, a minaret, a neo-Byzantine basilica, a
synagogue, a domed bathhouse, an interwar Moderne
high-rise, and a transplanted organ from Stalin's Moscow,
topped with a Kremlin spire. All of Sofia's histories –
Roman metropolis, Byzantine and Ottoman province,
interwar and communist capital – are on display, none of
it covered up with a veneer of 'European' good taste. The
only era that hasn't contributed much to the ensemble is
post-1989 Bulgarian capitalism, which has added only a
rather perfunctory angel atop a triumphal column, and a
lot of big adverts. Even so, the reaction of most architectural enthusiasts on getting out here would surely be:
'This is going to be fun.'

Exploring the area maintains the impression. You can't
do it chronologically, as no era dominates, at least not in the

Archaeology in the Hotel Balkan

The Largo

centre, but the earliest building is the Roman church of St George, an exceptionally early, fourth-century Christian basilica – a small, symmetrical rotunda of red brick, severe and ordered, with tenth-century frescoes inside, and surrounded with remains from Roman Serdika, which in turn are surrounded by that transplanted chunk of Stalinist Moscow, sitting in the publicly accessible courtyard of the Hotel Balkan, entered through a colonnade of neo-Byzantine columns and down a flight of steps. From the other side you can survey the Largo, the city's ostentatious Socialist Realist setpiece. Planned in the late 1940s and finished just after Stalin's death, it is a cousin to the likes of Berlin's Karl-Marx-Allee or Warsaw's Palace of Culture and Science but even more obviously Muscovite in its derivation. Designed by a Bulgarian team headed by Petso Zlatev, it has two flanking blocks, the TZUM department store and the Hotel Balkan, leading to a third, the former Communist Party headquarters, set in the middle of the wedge-shaped plan. If you've been to Moscow you'll know the idiom – rustication on the lower floors, arcading at the top, with a scattering of heroic statuary. The CP headquarters has been without its crowning red star since 1990, but the inspiration of the great spike at the top of its tiered neo-Baroque tower is easy to spot, a smaller cousin of Moscow's post-war 'seven sisters' skyscrapers. When you're standing in the middle of it, the Largo presents a total and totalitarian image, but it's only a fragment, easily escaped into the messier surrounding streets.

If this overpowering presence of an era usually considered shameful isn't enough, there are also a lot of Ottoman fragments left around in prominent places. The Archaeological Museum, just off the Largo, is a conversion of the fourteenth-century Grand Mosque. It's only lightly remodelled, and the original purpose is clear. Stone and brick to the street, the multiple domes of the interior house exhibits which are not as ecumenical as Sofia's urban planning, as 'archaeology' stops with the Ottoman conquest. However, much as the restorers of the churches turned into mosques under the 'Turkish yoke' peeled off their Islamic decoration and revealed the frescoes beneath, here the whitewash applied when the building became a museum is scratched off on parts of the domes so you can see the Turkish decoration peep out. On the other side of the Largo, there's St Nedelya, the best of Sofia's several nineteenth-century neo-Byzantine churches – big, heavy, powerful, and convincingly ancient-looking. Further north is the synagogue, overripe and eclectic, with a bulbous black dome and vaguely Moorish ornament – it's very large and prominent for a synagogue, which speaks well of Sofia. Opposite this is the slightly over-restored Central Market, opened in 1911: one part Victorian iron and glass hall, one part Balkan bazaar. Across the road is the Banya Bashi Mosque, a sixteenth-century design of the great Mimar Sinan. Inside, it's a disappointment, currently dominated by the ad hoc frames put up to stop the dome from collapsing, but as an urban object it has real grandeur, pulling the accidental ensemble together. Across a small green square is a bathhouse, recently converted to the Museum of Sofia, with more domes and more patterns and polychrome tiles. At midday, the overdriven speakers at the top of the minaret blast out a distorted muezzin, and Sofia is the perfect Balkan metropolis, with all the area's cultures and eras present and peacefully coexisting – architecturally, at any rate.

Sofia mosque

Sofia bathhouse

There's another, less interesting, more official city centre in Sofia, towards the ditch-like Perlovska river. It consists of several dull Viennese-designed civic and political structures, the brutal, stripped-bare early-Byzantine Hagia Sophia, and the pompous, opulent Alexander Nevsky Cathedral, designed by the prolific Russian imperial architect Alexander Pomerantsev. It's a gilded gift from Bulgaria's long-time ally, and as grossly, unimaginatively retrograde as Moscow's Cathedral of Christ the Saviour. Russian architecture is better represented by the Orthodox Baroque of the much smaller St Nicholas the Miracle Maker, just near by. Walk along the river southwards towards the peak of Mount Vitosha and you'll find more fragments of much later Russian imperial architecture, such as the Stalinist classicism of the Vasil Levski Stadium, the frequently defaced Red Army Memorial, and lots of monumental sportsmen, sportswomen and workers left around the river as heroic punctuation. The actual buildings here, and in most of central Sofia, are speculative interwar Moderne, with the occasional neat detail in the balconies and the stairwells, but otherwise a low-key vernacular. Then you're faced with a sudden interruption to these dense streets, thrown into a wholly late-twentieth-century zone of wide-open space and dissonant monumentality. This is the National Palace of Culture.

Aside from the Largo – built on a bombsite – central Sofia does not have much in the way of grand projects or imposing prospects, which makes the National Palace of Culture all the more dramatic. It blasts a huge hole through the city's fabric – although it should be noted it was built on the site of a barracks and goods yard rather than a

Balkan

Refugees are welcome at the National Palace of Culture

residential area. The obligatory very big square is currently under renovation, and the '1,300 Years of Bulgaria' Monument, an intriguing combination of Brutalism and Expressionist figuration, is literally falling to pieces, surrounded by campaign posters calling for it to be replaced with a reconstruction of the barracks' old war memorial. There is a counter-campaign to preserve the current monument.

The Palace of Culture was commissioned by Lyudmila Zhivkova, Bulgarian cultural figurehead and daughter of the Party's boss, Todor Zhivkov. Designed in 1978 by Aleksandr Barov and Ivan Kanazirev, it was finished in 1981, in time for the regime's '1,300 Years of Bulgarian Statehood' celebrations. Strictly as a work of architecture, it is an unresolved combination of monumental symmetry and

Brutalist angularity, with a steel frame clad in greying marble. Inside, there is much to enjoy in this complex, multifunctional building, a classic socialist 'social condenser' of overlapping spaces and intersecting zones. The octagonal plan is cranked inside into a sequence of spacious foyers, beautifully furnished with sculptural chandeliers and ceilings made up of octagonal panels. These are a much larger cousin to Denys Lasdun's complex circulation spaces in the (roughly contemporary) National Theatre, but with the addition of large quantities of modernized folk art on panels, murals and reliefs, with almost every level boasting, say, a wooden relief of frolicking nudes, or a mural on Bulgarian history. In each case, they're cleverly integrated with the architecture, and mostly avoid kitsch of the Socialist Realist or folksy varieties, although you couldn't imagine any of it in a Western building of the same period. Along with the spaces for theatre, music and art, there are several cafés. Some of these take the hipster approach favoured in ex-socialist Berlin or Warsaw, but there's also a Costa – the Palace of Culture is not subsidized, so parts have been parcelled off to the highest bidder. Terraces on the upper storeys give views of the city, with the centre's skyline dominated by the domes of the Alexander Nevsky Cathedral and the spike of the Party headquarters, and on the other side the suburbs, dominated by high-rise hotels and the slab blocks of the *microrayons*.

These are best reached via the Sofia Metro, planned in the 1970s as part of the same project as the palace, with its first stations opened in the mid-1990s – a timescale reflected in the Moscow Metro proportions and decorative details of some stations and the shopping mall materials of others. Extensions have been directly funded by the EU, and European Union station has been named in its honour. 'Europeanism' is, as in much of Eastern Europe, practically an official ideology – the conservative ruling party is called 'Citizens for the European Development of Bulgaria', a name which says a lot. Its leader, Boyko Borisov, is Todor Zhivkov's former bodyguard, which says just as much.

Sofia has walkable streets and lots of trams, but hasn't done much to maintain either. You can get a clue how this has transpired if you get out at James Bourchier station, in the Lozenets district. The area is dominated by the Vitosha New Otani Hotel, rather improbably designed in 1974 for a Japanese developer, by the only major international architect to have worked in the

Lenin and Sopharma

Bulgarian capital, other than Mimar Sinan – Kisho Kurokawa. As a high-rise it is decent enough, with a dramatic silhouette set against Mount Vitosha, but the interiors are standard luxury tat; perhaps just a little uglier than normal. Outside the hotel is chaos – shrill speculative apartment blocks, kamikaze car parking, broken or non-existent pavements. This is, apparently, where Sofia's new rich live, and it suggests they are not a public-spirited lot. The state of the city's social housing reinforces that impression. Sofia tripled in size in the communist era, incomers being housed in estates with optimistic names – Nadezhda (Hope), Mladost (Youth), Druzhba (Friendship). We opted for Youth. Aside from its decent connections to the centre (three Metro stations), EU funding doesn't seem to have arrived, so the panel-built blocks are in a melancholic disarray, with residents upgrading their own corners rather than the city reno-vating the entire buildings; the parkland and squares around are generously proportioned but scrubby and barely maintained. To the street are grim mini-malls: 'ALKO CENTRE' reads the sign over one of them.

The missing factor from the Serdika ensemble is the main missing element in Sofia's architecture in general – anything of note from the last twenty-six years of 'freedom' and capitalism. The most interesting recent structures we found were the Sopharma Business Tow-ers. These three office blocks on a podium, which also houses a shopping mall, are pleasant Fosterian corporate Modernism, and claim to be 'the first sustainable build-ings in Sofia'. Just behind them are more scrubby areas around panel-built points and slabs, and a former factory canteen – a simple Modernist building, with a mural of revolutionary scenes – which houses the Museum of Socialist Art, the statue graveyard that each post-socialist country must dangle as an incentive to Western tourists. It has a decent selection of monumental remnants, and is nicely non-didactic. Still, as a juxtaposition, it isn't quite so encouraging as the harmonious culture clash in the centre – here, there's an uneasy mix of financial swagger and poverty. Sofia feels a very easy-going metropolis: refreshing, in an area (and era) that is often neurotic and paranoid. As architecture, the socialist era has left it an ambiguous legacy, but as sculptures of workers are put in museums and the former workers' districts rot, Sofia is a capitalist city through and through.

5 Baltic

Aarhus is Nice

Aarhus is the second city of Denmark and the largest city in Jutland, the thin, crested peninsula that grows out of the top of Germany, and that makes up the bulk of the Scandinavian country. I had the pleasure – almost always a pleasure, in Northern Europe – of travelling there by train. In this case it wasn't for the scenery. There has been a minor craze in Britain for Denmark's apparently much more enlightened approach to cosiness, warmth, nature and whatnot, with books published on the subject being bought as guides to *savoir vivre*. The largest country of North-Western Europe – one which once had an adversarial relationship with Denmark, now mainly remembered in the phrase 'Danegeld' – often dreams of Scandinavia, and the nice things it apparently has. What surprised me, though, on the train between Copenhagen, on the archipelago in the east of the country, and Aarhus, on the north-east of the Jutland landmass, was how brusque Denmark had been with its landscape – a flat, marshy, grey expanse, bluntly bridged by causeways and concrete. Unlike in Sweden or Norway, there's nothing romantic about the Danish countryside. It is well managed, clean and clear, with nothing extraneous.

The railway station is as good as one would expect. It is a classical building of the 1920s, to the design of the architect of Danish Railways, K. T. Seest. It presents a familiar face to the street, with a formalized repertoire of columns and pediments, but the interior breaks with precedent to create an airy, cubic space, with residual classicism in the galleries of Corinthian columns on the top half of the two-level space. This is stripped classicism at its purest, where you're not meant to admire the opulence or abundance of the carving and the decoration, but the elegance and lushness of the facing material, the travertine frames around the doorways, the terrazzo floors, the unpretentious but meticulous brickwork. There is a McDonald's, and even that is made to look classy. From there, it's a very short walk to the main monument of Aarhus, and what is probably the only thing in the city (until very recently) that is known outside of it – Aarhus City Hall, designed by Arne Jacobsen and Erik Møller in 1937, and finished four years later, by which time Denmark was under Nazi occupation.

'Scandinavian design' became a cult gradually, sometime between 1930 and 1950; it is hard not to see it as inextricably connected with the way in which Denmark, Sweden and Finland (and to a lesser degree Norway and Iceland, with their inferior brand recognition) created their particularly peaceful, egalitarian, Socialism-inflected form of capitalism – through export drives, and particularly the export of highly finished, attractively designed consumer goods. The work of Arne Jacobsen, like that of Verner Panton or Alvar Aalto, is an internationally recognized brand, and in both cases, whether you've been to one of their buildings or not, you've almost certainly once sat in their chairs,

Aarhus City Hall

Jacobsen's chairs having had a little more notoriety since one of the more curvaceous examples was straddled by Christine Keeler in a 1963 photoshoot. The Modernism for export created in Scandinavia is usually considered 'friendlier', more 'organic' than the steel tubes and monochrome colour schemes favoured by Mies van der Rohe or Marcel Breuer, whose chairs are also more popular than their buildings. Aarhus City Hall is a very sophisticated and relatively early example of that shift. Consisting of a large, long volume topped by a clocktower, it is clad outside with a lustrous, icy, volcanic-looking grey Norwegian marble, but the clocktower has opted for the kind of cute, raised-eyebrow details that would make Scandomodernism such a hit in the 1951 Festival of Britain, with serif Roman numerals incised into the clock-face, which is attached to the concrete frame around the marble-clad tower. The result is both chic and jolly, as well as a sly engagement with historicism that avoids the lumbering literalism of most Neoclassicism. And the interior is just a joy: a multi-level gallery, like in a Renaissance office building, and rooflights cleverly incised into the barrel roof, with all the small details – the floors, the handles, the lamps and, of course, the chairs – designed with care and a casual lightness of touch. It has the honour rare in pioneering twentieth-century buildings of being superior to its many imitators.

After these two triumphs, one of local, one of international significance, Aarhus as a townscape is as pleasant, functional and forgettable as the train ride that takes you here. Historically, the point of the place is the port, the decline of which after containerization has been managed,

Gravity and grace

unsurprisingly, a lot more cleanly and carefully than has been the case in comparable cities in more Anglo-Saxon economies, but has transformed the city irrevocably none-theless. There are two parts of the centre which are frequented by visitors. The modern centre revolves around the city's river, which was first culverted, then reopened in the 1980s when inner city deindustrialization made rivers in port cities a little more attractive for promenading. The result is very nice. Very nice also are the buildings around it, polite little essays in all the important European styles – classical, Gothic, a little very very mild Expressionism and Modernism, around a nice little river.

Those longing for a little more vigour and drama can find it, of course. The Aarhus City Theatre of 1898 is a busy, very free-classical monumental building with a

Cold-weather café culture

crowded façade of terracotta, mosaic, mural and red brick, in what would in London be called the 'South Kensington style'. Its architect, Hack Kampmann, would later design the exceptionally stern stripped classicism of Copenhagen Police Headquarters, well known to viewers of *Borgen*. While both show a willingness to experiment within the confines of classicism, the Aarhus building looks a great deal less glowering. The other monumental structure stiffening up the townscape is Aarhus Cathedral, incrementally built between the fourteenth and sixteenth centuries. Though Denmark's cities were not 'Hanseatic' as such, the cathedral's particular version of brick Gothic is part of a trans-Baltic style you can find sticking up from the sea-fronting skylines of Lübeck, Gdańsk, Riga. The brickwork is blunt, square, hard-edged, and the green copper tower is totally confident, rising unfussily to as tall a spike as possible, so as to signal the city to seafarers as much as to signal the piety of the burghers. If you prefer your townscape cute, however, the 'Latin Quarter' – an amusing 1990s rebranding – of late-medieval and early-modern houses is great if you like the idea of start-ups and craft bars housed in a preserved fishing village.

As I may have already implied, Aarhus is not a city full of sights. Its buildings are never less than scrupulous and serious, nothing has been done carelessly or obnoxiously, and given that it is historically not dissimilar to, say, Cardiff or Hull, that seems much more impressive to an English eye than it might to a Danish one. However, in a city which has been re-engineering its economy from production and port-side industry to services, it is necessary to have 'attractions', things that would make people visit,

Spire as beacon

The Latin Quarter

and settle, from the surrounding area, or even from further afield. One example of this is in the city centre, where a square red Art Museum features a rainbow sculpture by Olafur Eliasson as its crown; but, unsurprisingly, most of the effort in this has been concentrated on the inner-city part of the docks, which have been transformed in the last few years into a new educational and residential district. Everywhere with a strip of coast in Europe has done this, of course, and it would be interesting to see if the fairest, most humane capitalism in the world has done anything significantly unlike what has been done on the laissez-faire quaysides of France or Britain.

The main road along the quay is lined with flamboyant bourgeois tenement buildings, florid and a little pompous, interspersed with bronzes of local worthies, tree-lined boulevards and another Hack Kampmann work, the squatly medieval Custom House. There are still wooden sheds here which sell locally caught fish – when I visited Aarhus, teaching a small group of art and architecture students, this was considered one of the main sights to which the foreign lecturer should be introduced. The townscape that I saw then, in 2012, half completed, has since then received its residents and its workers, and alternately snotty and excited reviews in the architectural press. Its centre-piece is 'the Iceberg'. Single-handedly attempting to introduce something into the Danish cityscape that it otherwise lacks – terrain – it does very efficiently what it is supposed to do, which is to create an image through which the city can sell itself as a 'destination'. It is very photo-genic, this assemblage of around ten mini-towers arranged so as to evoke a snow-capped mountain range, clad in

Constructing the Iceberg

arctic whites and blues. Its architects, CEBRA, are doing something similar to what the masons of Aarhus Cathedral did many hundreds of years ago: announcing the city to the sea, except the amount of people who will see it via that route is probably limited to the occasional cruise and, more often, the Filipino crews of the container ships. For residents, the views of the towers are actually accentuated by the seemingly totally whimsical, image-driven design, which as a side effect means that no tower blocks another. The semi-automated cranes of the port, in their clanking, linear, unstoppable motion add to the sense that, here, the city has shifted into another scale altogether, from warm, cosy and intimate to coldly modern, hard and futuristic.

The other parts of the Aarhus port redevelopment weren't as likely to grace magazine covers as the Iceberg. There are a neat, low-slung port centre by the long-running firm of C. F. Møller, who designed the vernacular-modern Aarhus University in the 1950s; a severely square-point block of student housing by the Danish firm Arkitema, in a smooth material that looks sandblasted, known as 'High Performance Concrete'; and the Lighthouse, a more rippling, curvilinear set of luxury flats with decorative, computer-aided balconies, courtesy of Dutch 'Supermodernists' UNStudio. All of it is in a gleaming white, which has obviously been chosen by the local planners as the common vernacular to unite all of these disparate essays in the 'iconic'. The public spaces are planned by Jan Gehl Architects, who are sought after by every local authority on the planet to bring their 'place-making' authority, hard won in the preservation of nineteenth-century Copenhagen to 'stop it becoming Stockholm'. So pedestrians and pedestrian spaces dominate in a way that they seldom would in Britain or Ireland. It is a complete package of design and urbanism, and is very much in the great tradition of Scandinavian design. Just as Jacobsen, Panton or Aalto put their small, historically unspectacular countries on the map through the mass production of their designs and the circulation of their images, so this too is about using architecture and media to market a city that would surely otherwise be seldom visited on 'City Breaks' due to the formidable expense of a meal or a drink. But just as the dream being sold has shifted from social equality to 'wellness', so the development of a luxury-flat complex has become the means of selling the city abroad rather than, as was the case in the 1950s, housing estates and New Towns. *Stunning developments* for export. As the developers of the Lighthouse promise – 'living the view'.

Dear Old Stockholm

Stockholm was my first experience of European city that felt socially 'different'. In 2003 I visited a friend in Björkhagen, a suburb resembling an exceptionally well-maintained post-war council estate lived in by only affluent people. A short walk from everyone's front door was a real forest, although we were fifteen minutes on the Metro from the centre of a city of 1.5 million people. Jagged crags shot out of the pavements, as if in the aftermath of an earthquake. A bare-brick church, a towering hostel, a supermarket and a state-owned shop that sold only alcohol were the other amenities. In the centre, we visited Gunnar Asplund's City Library, where a black frieze decorated with figures from Homer led up to a rotunda stacked floor-to-ceiling with books. In the evening, we went to a nightclub called Debaser, on an island under a tangle of concrete expressways. Here you could see bands and DJs as up to the minute as any in London or Berlin, except playing to an audience that were, at worst, very slightly tipsy. Advertising was rare, nobody looked poor, bread was black. There was a royal family, but they sent their kids to state school.

I've been back several times since, and that image of a functioning social-democratic city set in a wild yet controlled natural environment has never quite dissipated. But make no mistake, Swedish social democracy is declining, with the fastest-growing inequality in Europe; at current rates, it will be as unequal as the USA by 2050. Stockholm is also one of the most racially segregated cities in Europe, a

Approaching Stockholm Central Library

Paris-on-the-Baltic that exploded into suburban riots in 2013. Not unrelatedly, the Swedish capital has been 'enjoying' a real-estate boom. Rather than indict Stockholm, though, I want to praise it. Even aside from its social achievements, it's a heady topographical and architectural experience, which Swedish architecture's reputation for prettiness and 'empiricism' belies. Stockholm is essentially an archipelago of housing estates strung out across islands and crags. High, thin concrete viaducts carrying cars and Metro trains soar across lakes and seas, and crash in and out of valleys planted with maisonettes and peaks crowned with towers. Woven into every estate is a fragment of forest. Sometimes it's almost vertiginous, but you know you're never going to fall off the edge. That combined feeling of security and awe is rare and special.

A perambulation of Stockholm ought to start with the rather too preserved Old Town, Gamla Stan – narrow streets and seventeenth-century spires, with Baroque details on the ground floors. The street plan is medieval, and the palaces are Neoclassical. The very few tourists that make it to this absurdly expensive city are concentrated here. It is better from a distance, where it forms part of a carefully tended skyline along with Stockholm City Hall, where Ragnar Östberg pioneered the standard type of the early-twentieth-century municipal palace, particularly in the many reproductions of its stark tower topped with copper crowns. Designed in an invented 'traditional' Swedish Gothic full of Tolkien mannerisms, it opens itself out to the water with both a colonnade, an embankment and a secluded garden. Deeper into Norrmalm, the commercial centre, there are two other punctuation points on the skyline. One of them is Kungstornen, two masonry-clad skyscrapers of 1925, with Louis Sullivan-like tripartite designs, connected by a bridge, integrated as part of the design, with a street flowing below. Aside from the unique, retro-Futurist decor, it's worth noting that this is a concerted town-planning project, a good decade before the Social Democratic Workers' Party began their fifty-year hegemony as one of the most successful political parties in history. The other object on the skyline otherwise still dominated by Gamla Stan and City Hall is HötorgsCity. Built in the early 1950s, this is harder stuff, five glass towers in enfilade, a miniature Fifth Avenue.

The streets around here are the centre of Modernist Stockholm. There's Backström and Reinius's Åhléns

Municipal power

Capitalist planning – Kungstornen

department store, an object lesson in how to design a long windowless box with wit and charm, but more importantly there's the large complex by Peter Celsing that includes the rugged, classicized Bank of Sweden and the fabulous Kulturhuset. Placed somewhere spatially, typologically and temporally between the Royal Festival Hall and the Centre Pompidou, this long, simple yet labyrinthine glass volume briefly housed the Swedish parliament, when the Riksdag was being renovated. Imagine the Palace of Westminster relocated to a building one part Queen Elizabeth Hall and one part Elephant and Castle shopping centre, and you'll get some sense of just how radical the Swedish mainstream had become in the 1970s. In front is a large square and the meeting point of the city's Metro lines, and you notice something.

Social condenser – Kulturhuset

Gamla Stan and Norrmalm are overwhelmingly white, and yet this square is comparatively mixed. Take the Metro out from here and the contrast is greater still.

Stockholm's suburbs are the product of a conscious but rather complicated social project. The state, municipally and nationally, bought up land on a large scale to expand the city, in conjunction with the building societies and housing companies run by the trade unions and co-operatives who still build a sizeable amount of Sweden's new housing; the HSB insignia can be found on Arts and Crafts pre-war tenements and new, shiny neo-Modernist blocks; the KF co-operative's Constructivist headquarters, with its ribbon windows and cantilevered crane, still stands opposite Gamla Stan. Housing therefore had a lot of state subsidy and is largely rented, on a waiting-list system, but the universal welfare state here didn't, and doesn't, have 'social housing' as such, let out according to a means test. These suburbs were meant to be for everyone. They aren't.

Some of these suburbs are pre-war. Aspudden, for instance, is a company suburb built for Ericsson workers, intensely gentrified since the 1990s: it goes from mildly Art Nouveau tenements to low-rise functionalist blocks, and those fingers of forest leafing in-between. Typically, Aspudden is built around a church, the tiny Uppenbarelsekyrkan, placed on top of one of those volcanic outcrops. These churches are treated as much like community centres, concert halls or 'social condensers' as they are places of worship; certainly I've never visited a church less intimidating, although its central space, irradiated by polychromatic, abstract glass, is powerful. The

Uppenbarelsekyrkan

better-known suburbs date from the immediate aftermath of the war – Sweden was neutral, but was forced to run an austerity regime during the conflict. One early cause célèbre was Gröndal, commenced in 1944, where former hardline functionalists Backström and Reinius 'softened' their right angles and white walls towards pitched roofs, complex, cosy arrangements of blocks, bright colours and individualistic stylistic touches. It's lovely, and much less staid than its British imitations might have you assume. Larger and more impressive is Vällingby, almost a New Town, the first phase of which was finished in 1953. The casual scorn that the New Brutalists had for 'the Swedish retreat from modern architecture' is hard to sustain on acquaintance with it. There's such a lightness and warmth of touch, in Backström and Reinius's (admittedly often whimsical) fittings, pavings of the central precincts, and the placement of the towers and maisonettes, that it would be silly to object to the lack of rigour. Parts of it have been glazed over in a renovation by the prolific White Arkitekter, whose somewhat blank mild functionalism is a good indicator of where mainstream Swedish architecture is at today, roofing over an H&M featuring the famously zaftig Swedish mannequins.

In the 1960s, Sweden aimed to solve any remaining housing problems at a stroke via the 'Million Programme'. In Stockholm, this would ensure that every single inhabitant of the city would have their own spacious, sanitary space, in a block of flats with a community centre, a forest, a church and a Metro station. This really happened, and nearly everyone does have exactly that. Yet the Million Programme, achieved largely via massive use of system-building, has been heavily criticized for creating allegedly inhumane and monolithic environments. The first I visited was, coincidentally, soon after the 2013 riots – Flemingsberg. Home of Södertörn University and the Karolinska Hospital, it occupies a clifftop site above a motorway, and it did 'kick off' here that year. White Arkitekter's university buildings are decent contemporary Modernism, with that familiar mastery of landscaping, while the earlier hospital is thick, tubular Brutalism strung along concrete walkways; but what of the housing? Expecting some sort of Castle Vale or Aylesbury Estate, I was bowled over by its brightness and optimism, the amount of social amenities, not to mention its level of maintenance and the continued use of forested spaces

Volcanic landscaping at Södertörn University

always just around the corner. Aside from the undoubt-
edly larger scale of the housing – mostly in long slab
blocks – this was obviously from the same school as
Björkhagen, Vällingby or Gröndal. I also couldn't help but
notice that Flemingsberg was as black and Asian as Norrmalm or Sodermalm were monolithically Aryan.

That's even more the case in Husby, the suburb where
the 2013 riots started, and raged longest. While Flemingsberg is on the suburban rail, Husby is on the Metro. The
Metro, also, is pretty special: stations from the 1970s
embarked on a similar dialogue with the rocky landscape
to the housing estates, only flipped, so that each station is
like a cave, the tunnels rudely blasted through and then
painted and decorated with Surrealist artworks. When
out of Husby station, follow the very attractive little

arched bridges over the roads that serve it and you can see how similar, structurally, the Million Programme blocks can be to British (or Soviet) prefabrication of the era – large, corrugated panels, here stained into the same blush of red and yellow you find in the City Library. Just like in Aspudden, there are tables, chairs and benches in-between the blocks, and the maintenance – both by residents, on their balconies, and in-between, by the housing associations – is impeccable. Explore, and you'll find a swimming pool, community centre, lots of sports facilities, the obligatory forest fragments and then, again over the bridges, a change in typology, into brick-clad tenements and wooden terraces, intimate and utopian.

This is nobody's idea of a ghetto. In terms of style and maintenance, Span housing in Blackheath is the nearest

Riot-torn Husby

British equivalent, and there are middle-class employers nearby – the next stop on the Metro is the 'Swedish Silicon Valley' of Kista. Even so, Husby is the poorest part of Stockholm, with high rates of unemployment, and is overwhelmingly non-white. The effect is surreal. As one former resident of nearby Rinkeby told me, 'Stockholm is the most segregated capital city in Europe, and its slums are better maintained than Hampstead.' In a sense it is a victim of the Million Programme's success. Sweden has long had an enlightened asylum and immigration policy, and had plenty of decent housing for people to move to – and the cheapest and most abundant housing was in the Million Programme estates. The problem is not how people found themselves in Husby or Flemingsberg, but why they aren't being housed in the new estates in the city centre.

Stockholm, like so many European cities, shifted towards inner-city redevelopment in the 1980s and 1990s. You can see this at its best and worst in the Södra Station-området, where smart public spaces and parks surround a motley collection of blocks, from the neo-functionalist Konsum building to Ricardo Bofill's neo-fascist circus, with its concrete Doric colonnades, decorated to the doorways by that familiar HSB logo, a reminder that this comes from the same people that made Vällingby and Husby. Swedish housing recovered from this descent into pomposity and flash, however. Slightly further out is the rightly celebrated Hammarby Sjöstad, on an ex-industrial site, and recently completed. It's memorable not so much for its passable neo-Modernist architecture and its turn to a nineteenth-century block structure rather than the spacious layouts of the suburbs, but for its use of the

Middle-class Socialism – Hammarby Sjöstad

water and its wild embankments, which have taken on
the role of the forests in earlier estates – the result of a
strictly legally binding plan. In terms of creating beautiful, subtle and modern environments, Sweden really can
still do it. But these buildings are expensive, way beyond
the wallets of Husby residents; the housing associations
have to recoup the costs of their investment, and to provide deliberately cheap flats for 'social' tenants would
violate the rules of the system. Yet these are already
being violated, by the selling off of city centre flats on the
open market, which has created a huge housing bubble.
Sweden used to be – rightly – proud of the universal
nature of its welfare state, used by the middle class and
by workers alike, but what it might need now is some
affirmative action.

The Fortresses of Narva and Ivangorod

Since Russia's annexation of Crimea in 2014, there's been much talk of a 'New Cold War' between Russia and Europe. If that war has a symbolic border, it's the bridge over the Narva river that connects the EU, and the Estonian Baltic city of Narva, with the Russian town of Ivangorod. In the doom scenarios of the 'war' becoming hot, it's here that the first shots would be fired. The north-east of Estonia is overwhelmingly Russophone, and thousands of people here are officially stateless; a *casus belli* could be easily manufactured. On each side of the river are fortresses, reminders that this river has been a militarized border for centuries. In the week I visited, a NATO summit in Warsaw agreed to deploy troops to the Baltic, to militarize it yet further. But as sightseers look out over the bridge, and picnickers sit on either side of the riverbank, Narva–Ivangorod doesn't look like it's about to be the theatre of the Third World War.

Narva, like Estonia more generally, is the point where two very different versions of 'Europe' meet: Scandinavia, everyone's favourite welfare state consumerist utopia, and Russia, proverbially dark yet romantic land of poverty, dictatorship and prefabrication. The city was founded by Denmark in the thirteenth century, and then became one of the centres of the Teutonic knights. Russia built the Ivangorod fortress opposite at the end of the fifteenth century. Narva as it exists now, though, is the result of the late-seventeenth-century Great Northern War, largely between Sweden and Russia, for control of the

277

Baltic. Before the Second World War, the city, then part of an independent Estonia, consisted of a Swedish-built centre, in the Dutch Baroque style, a Swedish–Danish castle and a Russo-German industrial town; the population was Estonian with large Russian and German minorities. Only some of this survives today – Narva was pummelled by air raids in 1944, totally destroying the Baroque city. What you can see today is a very ordinary Soviet city, yet with the castle complex and the nineteenth-century industrial areas largely intact. The population, which has fallen precipitously since independence was regained in 1991, is over 80 per cent Russian, with Ukrainian, Belarusian and Estonian minorities. At the heart of it are those two opposed castles, glowering at each other across a fenced-off, heavily guarded bridge, an exceptionally picturesque image of division and paranoia.

It's a very long way in spirit, if not in actual space, from Tallinn, the Estonian capital. Though linguistically and socially divided, Tallinn is, along with Slovenia's

Narva river crossing, with Ivangorod on the left, Narva on the right

Ljubljana, the most convincingly 'Western' and affluent post-communist capital in Europe. Unusually for the ex-USSR, it has a lively architectural culture. At the Estonian Architecture Museum, a converted warehouse next to the impressive Modernist-Hanseatic blocks of the Roter-mann Quarter, I was told there wasn't much to see in Narva; the Baroque city, they said, was levelled after war damage, 'to demoralize the people'. Narva's historical politics are tense, as you immediately realize when you arrive at the station, a pretty typical piece of Stalinist Corinthian in limestone, severely dilapidated. Outside is a memorial to the two waves of deportation of Estonian citizens to the Gulag, in 1941 and 1949; the city is 94 per cent Russian speaking, but the memorial is in Estonian. It feels like it is aimed at the current residents, most of whom can trace themselves to post-war Soviet migrants. Street signs, similarly, are all in Estonian – I spotted two bilingual signs in the entire city, outside shops and information posts. The streetscape clusters around a miniature Stalinist 'magistrale', Pushkin Street, where small yet pompous blocks, with porticoes, towers, loggias and portals somewhere between eighteenth-century Petersburg and 1930s Moscow, mark either side of a pretty, tree-lined avenue. One portal is a little more elaborate, with rich Mannerist decoration – it later transpires this is a transplant from one of the destroyed buildings of the seventeenth-century city. Then, at Peter Square, you come to both the castle and the border.

This is looked over by a twelve-storey high-rise, an interesting design of prefab storeys capped with a sinister, Expressionist water tower in fluted brick; thanks to the current vogue for people renting out their flats to strangers, this is where I stayed. From there, you can get a view of how Estonia and Russia meet. On one side of the square are bastions built in the seventeenth century and the castle, its entrance marked by a Soviet obelisk to their war dead; and on the other, the strictly secured border point. High fences, running right alongside the castle walls, lead to a rectilinear, red-brick border post. It is unusual to find a historical fortress that genuinely also doubles as a real, and properly patrolled border. Queues of lorries are a seemingly permanent presence on the backstreets here, but on the weekend when I'm visiting there's something else also: Narva Motofest, where bikers from all over Eastern Europe congregate on the castle to drive their bikes in hairy fleets and, in the evenings, listen to some strangely appropriate heavy metal, wholly audible on both sides of the river.

The castles themselves are a great comparison in aggressive/defensive forms. Ivangorod Castle is earlier, a late-medieval design perched on a ridge, with high castellated walls and circular towers, sweeping impressively across the river; the slits for archers are aimed right at the squarer, higher Narva Castle, where the Swedish-designed battlements surround 'Tall Hermann', a partly reconstructed whitewashed tower with a neat little Baroque opening where you can poke your head out and glare at Russia. Just behind Ivangorod Castle you'll notice a late-Soviet housing complex which tries to emulate it, a long wall of flats leading to a 'fortified' tower. Inside Narva Castle are exhibitions and the Northern Yard, a little medieval shopping centre with wooden galleries and people in

Ivangorod Castle, on the wrong side of the border

period costume selling food and trinkets; the bikers par-
ticipate enthusiastically in making pyres for barbecues.
Nearby is Narva's Lenin statue, unusually not demolished
or sent to a museum in the 1990s, but moved here from
Peter Square. He currently points the way to the portaloos.

The castles are in good condition, convincingly antique
and sinister even without these weekend berserkers. The
Old Town is something quite different. Often, Stalinist
regimes were happy to reconstruct Old Towns – all of old
Warsaw, most of old Gdańsk and old Dresden, and much
of old St Petersburg are a matter of post-war replicas. Here,
though, only three buildings from the seventeenth century survive; it is hard to say whether this was to do with
their association with the once-dominant Baltic Germans,
a move to 'demoralize' ethnic Estonians, who became a

Old Narva

minority in their own city, or simply a utilitarian move, as was the norm in Western Europe, to prioritise unpretentious shelter for a small industrial city rather than wasting resources on a historicist fantasyland. But even then, the treatment of old Narva was drastic, verging on urbicide. The entire city centre is made up of standardized brick 'Khrushchevki' walk-up flats from the early 1960s, in an open layout, with scrubby playgrounds and car parks in-between. The fragments that survive are sad. There is a chubby, late-nineteenth-century multi-domed Orthodox church, an eerie presence surrounded by factories, and a rustic eighteenth-century warehouse, converted in 1991 into the city Art Gallery. It has an excellent permanent collection, awful temporary exhibitions and a heartbreaking

Orthodox Church of the Resurrection of Christ

room of paintings of the Baroque city, clearly once akin to Tallinn and its romantic Hanseatic skyline.

One single historic building was reconstructed – the town hall, designed in 1668 by a Lübeck builder, Georg Teuffel, with additions by Sweden's court architect, Nicodemus Tessin the Elder. It's very Protestant, symmetrical, upright and unfussy, and you could imagine it in some more affluent part of the Baltic, a Stockholm or a Hamburg, with its light, pretty tower and swaggering entrance. It's currently derelict, but opposite is the best new building in Narva, one which deserves better than that faint praise: Narva College, designed in 2012 by the Estonian firm Kavakava Architects. It's the sort of smart, oblique Postmodernism that almost gives the genre a good name. The front elevation, facing the town hall, is a concrete 'impress' of the destroyed Stock Exchange, in a similar Swedish classical style to the town hall; it is a façade, topped by an overhanging concrete roof, and leading behind to a peculiar experiment in angular geometry, with a regular red-brick grid interrupted by sprawling, overlapping glazed studios. There was, unsurprisingly, pressure to reconstruct the building 'faithfully', but more fidelity is paid here to the complex, scarred city that Narva actually is.

Similarly excellent is the Narva Embankment, completed in 2014, an EU-funded endeavour whose openness and public-spiritedness spreads under the blunt, fenced-off post-war bridge connecting to Ivangorod. It is the most casually impressive recent public-space project in this book. Reached via various staircases from the bastions and

Narva College and Old Town Hall

castles – some historic, some overgrown and informal, some new constructions in corten steel – it is a generous, comfortable esplanade, lined with benches, chessboards, playgrounds, including a new, fashionably geological Zahaesque youth centre. Wonder of wonders, it even features a new public loo. It ends at a little beach, and a curious geopolitical freak, where a 1950s hydroelectric station on the Narva side is actually in Russia. Walk up the staircase here, and you're in the industrial part of the city.

Once the most industrialized city on the Baltic outside St Petersburg, Narva was developed by courtesy of the long-disappeared Baltic Germans, who were moved to the Third Reich in the early 1940s to populate its '*Lebensraum*'. Several huge factories on Kreenholm Island were built, two textile mills and one bakery, all now either disused or turned to post-industrial purposes. A planned company town was built around this, inhabited by a multi-ethnic, working-class population. Around that, a little Stalinist suburb was built in the 1950s, with many small Baroque details recalling the unreconstructed Old Town beyond. It's the sort of urbanism now favoured, with shops on the ground floor, but these are almost all derelict. As is the grandiose Gerasimov Palace of Culture, marked by a pompous, full-height Doric colonnade. Heroes of the socialist revolutions of 1905 and 1917 are remembered with busts on plinths, standing lonely in a wildly overgrown but surprisingly well-used park. The company town itself resembles some transplant from the Ruhr, rough and red brick with stubby Gothic details, starkly arranged around small squares, where residents have hung their washing up – tall

tenements for the factory hands, more spacious and decorative blocks for the foremen, and an imperial Baroque
residence for the factory owner. The war-damaged tenements were partly spruced up in the 1960s, with modern
flanking blocks and a wonderful abstract mosaic accom-
panying a memorial to the revolutionary Amalie Kreisberg,
a social democrat who was killed by Tsarist forces in
1906. But the emptiness is inescapable, and the haemor-
rhage of population Narva has suffered is most obvious
here, making these memorials to working-class heroism,
stood in front of empty factories, incomprehensible and
anachronistic.

Doubtless the monolithic blocks on the outskirts were
more popular than these battered tenements. The suburbs
are a Soviet/neoliberal melange, the spaced-out slabs

The monument to Amalie Kreisberg

(some based on an elegant design by the great Estonian architect Raine Karp, originally for Tallinn) surrounding retail parks and a baffling quantity of furniture shops. This landscape is continued over the border into Ivangorod and Russia, for miles and miles. You'll find very little of the quality of the Narva Embankment out there, and nor will you find the outlet of emigration, so evidently taken by many inhabitants of the city. That's the dual promise the European Union made to places like Narva – we can make your cities better, and we can make it easier for you to get out of them. One part of that promise was made to Britain, too, and we decided we preferred our towns crap; the other part of the deal led to a hysterical reaction, whose consequences we now face. Here, they must regard our decision with the purest bafflement.

Vyborg: Finland's Second City, Russia's 208th

Seen in the very long run, the great Baltic success story, in terms both of architecture and of economics, is Finland. For a long time, it has been considered part of a wider Scandinavian axis of welfare state prosperity, which obscures the fact that its history is in many respects much more akin to that of Latvia or Estonia than it is to Sweden or Denmark. A hundred years ago, Finland – economically dominated by its Swedish minority – was a province of the Russian Empire, and a restive one. Revolutionary workers in Helsinki and the second city, Viipuri, were supportive of the Bolsheviks, and would fight – and lose – a brutal civil war for control of the country in 1918; many fled to the Soviet Union with the subsequent 'White Terror'. After a fairly quiet and affluent interwar period, dominated by the moderate Social Democrats, it was invaded by the USSR, who carved a chunk off the country; it then threw its lot in with the Axis powers. Unlike Latvia and Estonia it was not totally annexed by the Soviets nor by the Nazis, and unlike both its smaller neighbours it did not have a period of right-wing dictatorship – Finland had the curious honour of being the only democratic country in the Axis. Otherwise, its history is essentially that of its Baltic cousins. In 1945 the Red Army re-invaded, re-annexed the Karelian isthmus, and initially imposed a communist-led government. In theory, the result should have been like Latvia or at least Poland, leading to a similarly painfully disputed history. What resulted instead was a period of staggering economic growth, and notably the development of design and architecture as export and raw material for nation building. A large and popular Communist Party won a plurality at the polls at least once, but never dominated the various coalitions it took part in. Social Democrats and Liberals negotiated their way through the Cold War by trading with, and resolutely refusing to offend, the Russians. 'Finlandization', it was called. But one part of historic Finland was still left outside its borders, and of the 'West' – the annexed Karelian isthmus, and its largest city, Vyborg – Viipuri, as was.

Historically a multicultural but for centuries largely Finnish city, Vyborg has gone from being Finland's second city in 1939 to being the Russian Federation's 208th largest city in 2018. With St Petersburg so near by, it couldn't have become much more than a satellite town in what is still known as Leningrad Oblast. Originally, the Karelian isthmus was part of a Soviet Republic of Karelia within the USSR, which had the same legal status as Ukraine, Georgia, the Baltic Republics, and so on. Yet as Russian migrants came to massively outnumber Finns and Karelians, it was wound up into Russia proper, a denouement which many in places like Latvia, Estonia and Kazakhstan worried would be their own eventual fate, a total national disappearance. But while since the 1940s Vyborg has been almost totally Russian in terms of population, the architecture that has been left there is so overwhelmingly reminiscent of Scandinavia – and specifically of Helsinki – that the disconnect is head-spinning, an architectural cognitive dissonance. Whitewashed Baroque castle towers, grand classical office blocks, distinctive 'National Romantic'

Street sign on Lenin Prospect

early-Modernist commercial palaces and clipped, white-walled Functionalist residential flats – many of them in a highly distressed state – Vyborg looks like you might imagine Helsinki would after a long, drawn-out war. There is one major exception to this state of admittedly photogenic collapse, and that is Vyborg Library.

If you were to google Vyborg, you would find two things in particular being noted. One, is the city's status as the terminus of 'North Stream'. This was an interesting geopolitical wheeze, created by the German and Russian governments, whereby a pipeline will go directly under the Baltic sea from Russia's huge gas reserves, all the way to northern Germany, bypassing potentially restive countries like Latvia, Poland or Ukraine, not improbably so that the Russian government can boss them without worrying about gas supplies to Germany being cut off. The other thing you'll find is images of one of the major buildings designed by one of the five or so most praised architects of the twentieth century. The Vyborg Municipal Library, designed by Alvar Aalto incrementally through the first half of the 1930s, is of some archaeological significance in the great Finnish architect's career, for marking the second major shift in his work. Beginning as a classicist, which in Finland (as in Sweden) in the early twentieth century meant a quite open, experimental approach to the tradition, Aalto suddenly switched to a bare, elegant functionalism at the end of the 1920s, in buildings like the Paimio Sanatorium. At Vyborg – or, rather, Viipuri – that functionalism was inflected with local reference. In the library's public auditorium Aalto created instantly, in a single room, the idiom of moderate, 'organic' Scandinavian Modernism that remains influential to this day in every bit of applied wooden cladding on a modern building. It had a Russian fashion show on the day I visited, but that didn't distract much from the form. The library's restoration, which has taken nearly two decades, was lavishly funded by the Finnish government, who have brought the building back up to the very highest standards after decades of decline. The building, however, is not in Finland, and the result is uncomfortable.

In case there's any doubt, Vyborg Library is a brilliant work of architecture, and it's totally right that it be restored as it has been. Nestled in the city's municipal park, it is long, low and gleaming white, but it is inside

Vyborg Library auditorium

Vyborg Library reading room

that Aalto's personal style comes in. The main reading room is lit with dozens of round roof lights, so that every minute change in the weather – which changed a lot, just in the August afternoon that I spent there, from black to grey to white to blue – transforms the mood of the room. Recently, the finishing touch was put to the restoration, as Aalto's original curved wood balustrades were replicated, sweeping wilfully along the second level of this double-height space. In the auditorium is the distinctive ceiling, an arbitrary gesture, allegedly dictated by acoustics, where a delicate wave of wood – originally worked by local shipyard workers – was placed under the roof's concrete lid. After 1945, the building narrowly avoided being bulked up with stone and ornament in 'Socialist Realist' style, and had an inept but well-meaning restoration in the 1960s. Photographs in the library – which has an entire section devoted to the great man – show the scale of its decline by the early 1990s. Looking around, you'd never know that anything had happened, and you'd never know that you weren't in achingly affluent Scandinavia, but for the fact that most of the library books are in Russian. It is all a success, but it feels strange – a little fragment of egalitarian luxury in the midst of public squalor.

Vyborg's post-1945 architecture is not a credit to the USSR. A perambulation could begin at the good, grandiose, if standardized Socialist Realist railway station, exceptionally similar to stations all over Russia and Ukraine, with its coffered ceiling, chandeliers, and decorative features on revolutionary themes. In front of it is a similarly heavy block of neo-Baroque tenements, but next to that, something different – a row of yellow-rendered flats decorated with Expressionist gargoyles, freely and wildly carved in vertical strips; if you've ever been to Helsinki Central Station, you'll recognize the manner instantly. There is an excellent park opposite, with a waterside promenade and a view of the late-Soviet Hotel Druzhba, a minor essay in the 'cosmic' style; the main square, with its palazzos, Baroque remnants and Art Nouveau markets, is puzzling. The market, in a splendid barrel-vaulted hall, is full of gruff, aggressive traders trying to flog T-shirts of Stalin and Putin to a clientele of bored Russians and curious Finns; the architect's name, K. Hård af Segerstad, is inscribed into the stones of the entrance. A little effort has been made to be 'contextual', through a big hotel in a clumsy Postmodernist-nineteenth-century-commercial

All the 'Crimea is Ours' T-shirts you could ever want

melange, but the contrast with Narva is instructive. The 'urbicide' that happened there, in a city of a similar size and a similar history, never took place in Vyborg. Though it was bombed and then supplemented with a Khrushchevka here, a 1980s slab there, almost all of the historic city survives; and unlike in, say, Aarhus, what survives hasn't been smothered by over-the-top restoration. Far from it.

When I visited Vyborg, the city was hosting a film festival, named 'WINDOW ON EUROPE'. As indeed it is, and in a different way to St Petersburg itself, where the total nature of the planning, the colourfulness of the buildings and the overpowering presence of power created something as autocratic as it was European (and why wouldn't it be, built as it was in the age of Western Europe's absolute monarchies?). Here, the city created at the end of the Russian Empire is so obviously present, and looks so obviously 'European', that you feel like you're in a part of Western Europe that has fallen into Russia by pure historical accident. Unlike in Lviv, with its distinctively Hapsburg International Style, Vyborg's 'Western' architecture is not the local expression of a colonial style, but a typical turn-of-the-century attempt to express locality and nationalism – the architecture is not Russian Imperial but nationalist Finnish.

It is also exceptionally complete. There is Soviet infill, of course – alongside the river park, you'll find Soviet luxury flats next to the terrific and, unusually, restored Viipurin Panttilaitos Oy (Vyborg Deposits Ltd) building, the only other interwar Finnish functionalist work to have been repaired anything like as scrupulously as the Vyborg Library. It features on its roof a big sign reading

Viipurin Panttilaitos Oy

'Welcome'. It is not unlike many Modernist buildings built around the same time in then-Soviet cities, so one might hope that bringing up these buildings to the international standards displayed by the Finns at the library might have an effect on the way that modern architecture is treated more generally in Russia. In 1929, it would not have been clear to an observer that it would be Alvar Aalto, of all his generation, who would become a famous icon of modern architecture, designing in an increasingly personal modern manner right up until the 1970s. No Soviet Modernist ever got this chance, although the built work of, say, Moisei Ginzburg or Konstantin Melnikov from exactly the same time is every bit as strong and as confident as Aalto's, in many ways more so. Ginzburg or Melnikov didn't get the chance to develop as modern architects, forced instead either into a lumbering neo-Baroque or, to quote Isaac Babel, 'the genre of silence'. Very few of their buildings are restored, with most dilapidated, rotting or kitschified. Yet here, totally 'Western' buildings of the same period face the same.

The library and Viipurin Panttilaitos Oy aside, Finnish functionalism languishes in much the same melancholy state as then-contemporary Constructivism does in Soviet cities like Dnipropetrovsk or Nizhny Novgorod. The work of Uno Ullberg, the city architect in the 1930s, is one example. Like Aalto, he was a convert to Modernism: his earlier manner, a heavy, articulated Art Nouveau comparable to Eliel Saarinen or Charles Rennie Mackintosh, can be seen in the city's fascinating but horribly sad dockside side streets, where gutted, windowless buildings are common. The best of Ullberg's Art Nouveau period is the Khakman & Ko building, with its outsized rusticated masonry and jagged little bay windows. Ullberg would exchange this for the classicized Modernism found in the Vyborg Art School, which has been restored, but in such a way that the differences here with the work the Finns did with Aalto are exceptionally telling. The art school was repurposed to become a Vyborg branch of the St Petersburg Hermitage, and the building – which, placed on top of a historic fortress, has a beautifully clear view of Vyborg's port, with cranes dancing between its tall colonnades – was patched up. Coming alongside this was some more typical Russian kitsch, with a big blingy sign and Neoclassical statues placed around the building, as if to say: 'Here be culture.' The interiors, and the exhibitions, are nondescript.

Khakman & Ko

The Hermitage, Vyborg

Just next to the Vyborg Hermitage is the more aggressive, Constructivist-like Flour Mill, designed in 1931 by Erkki Huttunen, which is in so poor a state that, to the untrained eye, it could just be a utilitarian, Soviet port building. The same could be said about Olli Pöyry's chic, curved Karjala Insurance Company high-rise in the city centre, which would be long-since restored and considered a Modernist cult object were it in the centre of Manchester, Stockholm or Rotterdam. If nothing else, Vyborg makes it obvious that the poor condition of modern buildings in Russia or Ukraine isn't anything specifically Soviet or post-Soviet – these battered structures, with their messy replacement windows and flaky render, are just what International Style buildings look like when they've been forgotten for seventy years. In Lenin Square, a standardized statue of Ilyich looks down on what I was surprised, on looking up, to find was an ensemble of 1930s commercial buildings, which would when built have been chic and smooth, but in their worn-out, unloved state resemble second-rate 1960s buildings in a provincial Russian city. Which, of course, is what Vyborg is.

The placing of Lenin in the main square of the city isn't just a matter of the Soviets imposing their identity on the place. Lenin stayed in the city during his period in hiding on the eve of the October Revolution, with a Finnish comrade – as with the Baltic coast of Latvia and Estonia, the coast of Finland was friendly territory for the Bolsheviks. Because of this, Vyborg has one of the few surviving Lenin museums. It is in the south of the city, just out of the centre, past the main Soviet structure in Vyborg outside the railway station, an interesting but horrifically

The Vyborg Lenin Museum

dilapidated 1970s café and department store, with blocked-up spiral staircases and falling masonry. Then after a while you'll arrive at an area defined by Soviet and post-Soviet high-rise suburbia, with just one little street of wooden houses left, kept as a reservation, because, well, Lenin lived on this street. The houses are lovely wooden constructions, recognizable from the better-kept Old Towns of Aarhus or Bergen. The museum has had a minor make-over to make it mildly less celebratory of V.I. and his Finnish comrades, but it still features a relief plaque and statue of that iconic, bald-head-and-razor-goatee profile; the exhibition in the attic, based on the sort of photos of ordinary people posing in picturesque sites in their city that people might find in *their* attics, is much more moving. Making my way from there to the bus stop back into town, I found that I was surrounded by prefabricated high-rises identical to those I had seen on the outskirts of cities in Ukraine. To find yourself in the same district in two places a thousand miles from each other is a useful indicator that this here is the Soviet world, defined by the dominance of the concrete panel.

On enjoying the Vyborg Library, you could well hope that something similarly generous, scrupulous, thorough and complete happens to some of the neglected masterpieces of the twentieth century, from Le Corbusier's work in Chandigarh to Moisei Ginzburg's Narkomfin building in Moscow, to Park Hill in Sheffield. It is also gratifying that this municipal library remains just that, and a good one. But restoring a whole city – and Vyborg's architecture is rich and important enough to deserve that – is a much more difficult problem than restoring one great building by a very famous architect. That noted, to be candid, the awful state of Vyborg's architecture is not unattractive. With all the Old Towns of old Europe ruthlessly restored and furnished with souvenir shops and Costa Coffee, the atmosphere of Vyborg is intoxicating: the rotting plaster and the crumbling masonry on the cobbled steps down to the sea secrete the acrid stink of history, rather than the waxy, varnished smell of heritage. If you want to see what a great European city looks like when it falls on seriously hard times, Vyborg has few rivals – Hull, Riga, Bradford, Liège are its siblings, but in none of them is the fall so total. Nowhere else is the gap between the 'West' and the 'East' made so sharp through proximity, and that may owe something to the fact that post-war Finland was one of the

most 'Eastern' of Western countries, with its mass Communist Party, its left-wing hegemony, its New Towns,
nationalized industries, high-rise estates and Soviet-
oriented foreign policy. Being friendly with the Soviets
but keeping them at arm's length brought great dividends
in creating a humane, pleasant capitalism, something that
has been largely beyond ex-Soviet capitalism, whether it
defines itself as the repudiation (Estonia, Latvia and now
Ukraine) or the continuation (Russia, Belarus) of the
Soviet legacy.

Posters celebrating Victory in the Great Patriotic War
are plastered around Vyborg, and they show the battles
of Stalingrad and of Berlin, not the taking of Viipuri. One
should not be too sentimental about the plucky Finns,
who helped the Wehrmacht enforce the genocidal Leningrad Blockade, an action explicitly aimed at starving
millions of civilians to death. But the subsequent Soviet
annexation of this town made solely military sense, a
way of strengthening the border defences around St
Petersburg, to make sure the blockade couldn't happen
again. The taking of Vyborg itself, and – let's not forget –
the ethnic cleansing of its population, was just an
after-effect, the town happening to be on the bit of land
the Soviets wanted to build their defences. The city itself
was barely relevant.

If you leave Vyborg, as I did, by train, riding the short
distance to Helsinki, the experience is totally unlike leaving the former USSR to travel to Poland, Germany or
Slovakia, where the shift towards affluence is gradual
and incomplete. Here, you're shunted on a fast train
from the Second to the First World before you can say

'combined and uneven development'. What effect the gas that will be piped through Vyborg on its way to the German Baltic coast will have on the city is hard to say, but, given recent Russian precedent, don't expect much in the way of redistribution. Where do you think this is, Norway?

6 North Sea

Bergen – Come Follow Our Path

Bergen is a city that sprawls. This has already been signalled at the airport, where after a passageway featuring images of sky and fjord – 'honest, pure, raw', and the tempting 'come follow our path' – you find yourself in a passenger hall overlooked by an advertisement for the

Admiring the houses of Bergen

Bolig Partner Home Catalogue. Three possible flatpack homes you can buy are on the advert, all in sylvan settings, in snow-dappled marsh and forest, all of them detached. From there, public or private transport will take you through a series of under- and overpasses that swing through forested hillsides, each of them dotted with similar suburban houses – though usually more closely packed together than in the ads. At first, they seem completely random, but after a while, you can make out that they describe streets, rising and falling along the densely forested hills. Along the way, as well as admiring concrete highway engineering, you can take note of the many filling stations for electric cars. Evidently, it isn't only the North Sea that Britain shares with Norway, but a certain hypocrisy – a country that has become the richest on earth through selling oil encourages you to drive electric. If only our hypocrisy had such concrete results.

If Scandinavian countries like Sweden, Denmark and Finland provided tempting models and analogies for British architects and town planners in the 1950s and 1960s, since the mid-1970s the inevitable, and much more tempting, model is Norway. Not because, unlike the others, it has been emulated, but precisely because it hasn't. One of the many foundation stories of neoliberalism in Britain hinges on what the 1974–9 Labour government decided to do with the oil discovered in the North Sea at the start of that decade, an unexpected licence to print money which the UK shared, geographically and practically, with Norway. The relevant minister at the time, Tony Benn, suggested that the British state take ownership of the oil, and put the proceeds in a fund which could be used to fund social projects. Rejected, like so many of the 1970s left's 'loony' proposals for workers' control and technological innovation, the eventual tax receipts from the oil flowed abundantly into the Treasury nonetheless, and were used by the subsequent Conservative government to subsidise the mass unemployment created by a deliberate policy of class conflict and deindustrialization. By contrast the Norwegians, on the prompting of Farouk al-Kasim, the Iraqi-born head of the resources department in the state-run Norwegian Petroleum Directorate, tried to avoid the 'Dutch disease' of a sudden windfall followed by decline by managing the oil through a nationalized company, Statoil, and creating a sovereign wealth fund to manage and distribute the proceeds – which, among other things, meant putting the money away, rather than immediately spending it, whether on tax cuts or social programmes.

The result is that Norway is on most measures the richest country on earth, rivalled only by the USA, but with its income incomparably more fairly distributed. In the 2014 Scottish Independence Referendum, a poster was often seen in Glasgow reading 'SCOTLAND – THE ONLY COUNTRY WHICH DISCOVERED OIL AND GOT POORER'; but given that nine out of the ten poorest parts of North-Western Europe are in Britain, that's true in the UK across the board. The comparison with Norway is nothing less than an indictment, not only of Thatcherism, but of the terror of new ideas in the British Labour movement. Norway also stayed out of the European Union, due to a shared aversion to it on the part of an influential farming lobby and of the radical left and its dislike of a 'capitalist club', with two referenda going against joining. The somewhat optimistic notion, shared apparently by the current Labour leadership, that leaving the EU could lead to a shift to the left could be seen to be borne out by the Norwegian experience, and a 'Norwegian-style' membership of the EEA is the least obviously awful possible outcome for Britain, though at the time of writing it would seem an unlikely one. Norway is in Schengen, and keeping the migrants out was never part of the reason why it stayed out of the European Union.

In Norway itself, the effects of the oil bonanza – which, even now, is barely tapped, with the government usually only spending around 4 per cent of the sovereign wealth fund – is a little more unclear. It has made the country fabulously wealthy and comfortable, even by Scandinavian standards, but it has also helped create that sprawl around Bergen, otherwise a tightly packed city, crammed in a strip between mountains and the North Sea. Norway got rich late. Like Finland, it became independent (from Sweden) only in the twentieth century, and lacks the sort of large-scale post-war housing projects and New Towns that you can find in Sweden, Finland and to a lesser extent Denmark; it was also heavily damaged in the war, before being liberated in the south by the UK and in the north by the USSR. But otherwise it is similar to its neighbours – an extensive welfare state, a hegemonic Labour Party, an intelligent modern architecture with a sensitivity to landscape. What it has done since getting rich, in the 1980s, 1990s and 2000s, is not quite so far from Britain as one might assume. Though most of the social-security system instituted by Labour from the 1930s on is still in place, housing was deregulated in the 1980s. One result is the hillside patchwork of catalogue houses, each with their views of the sea from which the wealth that paid for them has come. The road infrastructure to connect this is massive and heavy, and no matter how much of it consists of electric cars, buses and trams, the result is suburbanization, to a degree that was surprising to me after the tightly focused planning of the other Scandinavian cities I've visited: Stockholm, Aarhus, Copenhagen, Helsinki. It makes a degree of historical sense, though, as in Bergen, at any rate, the historical architecture is not a matter of tenements and flats, but wooden houses that are lightweight, easily erected, easily dismantled.

The suburbs of wooden houses that survive around Bergen, from the eighteenth and nineteenth centuries, are attractive, if pretty-pretty. I stayed in one of them, Sandviken. A couple of little enclaves of flats lurk unobtrusively around streets of white clapboard villas, semis, detached, terraces, often around little squares, but mostly as casual as a colony of catalogue houses; then, just behind them, limiting the depth of denser development, are the mountains (above, funiculars give steep, vertigo-inducing views). The journey along the ridge above the port from here to the centre shows something else: inset into the cliffs are the blast doors of what look like military facilities, Cold War supervillain style. Norway may have avoided the EU, but unlike Finland and Sweden it joined NATO (the last Labour PM, Jens Stoltenberg, is currently head of the organization), and there is a surprising defensive aspect to the coastline, some

Sandviken, urban village

of it inherited from the Nazi fortification of the Norwegian North Sea littoral. The views from here, especially at night – where the blandness of the buildings matters less – are something. Bergen has, at least according to (a) my experience and (b) statistics, the worst weather anywhere in North-Western Europe, worse even than Glasgow or Belfast, with drizzly, icy rain around 70 per cent of the year. The resultant haze of dampness, yellow lights and ships slowly sailing in and out of the port is quite beautiful, if you've dressed appropriately.

The centre of Bergen is small but just about interesting enough, especially compared with, say, Aarhus; it has an *otherness*, created by the constant closeness of the port on one side and the forested hills, and the extensive streets of wooden houses. These include one delightful little gabled

Secret passageways

effort where McDonald's have been forced by the municipality of Bergen to eschew the use of the golden arches and,
instead, write their name in a polite classical serif; nearby, a
neon sign reads: 'There are a lot of good people around'.
Stronger stuff can be found in a few examples of National
Romanticism and a good crop of Modernist buildings. The
railway station and municipal library are Arts and Crafts
fantasies with dark chunks of rusticated stone and squat
roofs; the station has within an exhilarating iron and glass
roof, a miniature version of the great station halls of Britain
or Germany. Facing the port is the new fish market, combined with a tourist information centre, a 2012 design by
Eder Biesel. It is a long, cantilevered tube, clad in a sweet-
shop pattern of metal strips: the most obviously 'iconic',
tourist-inviting thing the city has done since acquiring its

Tourist information and fish

immense wealth, and even this is very small-scale. Further inland is the excellent Sundt department store, a Constructivist design of 1938 by Grieg Architects, with built-in avant-garde typography and razor-sharp ribbon-windowed floors, ending in an abstracted tower. There is also a cute, wrought-iron turn-of-the-century bandstand, which proved useful to shelter in on the December days when these pictures were taken.

Then there is the administrative and cultural centre of the city. It is organized around a lake and a giant concrete plinth, surmounted by a bronze statue of a former prime minister, Christian Michelsen, who negotiated Norway's independence from Sweden in 1905; his extreme height would seem to be dictated by the presence alongside of one of Bergen's few high-rises, the 1974

311

Bergen City Hall and a city father

City Hall, to a concrete Rationalist design by Erling Viksjø. On the other side of the lake is the 1934 Kunsthall, by a local designer, Ole Landmark, in a laconic, modernized classical manner that could easily be imagined over the border in Sweden; it forms an ensemble with later, more Brutalist extensions, looking out at a strapping female nude, who in turn looks proudly out over the mountainside suburbs. Just behind these is the Grieg Hall, designed in 1978 by the Dane Knud Munk, a long, black-glass curtain wall looking out on the pissing rain and a monumental crown of concrete for the auditorium. This is a lot of cultural and municipal infrastructure for a city closely comparable in its history and size to Norwich or Hull, and almost all of it precedes Norway striking oil, suggesting that an already extant culture of

Grieg Hall

concerted, patient planning might have helped it to accept Farouk al-Kasim's gratification-deferring proposals. It's also a great place to see the spread of little houses in an arc across the mountain, a much less tightly planned vista.

The part of Bergen that visitors are expected to visit – and that UNESCO has listed as a World Heritage Site – is Bryggen, once an entire city within a city run by the Hanseatic League, the German-dominated trading league that is occasionally compared to the German-dominated Union that Norway has opted out of. Bergen was the Hansa's northernmost *Kontor*, and Bryggen was where the north German merchants managed their outpost. What you can see there now – you will have to take my word for it, as the rain made my photos unpublishable – is an

313

extremely restored rebuilding in the early eighteenth century, after a fire, although on the original medieval plan.
To the street, and the harbour, this is a dignified enfilade
of tall, gabled warehouses, but the tallest, most turreted
parts are Victorian additions; the original Bryggen is the
clapboard maze adjacent, with houses inclining outwards
and inwards, with walkways and pulleys overlapping
each other, slicked into shininess by the constant down-
pour. It isn't the pretty wooden fishing village style of
Sandviken (or Aarhus's Italian Quarter, or the suburbs of
Vyborg), but the dense, busy logic of a commercial functionalism executed in yellow and red painted board.
Spatially exciting as it is, constantly opening up new
spaces, little squares and corridors, the restoration effort
is so relentless that any atmosphere it might have had, any
sense of its age, is negated by cleanliness and wildly overpriced organic burger emporia. The Hansa enclave leads
to the historical government centre of Bergen, and the
hardcore, burn-the-heretics horror of the Rosenkrantz
Tower, square, fortified and formidable. The Bryggen
Museum, collecting the various Viking and Hanseatic
finds uncovered in excavations of the site, housed in a
Brutalist complex designed by Øivind Maurseth in 1976,
employs a similarly gruff approach to form; it has absolutely no concession to make to the wooden gables of
Bryggen itself. As if to soften the contrast between the
brown concrete and the painted wood, a new hotel adjacent has been designed in a neo-medieval style, just like
it would be in Britain.

What you can't imagine in Dundee, Hull or Norwich,
though, is the Bergen School of Architecture, founded in

1986 as an explicitly social school, inspired by the theory of 'open form' developed by the Polish architect and socialist Oskar Hansen (the school's founder, Svein Hatløy, was one of Hansen's students). Its current home is a former grain silo, down by the docks at Sandviken. Although the structure has been stabilized, it has otherwise been left fairly untouched by the very different functions that go on in there now; among other things, the smell is still overpowering, and the lightweight stairwells designed to create storeys out of the sheer drops of the empty concrete shell are improvised and shaky. Walking through it, I was surprised to find complete houses constructed on the ground floor, by students – something extremely rare in architecture schools. These are not much like the catalogue houses advertised in the airport,

Inside Bergen School of Architecture

but are weird miniature constructions: huts, prefabs, kiosks, surrounded by detritus. The school encourages the sort of 'learning from' vernacular building tradition that has been fashionable in architectural circles for some time, but is much more interventionist about it, sending students off to India, Brazil, Mozambique and other countries that don't have sovereign wealth funds and elaborate welfare states, in order to learn from how they build in their own circumstances. Its openness is admirable, given how curiously closed Northern European architecture can be to much beyond a sober, tight-arsed Rationalism and a technocratic approach to politics. I had mixed feelings about the punkish, unsentimental, disordered world the Bergen School of Architecture seemed to be building for. It was exciting and politicized, to a degree deeply unusual in the architectural mainstream. It felt good to be there, enjoying the warmth of a futuristic, perhaps postapocalyptic, squat. I wondered, as I had in Stockholm, why poverty was so interesting to people in a country that has all but successfully abolished poverty within its own borders. Nonetheless, the future as driving your electric car up the hills into the forest, to a self-built anarchist villa colony, all paid for by a giant, publicly owned petroleum multinational – it could be worse.

Hamburg: Free and Hanseatic, Social and Democratic

In December 2013 and January 2014, there were riots in the German city with the largest proportion of millionaires per capita. So severe were they that – in a move that was widely ridiculed – the American embassy officially discouraged US citizens from visiting the 'Danger Zone', which consisted of a large swathe (including the tourist-centred red light district, the Reeperbahn) of the centre of the second-largest and richest metropolis of the most populous and most powerful European state. When I saw the news of these events, I realized straight away that I'd seen the main building on which the fighting centred before, and had walked around it three years

Red Flora

Opinions about the Social Democrats vary in Hamburg

before. This was and is 'Red Flora', a Neoclassical theatre
daubed in graffiti, painted yellow and used as a leftist
social centre since 1989, which was finally slated for
clearance and sell-off in 2013, with nearby squats facing a
similar fate, with the approval of the city council, controlled since time immemorial by the Social Democratic
Party of Germany. The protests, whether through their
violence or through their support in the wider community or a combination of both, achieved their main aim:
today, Red Flora remains a social centre and home of
faintly crusty club nights, whereas the unified German
capital's equivalents, such as the famed Tacheles, have
faced gradual erasure. Irrespective of the cause, to create
such turmoil in a city like this, and, moreover, to cause
a climbdown from the city council and developers, was

quite an achievement. Not only Londoners but also Berliners could be jealous.

I hadn't felt like this when I walked around Red Flora three years earlier; ambiguity and discomfort were much more my responses. I felt a similar uncertainty on returning to the city in the summer of 2017, a few weeks after the G20 summit held in the city had culminated in rioting, after, in what seems a transparent piece of provocation to the city's large and volatile political left, a huge swathe of the inner city was policed as a 'Red Zone', where protest or public action of any kind was banned. In each case, that same combination of admiration and frustration.

The first time I went to Hamburg, it was on the invitation of Unlimited Liability, a gallery which sells artworks cheaply to customers who must first sign a declaration that their income and savings are below a certain level, indicating the class tensions of the city pretty neatly. I was hired with the expectation that I would be able to discuss HafenCity (a Deutschlish compound, reversible to 'HarbourStadt'), one of the largest – according to some accounts the largest – inner-city redevelopment schemes in Europe, because I had published various deeply unimpressed things about similar projects in the UK, in London, Salford, Cardiff, Glasgow and my native Southampton. I don't want to put words into their mouths, but I got the impression that the people who had invited me to Hamburg did so on the assumption that I would denounce the scheme in the strongest terms, as I had done in print on the aforementioned British schemes. I couldn't. Although I agreed wholly with the political critique being mounted – that this was another redevelopment for the rich, another land grab, another insult to the notion of a truly social city – I knew that in terms of planning and architecture I would have been lying if I'd argued that this was anything other than impressive. In fact, I spent much of my time wandering around the former docklands of Hamburg wishing that the docklands of Liverpool, say, could have been treated with anything like the same sensitivity and intelligence. I simply couldn't get angry about HafenCity.

Hamburg's docks, though no longer at the old and much mythologized 'Free Port', are still very near to the city centre, and visible from much of it. You can get there via the Kontorhausviertel, the original central business district. This was planned after 1918 by the architect Fritz Schumacher, under the city's Social Democratic adminis- tration, and is a showcase of German Expressionism, a jagged, insurgent architecture, one of biomorphic forms, crystals and neo-Hanseatic intricate brick and clinker. Much of it is designed by Fritz Höger, an architect who would after 1933 become a fervent Nazi (they still didn't give him any commissions). The 'icon' of the Kon- torhausviertel, an image that anyone interested in the Weimar Republic will have seen at least once, is the Chil- ehaus, where accidents of planning – the oddly shaped plots parcelled out by Schumacher to various corporate clients – created an instantly memorable form, the pointed 'stern' of a dreamlike warship. Buildings in ports that look like ships, especially in the 1920s, are usually smooth and streamlined, and there's nothing chic about this dark, cranky, clattering, Nietzschean vessel.

Inside, the Kontorhausviertel's office blocks have atmos- pheric, wide courtyards: public spaces that could be

Chilehaus

Kontorhaus decoration

suddenly enclosed and gated off if necessary (an inside-outside approach to urbanism that Hansa enclaves like Bryggen in Bergen, or the Steelyard in London, had pioneered). Hamburg was tense in the early years of the Weimar Republic, and failed communications meant that an all-German communist uprising planned in 1923 took place here, and nowhere else; the street fighting was fierce, before the national headquarters called it off. The Kontorhausviertel's construction is only briefly noted in books on radical Hamburg, such as Larissa Reisner's *Hamburg at the Barricades* and Jan Valtin's panoramic *Out of the Night*, to record that a very large police station was the first building to be built there. Today it's a quiet area, the proximity to the dual carriageway that runs along the Elbe leaving it a little isolated, with the space in front of the Chilehaus, which should be some kind of Fritz Lang vortex of activity, lost to a car park. As the Kontorhausviertel developed over the 1920s into the 1930s, its architecture became less anxious, more conservative. Repetitive rectilinear blocks step down the main road, with a certain monumental presence, and retain the movement under and across in the arcades that run beneath it; and there's Nazi architecture just behind. The blocks of the Kontorhausviertel designed in the late 1930s by Rudolf Klophaus keep the scale and the courtyards, but lose the twentieth-century Gothic fervour, content with more conservative neo-Biedermeier details and big Dutch gables. What interest there is in Klophaus's Third Reich *Kontorhäuser* lies in the gentle realist figures that surmount the entrances to the offices and courtyards. On one of these entrances is a nostalgic gallery of Hamburg types of the late nineteenth century, charming in their detail and costume. Yet as time goes on these applied sculptures get closer to rote Nazi iconography – giant Neo-classical nudes, cold-eyed and serene.

The HafenCity is entered off the wide road that sweeps past the Kontorhausviertel. The first thing you come to is the Speicherstadt, a warehouse district equivalent in grandeur to Liverpool's Stanley or Albert Docks. They're flats and offices now, of course, but in the way they cleave to the water, they still create a rich atmosphere; several plaques still advertise suppliers of *Orient-Teppiche*, Oriental carpets. Some of the new structures defer to the Speicherstadt, like a clinker-clad car park which junks the spiky detail. New pedestrian bridges link the two versions of the harbour. A sweeping landscaping project by the Catalan–Italian architect Benedetta Tagliabue weaves

Speicherstadt

together a series of small plots, with offices and/or flats along each bit of dockside, more wilful stand-alone architecture at the edges. Tagliabue's landscape architecture is far and away the most original part of HafenCity, and part of what makes it so enjoyable. Lamp posts fool the eye into seeing them swinging around, tracing peculiar waves through the place, perhaps so as not to have any bourgeois strung from them. The sun was shining on each of the weeks I've spent here, which was lucky, as Tagliabue's terraces provide little shelter from the north German rain (although there are plenty of cafés to hide in).

The nomenclature of the area reinforces a certain imperialist theme park air: everything is Vasco de Gama this, Marco Polo that, Magellan here, Sumatra there. Local press have called the place an 'architectural zoo',

Lamp posts of HafenCity

which implies a little more spectacle than is actually offered. Most of it is straightforward if mostly very well-made mild Modernism, tightly controlled. As in the Kontorhausviertel, the architectural effect of planning edicts is easy to read. Along each quay you find ten or more blocks, all roughly of the same width and height, each terminating in a tower. The individual blocks are detailed in a variety of styles, with vaguely Hanseatic/Expressionist clinker, Miesian steel, bright render and so forth, in order to give the effect of variety within carefully controlled parameters. It's all very Teutonic; the strongest parts are by local firms, like Bothe Richter Teherani's vigorous China Shipping HQ. Not all of it is admirable. Erick van Egeraat's blocks make a particular fuss of themselves, the only obvious continuation of Expressionism (with one major exception, which we will come to presently) in the area. A tower for Unilever by Behnisch nods more towards Oscar Niemeyer, all feminine biomorphic curves which the great man would probably tell us are inspired by the beautiful buttocks of the Brazilian woman and the heroic struggle of the Cuban proletariat, but which here look more like the Costa del Elbe. It consists of offices and penthouses, and is advertised as 'Marco Polo Tower – design for Millionaires'. It's all build-up to by far the most expensive and controversial project in HafenCity: Herzog & de Meuron's Elbphilharmonie.

The Elbphilharmonie is the large swooping thing at the end of the rectilinear blocks, completely ignoring their context of neatness and self-effacement. It consists, respectively, of a hotel, car park, luxury penthouses and a

HafenCity from Hafenstrasse, leading to Elbphilharmonie

concert hall (curiously the name only mentions the concert hall). The building is a preposterous Caspar David Friedrich clifftop, billowing and crashing atop a square, red-brick 1960s warehouse, the Kaispeicher. It was not initially part of the HafenCity plan at all, but the private project of two local 'business leaders' who personally commissioned Herzog & de Meuron to draw up a 'landmark' scheme for the site, and claimed that they would pay for the execution, holding many fundraising dinners among Hamburg millionaires in order to pay for it. Needless to say, it soon proved to be much more expensive than expected, and the enormous cost was offloaded onto the city council. The cost has risen over fivefold, and is hence a matter of some controversy in the city. At least some of this is surely owed to the complexity and extravagance of the design, with each glass panel of the new building an oculus-shaped artwork in itself, and the earlier warehouse having to bear its enormous weight. By summer 2017, however, it was finished, and ready to play host to the leaders of the planet, at the G20 summit, deep within the protected Red Zone. The rest of the year, it's a 'public' building, although you have to pay to get to the viewing platform that runs between the Kaispeicher and the bubble-glass extrusion designed on top of it (notably unlike the viewing platform on another Herzog & de Meuron building, the Tate Modern Switch House in London). In August 2017, I watched, on Tagliabue's terraces below, as the wind blew the wig off one unlucky ticket holder on the platform, landing on the steps down to the Elbe.

As an architectural conceit, there's something curiously familiar about the Elbphilharmonie. Not only the town-planning context of rectitude topped by spectacular landmark which can be seen in numerous regeneration schemes, but also the building-eating-another-building motif, also used in Zaha Hadid's even more aggressive glass addition to the Port Authority building in Antwerp. This motif can also be connected to the failure of the German revolution, as the earliest example of it is the Mossehaus in Berlin: here, a press building held by the Spartacists in the January 1919 Rising, partly destroyed by bombardment, was given a streamlined concrete structure in the front and on the upper floors on rebuilding in 1922, not replacing but contrasting with the Wilhelmine building underneath. Meanwhile, the Elbphilharmonie's jagged, crashing form has more than a hint of Gropius's

Monument to the March Dead, his memorial to those who died in the General Strike against a right-wing putsch in 1920. The disjunction between the sober and unremarkable Kaispeicher and the glass mountains above is especially curious, spectacular entertainment rammed into dour industry. When I first visited in 2010, I spotted advertisements around the building site for the workers tasked with building the thing: not only for jobs but for housing, bedsits, not flats in the Monte Carlo tower. Many of these were in both German and Polish, so readable by the *Gastarbeiter*.

Hamburg started building decent housing for workers during the Weimar Republic; the largest estate built then can be found out in the suburbs, at Jarrestadt. Master-planned in the late 20s by Fritz Schumacher, who also master-planned the Kontorhausviertel, the architect was Karl Schneider, a member of the 'Ring', the Weimar-era circle of committed modern architects, and later an anti-Nazi exile. There's not much in the way of fancy Expressionist detail, just simple brown and purple brick with clinker embellishments around the entrances – here, we're very far from the Chilehaus's phantasmagoria. Suddenly, everything has become clear, rational, airy and sunny; but it is stark, something which must have been especially obvious when it was built, before the greenery had the chance to grow up around the buildings. In some accounts, such as Manfredo Tafuri's *Architecture and Utopia*, Jarrestadt appears an image of interwar Modernism at its bleakest. This austere appearance is likely because the place was built with fairly minimal funds, on the principle of the 'existence minimum', i.e. everything necessary

Social Democratic Jarrestadt

and nothing further. According to some accounts, the blocks were also at slightly too high a price for the really poor in the area (Barmbek, then as now a working-class district): deliberately so, as they were intended for the 'deserving', the 'hard-working families' as they'd be called now in the UK, and, in its contemporary context, those who voted Social Democrat rather than Communist. What is similar to the Kontorhausviertel is the sense of free space – movement below, through and across space, without gates and fences. It is a very attractive counter-model, both to HafenCity and to the anarchist urbanism of Hafenstrasse, needing neither the large quantity of money it takes to live in one, nor the utter and total commitment and questionable approach to material comfort it takes to be able to enjoy living in the the other.

329

Hafenstrasse is the centre of an area that was squatted by anti-fascists in the 1980s, and never quite went back to 'normal'. St Pauli is best known as via the notorious/ famous Anarchist football club, and is the home both of the famous sleazy Hamburg known in Beatles biographies and to what is left of Autonomous Hamburg, the dockside city as a prefigurative enclave of anarchist urbanism. The famous streets where sex is sold and where the Beatles played to early 1960s hipsters are not enormously interesting, however much a frisson is still produced by those names – Grosse Freiheit, Reeperbahn. There are some imaginative neon signs, and some shops with strikingly non-erotic names ('Paradise Point of Sex'), and a statue group of the Fab Four, rendered as steel silhouettes, where rough sleepers congregate. Walk towards the port from here and you get to Hafenstrasse, a major holdout of the anarchist city, with several tenement blocks still squatted or run as social centres. In 2010, the slogans alternated from German to English to Spanish: 'World Peace is Dead', 'Viva la Anarchia', 'Freedom for All Prisoners – No Prison No State', 'Against the Domestication of Humanity, for a Life in Freedom', in a red speech bubble rising up into a fist, punching a star. In 2017, most slogans and banners were directed at the G20, not far away in HafenCity. Stickers read: 'We Don't Call The Cops', 'Glasgow Celtic Anti-Fascists', 'Tourist Go Home', and one stencil drawing attention to the area's position as semi-official non-official space, 'Authorized Graffiti Area'. Topographically, Hafenstrasse is blessed by a raised position over the port, so you can see the cranes, an Amazon-branded boat reading 'ALL YOU NEED IS

LOVE', and the city's most famous building, the St Pauli Piers. These utilitarian dockside structures – landing platforms, tunnel entrances – are arranged into a sickly skyline of green *Jugendstil* domes and craggy rusticated towers, Hamburg's iconographic equivalent to Liverpool's Pier Head.

A civic notable in Hamburg said of the HafenCity that the place's obsessive cleanliness, privacy and security were there for one principal reason – 'this isn't going to be another Hafenstrasse'. This isn't rhetorical disdain, it is serious. In August 2017, on a Saturday night, groups of police constantly stomped around in gangs, on a loud and aggressive permanent patrol. The intention was clear – we cannot expel you, but we will make it clear we do not want you. So in what follows I don't intend merely to unfavourably contrast the state socialist approach of the Jarrestadt to the ad hoc anarchist model of Hafenstrasse and St Pauli – they are beleaguered, and need all the help they can get. Obviously, while it strikes me the latter is a far more convincing model of an egalitarian city, less about particular and not universally held tastes and subcultures, both places are necessarily limited incursions into the city of profit. As an enclave, Hafenstrasse is not merely a matter of protecting what has been squatted and acquired, but what happens here can potentially be expanded, can have an effect on the wider city. I once wrote a critical blog about what I found in Hafenstrasse, and therein I assumed one new building in a line of nineteenth-century tenements was a block of yuppie flats, as was practically everything else there that was new. Actually, I was extremely tersely told in the

comments box, this was a school, which had been fought
for by the radicals in the surviving squatland. Perhaps
my mistake was due to the fact that they'd forsaken
the possibility of covering it in stencils and tags. Not
constrained by a concern for legality, land values mean
nothing to squatters: if a space becomes available, it's
there for the taking.

This turns much of central Hamburg into a battle-
ground. Some of it is placid – the shopping streets, and the
calm vista of the Alster lake – but it can suddenly shift, as
I saw on a walk round the city centre with some local
activists in 2010. A Wilhelmine hinterland slated for demolition was quickly reappropriated, and a programme was
established. The apparently chaotic, untamed, newly
claimed space faced an area of seamless, icy business
urbanism, and it did so with an unsurprising aggression.
Chalked on a blackboard in a prominent place in the occupation was a declaration which seems aimed at my
objections. Roughly translated from the German, it read:
'If architecture can only commit to the bourgeois model
of private property and society, we must reject architecture . . . Until all design activities focus on primary
human needs, until that time design must disappear. We
can live without architecture.' The quote is from Adolfo
Natalini, of the Italian architectural satirists Superstudio.
This other urbanism seems to follow capitalist development around the city, nagging at it. Loomed over by
another Expressionist skyscraper, near the Messe, the
Trade Fair beneath the Hamburg TV Tower. Business-
land and squatland are at some sort of stalemate. 'Death
to Industry', 'Fuck Messe'. A mammoth Nazi bunker has

Instant autonomy

become a general space for the creative industries. Anything in Hamburg, no matter how bleak or how
unique – Cold War bases, *Jugendstil* department stores,
actual wartime bunkers – can be taken over by capital
and by squatters and turned into an office block or a social
centre much like any other. Long may it be so.

Modernist Randstad

Bearing in mind the imprecision of all analogies, the European country that is historically, economically and culturally closest to Britain is not France, Belgium, Norway or Germany but the Netherlands. A largely Protestant country with a reputation for mildness and liberalism belied by an overseas record of imperial plunder and massacre; an overwhelmingly urban country where most people speak a derivative of a western Germanic dialect; and, most of all, a peculiarly capitalist country. Before the baton was passed to London (and from there to New York and, presumably sometime soon, from New York to Beijing), Amsterdam was the heart of a world capitalist system as early as the seventeenth century, its stock market causing ripples in every corner of the globe (even before the armies of its companies captured places as far away as Surinam and Indonesia). Like the City of London, Amsterdam was a pioneer in making money out of money. Their decline has been longer and slower than 'ours', beginning in the early eighteenth rather than late nineteenth century, but even the most casual acquaintance with both countries would suggest they did far better in cushioning the fall. But perhaps the biggest similarity – and difference – has been in the approach to city building.

Amsterdam has no Versailles – not even a Buckingham Palace (and nor, really, does the royal seat at The Hague, where the palace is relatively modest). It has no Champs-Elysées, no Gran Vía, no Hapsburgian boulevards. Urban monuments to the powers that be, royal or republican, do exist, but they are harder to find than in London or Brussels, let alone Paris, Vienna, Madrid or Moscow. This does not deter visitors. What people go to see in Amsterdam or Delft is a continuous work that combines town planning, engineering and speculation – the crowded but regulated bourgeois tenements along canals that were laid out at the end of the seventeenth century and extended into the twentieth· It is a project far closer to Bloomsbury, Bath, Edinburgh or Dublin than it is to the monumental planning of the absolute monarchies in France, Austria–Hungary, Spain, Germany or Russia, which are sometimes considered to be the root of European urban success. In Dutch cities there are no axes, no vistas, and the streets, whether winding or straight, lead to what are mostly under-designed, under-scaled civic buildings. Because of all this, walking round the cities of the Netherlands should in fact be the best place of all to work out when, where and if there was a real divergence in urban culture between Britain and 'the Continent'.

Because a parting there most certainly has been. If you were to peruse the architecture websites and aggregators – let's say, the illustrated online database MIMOA, which collects notable or award-winning contemporary projects across the world – you'd find that Amsterdam's entries are about equal to those of London (a city ten times larger) and Rotterdam's at least ten times those of comparable cities like Birmingham or Manchester. If such a list existed in 1917 rather than 2017, this would hardly be possible. Victorian/Edwardian architecture in

Rotterdam, Amsterdam or The Hague is actually less original, less experimental, less impressive than it is in Liverpool, London or Glasgow: typical examples, like the dock offices of Rotterdam or the civic buildings of late-nineteenth-century Amsterdam (the railway station, the Stedelijk Museum and the Rijksmuseum, two of them by the same architect, Pierre Cuypers, all in the same upscaled version of seventeenth-century Dutch Baroque), pale by comparison with British equivalents. The shift seems to have come in the aftermath of the First World War, in which the Dutch stayed neutral; and from then on the two countries sometimes veer back near to each other, and then part again. At the moment, they would seem at a glance to be very far away indeed. Here, I want to try to test that impression against the sprawling con-urbation in which nearly half of the population of the Netherlands live – the 'Randstad', or Rim City.

From the North Sea to the German border, the towns and cities fade into each other, each with their own satel-lites, separated by strips of industry or skinny, bleak agricultural green belts; Hook of Holland becomes The Hague which becomes Delft which becomes Rotterdam which becomes Utrecht which becomes Amsterdam, which itself has its large satellites and New Towns, like Almere and Hilversum. More than Greater London, Greater Manchester or the West Midlands, the Randstad is a tightly regulated sprawl, with nothing allowed to grow wild, few picturesque rural spots – when taking a photo of a windmill, you'll have to mind you don't get a row of pylons or a refinery in the picture by mistake – and this is one big difference with the UK. Both countries are overwhelmingly urban in terms of where people live, but only the Netherlands is in terms of land use, and that – plus the necessity in Holland of suppressing nature with dykes and canals lest the cities be drowned – explains Britain's greater attachment to its far more diverse countryside. This, at least, is something about which we might not be envious.

The first big divergence comes with the architectural and applied-art movement known as the 'Amsterdam School'. In Amsterdam, if you walk around working-class districts of the nineteenth century, you'll find stark, tall tenements that are more identikit, straighter versions of the tenements of the Dutch golden age, retaining the height, density, narrow twisting staircases and the pulleys at the top so you can get things in and out – but no more unusual or distinguished than industrial housing in Britain around the same time (British workers were on the whole likely to have better housing, less over-crowded, more likely to have gardens), and you'll find far less Art Nouveau experimentation than in Brussels or Liège. They're pleasant and a little gentrified now, but the streets of Jordaan or De Pijp must have been grim and noxious a hundred years ago. In architectural histories, the unprecedented nature of what comes next is usually ascribed to the influence of the architect H. P. Berlage, whose work, beginning with his Amsterdam Stock Exchange, showed an unusual combination of Arts and Crafts bluffness and a love for early-modern-American architecture's experiments with structure. But the Stock Exchange wouldn't look out of place in Victorian Birmingham. What most definitely would is the

Scheepvaarthuis

Scheepvaarthuis, built in 1913 to the designs of Johan van der Mey, Piet Kramer and Michel de Klerk. This is a corner office block, built for various shipping companies, between the docks and the railway station. Its brickwork is intricate, but not conventionally Gothic, in a jagged idiom that seems to have come partly from Expressionist painting (Van Gogh has fancifully been proclaimed an influence) and from the sharply sliced intersecting volumes of Frank Lloyd Wright. It's modern, but as ornamental as anything Victorian – more so, with troll-like personifications of the Oceans moulded in granite into the façade. Inside, a partly glazed atrium exploits the novel construction, and serves well for its current incarnation, an obscenely luxurious hotel.

The Amsterdam School is best known for its social housing, which as in Britain was first built en masse in the Netherlands in the 1910s and 1920s; but as in Germany the bulk of it was built by subsidized building societies and associations linked with the trade unions and the socialist parties, rather than directly by the state. The estate that even tourists make their way to is Het Schip, the other side of the railway station to the Scheepvaarthuis. Built in 1917 to the designs of Michel de Klerk, and still functioning as social housing, 'The Ship' (see the pattern?) was experimental even at the time. You can see its ancestry – asymmetrical arrangements of towers and turrets from Gothic, meticulous brickwork from those Baroque canalside tenements, but everything else is new. The façades morph constantly. Your eyes trace past first a

The ship

corner moulded into something resembling a face, with the entrance in the yawning mouth (or is it a handlebar moustache?), past a cantilevered gable like a giant red-brick wart; stand up from this and you'll notice that the complex has the profile of some kind of longboat, hence the name. The obsessive brickwork is close to the Kontorhausviertel in Hamburg, but less harsh, with a variety of surfaces and shapes – dark-purple clinker, English-style bright red, a deep brown, a lurid orange, each of them laid with long, thin bricks into patterns. This isn't just superficial whimsy, a jolly façade over the usual barracks, but, as Reyner Banham puts it, 'space architecture', based on the plasticity of the buildings and the definition of collective space; the building's different functions are articulated with a completely three-dimensional mastery. There is a museum flat inside you can wander round, and also inside the original post office. A moulded truncheoned fist with 'FORBIDDEN' marking the non-public spaces of the latter shows that all this apparent cutesiness could mask a mordant humour.

Het Schip, through its placement just slightly north of tourist Amsterdam, can be mistaken for being a private eccentricity, but its ideas actually dominated mass housing and planning here for a decade. In the late 1910s, H. P. Berlage was tasked with designing an expansion plan for Amsterdam, beyond the workers' district of De Pijp; the resulting 'Plan Zuid' – Plan South – is one of the most pleasurable expanses of architectural scenery in Europe. The plan was for a grid of tenement flats, fairly traditional but for large green courtyards inside (something seldom found in the 'rental barracks' of the nineteenth century), along canals and with schools, libraries and cafés mixed in; the ground floors were 'active' in the contemporary sense, some with nurseries, some with shops, but with doors to the tenements opening right onto the street, which remained the focus – increasing in importance, in fact, given the way the architects constantly emphasized corners, doorways, windows, balconies. One of the earliest parts of it, De Dageraad ('The Dawn', developed by a socialist building society of the same name), was carried out in the early 1920s by Michel de Klerk and Piet Kramer, in a version of Het Schip's strange, tactile Expressionism. This estate also has a (smaller) museum of itself, and is defined by wave-like corners of billowing brick, treating this tough material with improbable plasticity, scooping and spreading it like it was concrete. Again, it can veer into the twee – De Klerk's high pitched roofs rhetorically invite people to dance around them in dirndls – but it would be pointless to resist something as powerful and rich as this. And it is all – still – social housing, outside the market. It is an improbable achievement.

In terms of who it was for and when it was built, the real comparison to make is of Plan South with the ribbons of council and private semis around every British city. They have things that Dutch housing from the time does not: private gardens, staircases you can carry things up, and that apparently all important up-with-the-drawbridge sense of privacy. Some of these things are nice, but I would challenge anyone to go from Penge or Wythenshawe to Amsterdam South and honestly say that they prefer the English suburb. However, the millennial

The Dawn

utopianism of Het Schip or De Dageraad did not dominate Dutch housing, even at the time, although the
general standard remained high. Much of Plan Zuid is just
middle-class housing, built by developers – albeit on
heavy manners from the local authority – and it gradually
shifts into a more familiar Modernism. If you go to
Amstel station and cross over the Berlage-designed
bridge, towards Victorieplein, you can see block after
block of this lush, exquisite housing. At Plan South's centre, in the middle of the square, is a high-rise, defined by a
full-height glass stairwell. One of the earliest high-rises in
Europe, this is the Twelve-Storey House, designed in 1930
by J. F. Staal. The Expressionism and Romanticism have
been purged, and instead you find what is in some ways

an equally exciting approach, based on elegance and high-tech modernity rather than impossible feats of craftsmanship and eye-dazzling metamorphoses. This is, however, an approach much more associated with Rotterdam.

The countermovement to the Amsterdam School – its successor, in many ways – was De Stijl. As an art movement, it favoured primary colours and straight lines and spawned Piet Mondrian, who left in disgust when its founder, Theo van Doesburg, began to employ diagonals. The extent to which there is a De Stijl architecture is disputed among the historians. The only building which meets all the criteria of De Stijl is the Schröder House in Utrecht, a geometrical experiment in interpenetrating volumes which is the only building to really fit the claim

The 'skyscraper' of Amsterdam South

made by the bloviating Australian TV presenter Robert Hughes that modern architecture involved 'living in a Mondrian'. There were, however, many architects associated with the movement at one time or another, among them J. J. P. Oud, who was once mentioned in the same breath as Le Corbusier and Mies van der Rohe as a modern master. Oud designed two large working-class estates in dockside areas of Rotterdam, only one of which still survives. The one that doesn't is in Spangen, still the poorest part of the inner city. Here, Oud designed a series of brick, deck-access flats whose façades were as flat and regular as those of De Klerk and Kramer were expressive and protuberant. They were demolished in the 1990s, something that is deeply unusual in the Netherlands, a country that generally preserves its Modernist heritage to an almost comic decree (in fact, modern buildings might be reconstructed if damaged by war or development – Oud's photogenic, poster-like Café de Unie in the city centre is a reconstruction, on a different site to the original). They hadn't been renovated, and were replaced with simple brick cube-like houses and flats, vaguely in the De Stijl tradition. The only building of his surviving here is a toy-like cube structure that appears not to be used for anything. The rest of Spangen is more interesting.

The architect Michiel Brinkman designed the Justus van Effen complex, again for a socialist housing association, in the early 1920s, around the time Kramer and De Klerk were designing their voluptuous brick fairylands. Here, all lines are straight and hard, and all the architectural focus is on space and circulation. The complex consists of a series of courtyards leading into each other,

Interwar streets in the sky

Purism at Kiefhoek

wide and spacious, with much more openness and air than in any of Plan Zuid; and its defining feature is a continuous concrete walkway, sculpted like an extruded Modernist relief. This is all closer to Brutalism than to the architecture of the 1920s, a fixation with public space and its extension upwards; it's a shame the spaces between are so stark, bare and scrubby, making the place a little institutional. Apparently, the area has a formidable reputation, but it looked in good condition and well-used – it is, however, much less white than some of the rest of Rotterdam, a development the architects would not have anticipated, nor probably considered relevant.

Oud's second, surviving, estate, Kiefhoek, is in a less eerie district, further from the docks, and makes a fine case for calmness and elegance. Its smoothly curved icing-sugar-white surfaces earned it a prominent place in Philip Johnson and Henry-Russell Hitchcock's 1932 book *The International Style*, which helped create, perhaps better than any other, a Modernism purged of the social, and purged of any interest in the immediate surroundings of a given building. Kiefhoek consists of tiny terraces, painted in the De Stijl colours – crisp yellow metal window frames, red doors and white stuccoed walls. These are overshadowed on all sides —a neo-Gothic church here, skyscrapers there, brick tenements hard up against the gardens. It feels like an enclave, not socially – similar people seem to live here to the more workaday area around – but architecturally. That's because the project of rationalization is carried out with such doggedness that it extends to the lamps, the railings, and a hysterical church, a white cube with a

Rotterdam Constructivism

chimney that could easily pass for a boiler house. If actually visited rather than viewed through the original photos, the estate – still a functioning area of social housing, not perceptibly affected by gentrification – ceases to be just a pure, Platonic series of volumes in space, but becomes a polemic. Not so much against the pretension, craftsmanship and cuteness of the Amsterdam School, but an anticipatory argument over what sort of a city Rotterdam is today.

This purist Modernism remained avant-garde, and didn't become a dominant presence in the Dutch second city in the way the 'School' dominated Amsterdam. A lot of the ordinary architecture of Rotterdam is in a somewhat milder version of the Amsterdam School, as is

the case with many other Dutch cities, the lovely Boij-
mans Museum being one of Rotterdam's best examples.
The acknowledged masterpiece of interwar Rotterdam is
not a housing estate or an office block, but a tobacco factory for Van Nelle, designed by Johannes Brinkman and
Leendert van der Vlugt, with some assistance from the
Bauhaus teacher and communist Mart Stam. The hardline Modernists of Rotterdam developed out from under
the rather personal slogans of De Stijl and adopted, as in
Germany, the more prosaic slogan 'Het Nieuwe Bouwen'
('the New Building') by the end of the 1920s. This is a
classic work of that shift, which is closer to the imaginary
projects of Russian Constructivism than to Oud's polite,
stuccoed cubic and curved terraces. Long since disused
as an actual tobacco factory and turned over to various
'creative' industries, it is close to the city centre if somewhat fiddly to get to, but when you get there, it is
jaw-dropping. A small glass block curves along a semi-
circular approach into a monumental concrete and glass
volume, capped by a glass rotunda and a giant 'VAN
NELLE' sign – and long glass walkways like robotic legs
jut out at angles towards the smaller engine rooms. The
architects will doubtless have justified everything on
functional necessity, and some of the motifs are borrowed from the American factories of Albert Kahn for
Ford and GM, but this is a project of aesthetes, with each
asymmetry precisely calculated, the walkways and the
precariously balanced top-floor rotunda the result of
architectural dreaming rather than the processes of
tobacco making.

What makes the interwar Dutch achievement so

The birth of Dudokery

extraordinary is that within the same decade two projects that were in their own way as extreme and as radical
as Het Schip and the Van Nelle factory were both carried
out, not just as isolated experiments but on a serious
scale. This is where the difference with British practice is
glaring, largely because the 1920s were probably the most
aesthetically conservative in the history of British architecture, a period of peak-of-empire Neoclassical office
blocks and tail-end-of-Arts-and-Crafts suburban housing:
even grand projects, streets like the Headrow in Leeds or
New Towns like Welwyn Garden City, were, stylistically,
exercises in architectural Toryism. However, it wouldn't
quite do to suggest that the Dutch architecture of the
interwar years had no effect on Britain; quite the reverse.

Berlage built a small office block in the City of London for a Dutch company in 1916, though it had no successors. Instead, in the 1930s, another Dutch modern architect, who never built in Britain, became one of the most influential designers in the UK: Willem Marinus Dudok. Every time you see a 1930s modern building of precisely laid yellow brick and cubic volumes in a British town or city, you're seeing an architect who had seen Dudok. Schools, Tube stations and borough halls in London, pithead baths and Co-ops in the north, and sundry Odeon cinemas everywhere, all are iterations of 'Dudokery'.

Dudok was the city architect of Hilversum. This town has had a few incarnations: a small medieval satellite of Amsterdam, then a bourgeois garden city of villas set in tree-lined lanes, and then a centre for the Dutch media industry (first radio, then TV). It was in this last incarnation that Dudok designed an expansion that was a total project involving original designs for housing (both social and private), schools, shopping parades and much else; but most of all a town hall of prodigious size and influence. Hilversum is not nearly as enjoyable to visit as one might expect from acquaintance with its architectural rep. On a Sunday it is utterly dead, and its high street of closed chain stores is as grim as a Luton or a Doncaster. Dudok's style shifted over the decades he carefully cultivated the city, and much of it is the Amsterdam School scaled down, a change in emphasis which stresses the twee side of the school – long, low terraces for the workers, more elaborate for the bourgeois, all with a language of steep roofs and pretty details. There is also what appears to be a police station for Hobbits. Here, with the urbanity of Amsterdam reduced to cottages and terraces rather than monumental housing complexes and bridges, you can see the school's heritage in the English Arts and Crafts – in places, you could be in Letchworth or Wythenshawe. This is not what Dudok's fame and his RIBA Gold Medal were earned for – that's that town hall, which is usefully signalled by signposts everywhere asking you to follow the 'Dudok Route'. When you find it, it is in its more conservative way an achievement as impressive as Het Schip or Van Nelle. An asymmetric composition in front of a decorative lake, rising in multiple levels to a tall clocktower, it is exceptionally photogenic. The composition, of cubes and rectangles slotting together, as if in a Malevich or Mondrian painting, is via De Stijl; the meticulous brick detailing and lush craftsmanship is via the Amsterdam School, a very deliberate synthesis. It also lacks the sort of things which made modern architecture scary – the almost dystopian machine-world of the Van Nelle, or the feeling of being in someone else's fantasy in Het Schip or De Dageraad. A compromise: no wonder it was so popular in Britain. Dudok's synthesis would also affect Dutch designers in the 1930s. For his last work, the Gemeente Museum in The Hague, H. P. Berlage adopted a version of Dudokery and abstracted it further, stretching out the walkways and piling up the cubes. Aptly, it houses a large Mondrian collection.

After 1945, this narrative of Dutch pioneering and British following is no longer quite so tenable. The Netherlands was occupied by Nazi Germany. Dutch Jews were exterminated – despite a General Strike in Amsterdam in protest against their deportation, one of the

Berlage's last work, the Gemeentemuseum

extremely few protests against the Holocaust. Thousands of Dutch citizens starved to death near the end of the war. The act that had the biggest urban effect, though, was the comprehensive bombing of Rotterdam. Done in order to demonstrate the futility of resistance, this was at the time, in 1940, the most complete erasure of a city that had taken place up to that point, although what would happen later on the Eastern Front would surpass it. Rotterdam and Coventry were closely comparable, and were in fact often compared; and in the aftermath of their near-obliteration they did, more or less, the same thing. They built new housing estates and garden suburbs (Tile Hill, Hoogvliet) and pedestrian precincts. Rotterdam's Lijnbaan precinct is barely distinguishable from its Coventry cousin, bar – with by now tedious inevitability – infinitely better care and maintenance, courtesy of a recent renovation which annoyed some preservationists for reasons I couldn't quite fathom, as it still looks as 1950s as can be: just clean and nice and with lots of people in, none of whom look sick and defeated. One reason why it has succeeded by comparison, other than the unique awfulness of Britain, is a key difference in planning. The Lijnbaan and the area around it is not monofunctional, isn't just shops; all around the pedestrianized streets are mid-rise flats, in the same brick and concrete grids. The rear ground floors of these blocks of flats were given over to workshops and workplaces. Even then, some parts of the reconstructed city are far too severe – the Blaak, for instance, is a Soviet-style boulevard without the monumentality to make it worth while, windswept and corporate. The memorial

1940 Square

part of the reconstructed city, Plein 1940, is more simple than Coventry's cathedral complex (Rotterdam's impressive Gothic cathedral was the only major city centre building to survive the bombing). It's just a wide, empty square overlooking a canal, centred on Ossip Zadkine's memorial of a figure gesturing in horror, the centre of his body blown apart.

Both Amsterdam and Rotterdam built new suburbs in the 1950s and 1960s. 'Garden Cities', they were called, though they're more closely connected with their parent cities than the British exemplars like Welwyn, Letchworth, Stevenage and Harlow. You'll often see them coming into either Amsterdam or Rotterdam from Schiphol, where they look a little chilling, severe grids of low-rise slabs and mid-rise towers, often painted in the De Stijl colours. Hoogvliet is around twenty-five minutes out of the centre on the Rotterdam Metro, past a green belt, and at first, you could be in absolutely any post-war peripheral estate in Britain (again, maintenance aside). Most of it is clipped little terraces around squares, with canals and ponds and lots of trees, and there are a few taller buildings to offer definition to what would otherwise be a vague landscape. First phases are the mild Modernism of the 1950s, and later parts are alternately more stark, as you'd find in the harder estates of the London County Council, or closer to a sort of 'vernacular', similar to what you'd find in later, 1970s New Town architecture, attempts at being both modern and homely. There is a shopping precinct, with an incongruous combination of a massive surface car park and lots of parked bicycles. The shift that also happened in Britain towards

The not-particularly dystopian Bijlmer

Brutalist monumentality can be seen in Amsterdam's peripheral Bijlmermeer, which has become somewhat notorious as one of Europe's great 'failed estates', comparable to, say, Manchester's Hulme Crescents. I can't comment on what it would have been like a decade ago, but visiting the complex recently – part of it has been demolished, and the rest renovated – it looked very nice indeed. What it does is both more futuristic and more verdant than the simpler Modernism of Hoogvliet. 'The Bijlmer' is a series of snaking blocks connected by walkways, around a dense, tree-filled landscape; residents have done a lot of the planting themselves, in their balconies. It's very fine, but only the maintenance differentiates it from, say, Thamesmead or Park Hill. After this, though, Dutch and British cities would diverge again.

Both of these models – placid New Towns and monumental, urban Brutalist complexes – were rejected by
protesters, and increasingly by 'public opinion', in the
second half of the 1960s. Unlike in Britain, protest movements then left a decisive and irreversible mark on the city.
The marginal ideas of semi-Situationist urban activists like
the Provos – such as a city whose major form of circulation
would be by foot and by cycle rather than by car or Metro,
or a city where you could if you so wished smoke pot in a
café for that purpose – have been accepted now for decades. And while Amsterdam would seem to lend itself
to this through its tight structure, you'll also find great
fleets of bikes in spacious, Modernist Rotterdam (even in
Hoogvliet), a reminder that this was the result of activism
and choice, not some sort of cultural or formal determin-
ism. People made Dutch cities nice, and there is no reason
why Birmingham or St Petersburg could not be treated in
the same way.

While it may have stopped some big projects of demolition associated with the Amsterdam Metro, this intangible
change had few obvious architectural effects: there is no
'Provo' architecture. What there is, is the Dutch modern
architecture occasionally called 'Supermodernist' or
'Super-Dutch', and it is this stuff that fills websites like
MIMOA. Firms like the Office for Metropolitan Architecture (dominated in the press by the designer and writer
Rem Koolhaas), Mecanoo, MVRDV, Erick van Egeraat *et
al*. favour a modern architecture which has thrown
Rationalism and utopian projects aside for spectacle, daz-
zle, engineering extravagance and façade experiments
that generally avoid the explicit historical reminiscences

associated with Postmodernism. Along with these, there are other Dutch designers such as Hans van der Heijden, whose architecture combines De Stijl's Rationalism with a more classical sense of repose and continuity. This means that 1980s–2010s architecture in Rotterdam and The Hague seldom has the same feel that Birmingham or Liverpool has of, first, terrified anti-modernity followed by developers' offcuts, but they have a similar approach to overdevelopment and density, something especially obvious in recent years. Rotterdam has taken to Koolhaas's idea of hyper-dense urban 'delirium', and built the major skyscraper city of Northern Europe; increasingly, the administrative-bureaucratic metropolis of The Hague has followed suit.

You can see traces of 'Super-Dutch' in something like Piet Blom's 1984 Cube Houses near Blaak Metro station in Rotterdam, which is otherwise a late outgrowth of 1960s utopianism, with a 'tree' of diamond-shaped living pods cantilevered out between the city's market square and an old dock-turned-marina. As much as architecture to be lived in, this is there to be gawped at, modern architecture as tourist attraction. Here is a very different approach to hard, angular works like OMA's early-1990s Rotterdam Kunsthal (literally 'Art Hall'), which uses brittle materials and spatial distortions to take the classic Modernism of the 1920s into more aggressive, wilfully confusing territory. There have been few Dutch Postmodernists, but they have been keen to invite others over from elsewhere – in The Hague alone, there is a 'Blitzcrete' shopping centre by the English eccentric John Outram, a 'Nonument' by British neo-Postmodernists

FAT and some Dutch house-shaped skyscrapers by the late American Postmodernist Michael Graves.

A massive quantity of Fun with a capital F has surged into the Randstad. Rotterdam fills its post-war open spaces not with whoever might be today's Zadkine, but with giant statues of Gundam or of garden gnomes. New city centre buildings range from the actually rather clever 'bathtub' of the Stedelijk Museum extension, which sleekly links the pompous Gothic Museum to the land-scaped museum park, to MVRDV's utterly horrible new Market Hall. This huge structure consists of a blobular office block around a scooped-out open space filled with chain restaurants, its daringly engineered ceiling covered with a mural of the sort of ordinary fare you could buy in a different market, one that doesn't revolve around a Jamie Oliver restaurant. In Rotterdam, though, the main ques-tion is that tangle of skyscrapers. Everyone has had a go, enough architects to fill a *1000 Modern Buildings to See before You Die* book – MVRDV, Renzo Piano, Álvaro Siza, Will Alsop, and dozens of others have done their whimsical high-rises. It is quite exciting in places, and certainly more so than Zuidas, Amsterdam's own, much more conser-vative and rational version of the same, at a Canary Wharf-style specially separated, master-planned site; but it can be oddly depressing, ideas thrown randomly at the wall. Accordingly, the best of these skyscraper complexes might be OMA's recently completed De Rotterdam, one of the most sinister buildings in contemporary Europe. As with many Koolhaas projects, you can see it as a dialogue with twentieth-century high Modernism, here with Amer-ican International Style designers SOM's three chilling

Corporate Dystopia – OMA, De Rotterdam

grid-like towers on the docks near Spangen, built in the 1970s. Here, that has become a massive volume intended to resemble three post-war glass skyscrapers shoved into each other, the World Trade Center undergoing a nervous breakdown. It looms over the centre of Rotterdam like a supervillain's lair.

Amsterdam has better things. The docks around the IJ, and the islands of Borneo and Sporenburg, have been filled with decent modern architecture in a manner that very closely resembles Hamburg's HafenCity, while Hans Kollhoff's new skyscraping government buildings in The Hague are images of metropolitan suaveness and bureaucratic opacity. A few years ago, I would have thought buildings like these impossible in Britain, but London, at any rate, at places like King's Cross, is moving

New Amsterdam

to imitate them, with regular brick volumes, classical proportions and clear, sensible public spaces. And they are imitating us, by tearing up their post-war social-democratic legacy for property development and social cleansing. Of course, they're doing it 'better' than we are, but the effects seem oddly similar, as the response to in-equality and instability is expressed through racism and paranoia. We have Nigel Farage, they have Geert Wilders, a preposterous Max Headroom lookalike whose explicitly racist politics is presented as a defence of Dutch tolerance and racism. Willders' political career emerged from 'liveable city' movements in the racially mixed sub-urbs of Rotterdam and Hilversum. Social housing is under attack here, both as concept and as practicality, although without the extreme speed and violence the British have become accustomed to since 1979. In Holland such change moves not via attack, but through consensus. What is happening at Hoogvliet shows this especially.

The interstices of the New Town are filled with new private housing, much of it very good, and unlike in the UK in obvious architectural dialogue with the old New Town – good brick houses, and even three new high-rises that could from a distance be direct remakes of towers from the early 1960s. Only one lone skyscraper in the middle of the New Town has the British sense of 'fuck you' in its placing in the middle of social-democratic space. The best result of all this is a thing called 'Heerlijkheid Hoog-vliet', a social centre in a park where Hoogvliet meets the

The Surrealist community centre

towers of an oil refinery, part of Rotterdam's vast port. Designed by FAT with Dutch historian-architects Crimson, it tries to bring together the attempt to make the new town fashionable and appealing to middle-class incomers with something useful for its social-housing residents. It does this by a bizarre and genuinely daring combination of traditional civic gestures – an approach bridge, a monumental profile – with pop art and Postmodernist ideas, such as a wooden skyline mirroring the oil refinery, and a cluster of yellow 'trees' billowing around the entrance. As social democracy dies here through consensus rather than through a declared class war, this building tries to achieve its synthesis through a combination of humour and civic pathos. The slogan of the project is 'WIMBY', an acronym for – in English, no less – 'Welcome In My Back Yard'!

In Praise of Hull

Alan Bennett noted that London-based writers regarded the city that Philip Larkin made his home as if it were some desperate place at the ends of the earth. The great poet, vicious reactionary and porn aficionado was, Bennett stated, granted endless kudos for living there, as if Hull weren't one of the largest cities in England, with a good university, a decent art gallery, a developed civic culture and a train that could get you to London in two and a half hours. It was and is far less remote from London than the country retreats that are advertised in the back pages of the literary magazines, and it's a short distance from York, which is never regarded with the same awe at its remoteness, provincialism and poverty. But there are the physically remote and the psychologically remote. Kingston upon Hull was, in the Middle Ages, in the ideal place for a British port to be: facing the North Sea, like Newcastle upon Tyne, Boston and London. Like the last two of these (and, ahem, King's Lynn), it hosted one of the English outposts of the Hanseatic League, the German-dominated transnational trading network that worked its way through the Baltic and North Seas. Hull is, of its very nature, an international city, and the less international Hull has become, the more it has suffered; the Brexit vote here was immense. It is, in the year of writing (2017), the UK's official 'City of Culture', but the problems it has to cope with – and will have to cope with when all the European Union Objective 1 money that sustains what is left of its economy is removed – are gigantic. Yet putting Hull here up against the various European cities in the book is not a joke, and is not intended to be an easy contest, putting a 'crap town' next to Hamburg or Stockholm or Porto. In architectural (and many other) terms, Hull is one of the most interesting cities in Britain, which makes its decline helpful if we're trying to work out in what way Britain is or isn't part of a comparative 'Europe'.

The decline of the UK's Atlantic ports – Liverpool, most of all – is occasionally dated to Britain's mid-1970s entry into the European Economic Community, the creature that eventually became the European Union, which, along with the end of the British Empire, meant that the Atlantic became less central to British economic life, and

Welcome to Hull, UK City of Culture

the Channel and the North Sea more so. If this is genuinely the case, joining the EEC seems to have helped Hull little. The positive effects were much more visible on London (from the mid-1990s on, finally on a rail route to Europe, and, under deregulation, with a financial sector able to do the dubious things European banks wouldn't do); on the container ports of Southampton, Tilbury and Felixstowe; and on Scotland, whose waters had the British part of the North Sea oil deposits, and where some wealth at least has rubbed off on Aberdeen, Edinburgh and their suburbs. In fact, it faced new and unexpected problems – the one people mention most in Hull is the effects of the Common Fisheries Policy on a local economy that was based as much on fish as shipbuilding.

Like eastern England more generally – with the obvious exception of London – Hull hasn't faced twentieth-century mass migration on anything like the scale of Liverpool, Bristol, Birmingham, Greater Manchester or the West Riding of Yorkshire. In fact, it is better remembered as the entry point of East European, often Jewish, escapees from poverty and pogroms between the 1880s and 1910s, who were just passing through on their way to settle in Leeds, Salford, Liverpool, or further afield in the USA and Canada. Accordingly, the sparse immigration Hull has experienced in recent years has been the direct consequence of the accession to the European Union of various post-communist countries since 2004 – a Polish shop here, a Lithuanian flag there, someone speaking Bulgarian on the bus. Unlike those of a hundred years ago, these East Europeans have decided to make lives here. Of course, their arrival hasn't even slightly managed to make up for the population loss the city faced after the Second World War. The east of England – again perhaps oddly, given that it is the part of the country most directly affected, for hundreds of years, by the proximity of continental Europe – has formed a formidable Brexit bloc, impervious to arguments about how reliant certain northern parts of it, especially Humberside and Teesside (and certainly Hull), are on EU cash injections.

Hull is often used as a synonym for those 'left behind', as the euphemism goes, straggling along as London goes full throttle. This extended into the way Brexit was reported, particularly by those hoping it might spur the Labour Party (long dominant in Hull, bar a brief period of Liberal control in the 2000s) to move towards some sort of nativist 'Socialism in one country', with renationalized railways and controls on immigration. In the words of one of the party's senior politicians, Labour had become 'too much Hampstead, not enough Hull'. The vote for Brexit in the city was thumping – 67 per cent, despite the fact that one of the city's MPs, the veteran Blairite Alan Johnson, was officially the leader of the 'Labour In' campaign (it's worth noting that in the same year there were huge rallies in Hull in support of Jeremy Corbyn's re-election campaign). There was obviously bigotry in all this – baffling, maybe, given that by all accounts many of the shops now housing *Polskie Sklepy* were previously derelict, and that the city has lost 50,000 people since the 1940s, but there it is, a testament to the xenophobia of British political discourse and the occasional awfulness of human beings. Equally plausible is that it was a vote against a smug establishment talking of a post-recession 'recovery' which never made it here, with one in four unemployed.

Exaggerated as it is, the perception of Hull as distant and insular has some truth to it. It is the end of the line on the rail network, not somewhere trains pass through, but where they wind up. Its famous cream phone boxes are a statement of cussed municipal independence, built by the local authority, who controlled the phone network here rather than the government. In the 1978–9 'Winter of Discontent', strikes in Hull were so huge and so extreme that the city practically blockaded itself and ran as a city-state for months. But if it feels disconnected from the rest of the UK – even from the rest of Yorkshire – it has close historic connections to the Netherlands, Scandinavia, Germany. Some of the attractions of the Capital of Culture in 2017 tried to draw attention to this. The Queen kindly lent the Ferens Art Gallery a Rembrandt painting of a shipbuilder and his wife; in the gallery, the painting was accompanied by urban land-scapes and maps of seventeenth-century Rotterdam and Hull, showing their visual similarities and trading links, under the slogan 'REMBRANDT IN HULL?' – he had visited the city early in his career, it transpired. A more convincing place to see this historic affinity is in Hull's major building, Holy Trinity church, a late-medieval design of more interest than many cathedrals.

Its short but delicate, lightweight clocktower is one of many fine things on the Hull skyline, but it's the interior that is really distinguished. The church is Perpendicu-lar, in the terms used by architectural historians to define English Gothic architecture: long, low, spacious,

Walter Crane's windows in
Holy Trinity

ethereal, a little uncanny, stripping away any superfluous
heft with thin arcades and pulsating expanses of polychromatic stained glass. The tracery of the windows
behind the choir is organic, great curved lines whipping
round and intersecting. Some of these have glass by the
Arts and Crafts artist and passionate socialist Walter
Crane, and the vivid, almost harsh colours – the sharpest
greens and reds – and elongated, abstract bodies point
towards German Expressionism, an atheist and Marxist's
idea of religious ecstasy. Other fittings are more whimsical, as with the pagan beasties carved at the ends of the
benches, a bearded green man mounting a lion, birds
growing out of the arms of cold seats. There is also a
questionable eighteenth-century painting by a French

artist (and a Dutch gold statue of King Billy just outside), but it is the memorials that make it obvious what an international city this is, and always has been. Not just all the mariners whose gravestones you walk over, but the Georgian memorials to Scandinavian dignitaries (the family of William Good, Danish consul and 'Knight of the Dannebrog'), and also the shipwreck memorials, recording all of the obscure places where Hull sailors in fishing boats had died obscure deaths. 'The gallant crew of the D.T. *Gaul*, lost with all hands off the North Cape of Norway' in 1974, 'the gallant crew of the S.T. *Ross Cleveland*, lost with all hands save one, in Isafjord, Iceland', 1968, among others. 'Safely anchored', they read. The sea here is not a balmy gateway to southerly climes, but a lethal adversary, and that may explain a few things.

A blast of cold North Sea air certainly blows through some of the architecture here. The first thing you see on the train from York that announces entry into the city is the 1970s Humber Bridge, an ambitious single-span suspension bridge, once the longest single span in the world, a design of impressive minimalist rectitude. Then partly disused industry, terraced houses, and a series of recently renovated tower blocks in enfilade lead you to Paragon Interchange. It's aptly named, consecutive arched glass sheds leading to a good, restrained new bus station by the architects WilkinsonEyre, well integrated with the train station, whose classical canopies are now the bus waiting rooms. Everything feels under-used, although (especially by British standards) the station is clean and attractive. The street you come to encapsulates one of the problems with Hull. Ferensway – named after a local Liberal politician and civic philanthropist – was carved through the city as slum clearance in the interwar years, as one of several English attempts at Parisian boulevards that were cut through between the 1880s and 1950s, in London, Leeds, Welwyn, Birmingham and elsewhere. Apart from maybe the rebuilt Regent Street in London, none are remotely convincing: none feel like the sort of imperial boulevards that you'll find in most big continental cities. Already in the 1930s planning like this was attacked for being bombastic, reactionary and dangerous for running heavy traffic and pedestrians alongside each other. All these accusations were of course true, and maybe because of that what we have is often in fragments, a few pompous blocks around dual carriageways, without the trees, ground floor shops, apartments above and the sense of civic coherence that actual Haussmannism usually meant, whatever else can be said about it. At best, the result is just architectural incoherence, such as at Birmingham's Corporation Street or Shaftesbury Avenue in London, and sometimes that incoherence is more fun than a limestone monolith. The worst outcome is something like Ferensway, an over-engineered, pedestrian-hostile gash through the city inadequately supplemented with a clutch of thin-lipped neo-Georgian blocks, pieces of a jigsaw which, no matter how pompous it was, would have been better completed than left in scrubby, shabby shards.

On Ferensway are Hull's best and worst new buildings. The former is the Hull Truck Theatre, designed nearly ten years ago by Wright and Wright. It is a small but intense building, brown engineering brick and rough surfaces, a bare concrete frame, for a theatre company.

New New Brutalism – Hull Truck

Since it was built, the excellent original red and white signage has been replaced with something more Clipart, but it looked in good condition both times I visited it, in 2016 and 2017. There's also a pleasant café/restaurant spilling onto the square outside. Drinks are at London prices and the show is *Educating Rita*. At least as architecture, it's much better than the modern theatres of bigger, richer cities like Edinburgh or Leeds. Next to it is another arts building, the Albemarle Music Centre, a cheaper, more gimmicky design: together, though, the pair form a strong ensemble. It's the way these are placed alongside the other buildings built as part of the same plan that is distinctively British – the cultural part is clearly a sort of 'offsetting' of an overbearing commercial development. The redevelopment of this part of Ferensway, near the end of the New Labour boom, was dominated by the St Stephen's Shopping Centre, a dull and oppressively tacky enclosed mall, to which these were the civic figleaves: something actually mandated by the British planning system, where councils are instructed to let developers get away with things unthinkable in Bergen, Hamburg or even Narva if they set aside some funding for a public purpose elsewhere. The worst part of it is the woefully inept Holiday Inn, cruelly underthought and desperately cheap, the hotel corp evidently considered so important that planners didn't dare hold them to a decent design, but let them foist a standardized plan on the city. It's a disfigurement of an otherwise superb skyline, one which is, infuriatingly, probably most seen from the Inn's shitty, poky rooms, as east Yorkshire's flat, marshy Dutch/north German/Polish landscape makes views and panoramas rare.

Cross Ferensway, though, and you're into Hull city centre, which is much more rewarding. Within Britain, Hull was the most bombed northern city in the Second World War, another consequence of its proximity to Northern continental Europe. The replacements for the Georgian and Victorian streets that were destroyed are in the unnamed style which determined rebuilding in similarly flattened Southampton, Plymouth, Swansea and Sheffield – though not more confident, Modernist Coventry. It has no equivalent on the Continent, although it bears faint resemblance to the axial classical planning of post-war Le Havre or East Berlin, albeit with the scale much smaller and the voltage turned down considerably; it's conservative, but not totalitarian. The style is usually

Post-war compromise

used for shopping streets, and there's seldom much of a mix of uses. It sits somewhere between Modernism and Traditionalism – not much ornament, usually flat roofs, flat brick surfaces interspersed with Modernist curtain walls set into Portland stone, or with residual classical columns fitted onto the concrete and steel frames below. Behind are bins and car parks, sometimes reached through Neoclassical archways. The results were described by the planner-writer Adrian Jones as looking like 'a grittier Welwyn Garden City'. There was an ambitious plan for Hull by the cult Neoclassicist Edwin Lutyens (one of the few architects of the twentieth century to get to design an entire new capital, New Delhi) and Patrick Abercrombie, planner of London, Plymouth and Haifa, but it was never implemented. Instead, there are the old streets, just with new-old buildings, and staid as it mostly is (two major exceptions – the unexpected Moderne chic of the House of Fraser, and the sprawling BHS, with its wonderful, glimmering green and gold 'Three Ships' mosaic – currently threatened with demolition), it isn't bad townscape – but it did mark a failure of planning, the preference after the war to just rebuild on the old plan and leave ownership in the hands of the same people.

The positive effect of this is that the new streets connect very easily and simply to the old, and these are superb. Many of the Victorian survivals are of the very highest quality, although their condition varies: the short neo-Gothic Paragon Arcade is a little sad, but Hepworth's Arcade is a glittering space, as intriguing as any Parisian *passage*, and is gratifyingly full of independent record

Hepworth Arcade

shops and similar things that have started to disappear from both richer and poorer British cities (though the pricing suggests it's aimed straight at collectors, with one eye on eBay and Discogs, and one on browsers in an arcade in Hull). The Arcade leads through to the Covered Market, and from there the expansive docklands. The streets of 'Hull Old Town', as it is branded, are full of passages and alleys, seventeenth- and eighteenth-century streets, winding or Palladian-straight, framed by archways, often cobbled. There are a few Georgian terraces to be found too, as fine as Liverpool and Dublin, though more fragmentary. What makes walking round the centre of Hull particularly enjoyable here is actually the *absence* of a plan, of any tidying up. An accidental ensemble of Georgian porches, Dutch gables and florid Victorian dock offices will be hard up against a concrete car park or a derelict office block. It is all a sign of failure, so one ought not to enjoy it, but I do – a townscape with a certain amount of give. But knowing that only two or three demolitions (such as of Kingston House, Maxwell Fry and Jane Drew's lone, knackered-looking office block) would make the centre look basically pre-Modernist must make doing so rather tempting. Then you could turn back the clock a little, to the time before the bombs (and also the time before free healthcare, council housing with central heating and hot water, universal suffrage, trade union rights, etc). Why would you want to do this? The main civic square of Hull offers a clue.

Little in Hull is dominating in scale. It is not a sublime classical city, like Liverpool or Glasgow, nor does it have the post-1945 monuments to the forgotten future that

make Sheffield and Coventry so thrilling and poignant.
Even its grandest buildings are not huge, but their recognition of the city's actual proportions gives them
immense power in the townscape. Queen Victoria
Square – a triangular 'square', an Edwardian product – is
an exciting space, where all the main streets converge,
one of those places which pedestrianization would probably ruin a little, although between my first and second
visits to the city this is what happened. In the square's
centre is one of those obsessively detailed Victorian
sculptural groups, where a meticulous story is told in
voluptuous kitsch, trident-wearing sea maidens holding
domes and ships with Victoria herself surmounting it all.
Around this is a series of domed civic buildings. The late-
Victorian Dock Office, now the Maritime Museum, has
four of them, on top of a lushly ornamented Italianate
sandstone hulk; the Edwardian City Hall has one huge
copper dome, and commercial buildings around have
their own smaller domes and domelets, deferring to
these, as does the Neoclassical Ferens Art Gallery, which
with its good manners and portland stone seems to want
to be in a politer, duller city.

All these are slathered in sculpture and ornament, and
you can sit on the monument in the middle and take it
all in, a heady experience of late-imperial grandeur and
excitingly bad taste. It is all partly the product of the fact
that the mayor of the Edwardian city, the Liberal Alfred
Gelder, was himself an architect, and a felt lack of a civic
heart was redressed with gusto. The early-twentieth-
century effort to give Hull the civic grandeur it deserved
as third port, at the time, after Liverpool and London,

City Hall

was wildly successful. The oddest of its monumental buildings is Hull Guildhall, a short walk away from Queen Victoria Square, nearer to the later Queen's Gardens. The front façade is a disappointment, a vision of the killed-by-kindness neo-Georgian bland that would have far too much influence on twentieth-century Hull. Its side façade, however, facing Alfred Gelder Street, is stupendous: a stomp of rhythmic, bulging pilasters, topped with towers bearing hysterically active statues of seabound figures on Wagnerian ships, about to blast off towards the North Sea – not 'Rule, Britannia' but 'Ride of the Valkyries'. There are all manner of reasons not to like this building – no doubt about it, this is the aesthetics of imperialism in full roar, all its iconography practically

377

bellowing its intention to rule the waves at you – but it is as thrilling as it is ethically questionable. Hull circa 1914 was clearly bent on being one of the great cities of the empire. Stripped of this ambition, the city is a cul-de-sac – unless it manages to reconstitute a new identity, based on taking something from the people who have moved here and the countries it trades with, something which it now seems exceptionally unlikely. On the 1980s and 1990s buildings opposite the Guildhall are more 'To let' signs in one place than I've ever seen.

Opposite is the city centre's most convincing twentieth-century space. Once a dock, Queen's Gardens was transformed into a sunken park in the 1930s, and redesigned with abstract concrete reliefs to its walls by Liverpool

The Wagnerian classicism of
Hull Guildhall

Metropolitan Cathedral's architect, Frederick Gibberd, in the 1950s. It's as good a Modernist public space as Queen Victoria Square is a classical one, with a real sense of openness, ease, and lushness, with its fountains, placid pools and enclosed gardens – seeing the domes of the Dock Offices rise through the trees here is one of the great civic moments of any British city, a vision of order, clean air, rationality, something the surrounding will-this-do architecture foisted on the city since the 1980s (the BBC's effort is especially pathetic) can't quite ruin. The gardens, though subtle and modern, are arranged on an axis – on one side the Dock Offices, on the other, the Brutalist mass of Hull College. On a square linking the college and the gardens is the Wilberforce Column, built for a different site near the Dock Offices, but moved

A quiet corner of Queen's Gardens

here in the 1950s. The politician and anti-slave trade advocate William Wilberforce was once the MP for Hull, and this dramatic, blackened sandstone Doric column, leading up to a toga'd statue of him, is impressive and absurd. Like a lot of monuments to and talk of Wilberforce, there's something slightly offensive about it – the country which made the most money through the slave trade, which funded those Georgian streets (and so many others), makes great display of its belated abolition of the same, and asks the world to be grateful. What I am grateful for is that just behind the column is Gibberd's college building, a Corbusian abstracted grid, with a psychedelic relief by William Mitchell, on scientific and Surrealist themes, unidentified ceramic lifeforms. Next to that is a dull but worthy Brutalist pavilion housing the art and architecture departments. From here, you're almost at the rivers and docks that the city grew around.

There are a couple of possible routes to the rivers Hull and Humber. One is infuriating: the straight line from Holy Trinity church to the Humber, where you have to pass a dual carriageway filled with lorries, and built in the 1980s (there are proposals to put it in a tunnel, which hopefully will go through), to a quiet but vigorous space of Georgian warehouses, empty spaces, a wonderful Edwardian public loo (again, unusually for the UK, still in use) and something called the 'Hull and Humber World Trade Centre', a small and pleasant office block resembling Norman Foster's more classical side. Where this meets the Humber estuary, there are some clever, discrete squares and piers to watch the ships go by from (or not). The Humber is bracing, its great expanse lined with cooling towers and container cranes, the only place in Hull that speaks of the sublime rather than the dense and rough-edged. That comes back when you get to the shallower, narrower River Hull, but before you do, you get to The Deep. This was Hull's 'Bilbao Effect' gesture in the Blair years. The funding of ambitious public buildings in towns like this is maybe something that people will remember New Labour well for, though at the time it always seemed – and to me still does – like the carrot offered along with the stick of privatization, casualization and the expansion of the market into every bit of civic and personal life, something which I find hard to forgive. But the building is great, on its terms. The Deep is basically an aquarium with a café, but the design by Terry Farrell makes it into a monument at the confluence of the rivers, with the sort of Expressionist drive, the

The Deep

crash and bang and plunge headlong into space, that resembles a little the spirit of Hamburg's Chilehaus, although naturally the detail isn't on the same level: a faintly generic titanium cladding, vaguely resembling scales, with a skeletal glass point at its thrust-out corner. It would be hard now to imagine the meeting point of the rivers without it.

Along the Hull, tall warehouses, some of them converted into flats, stand by a satisfyingly rickety board-walk, and a marshy, muddy river with a pleasingly harsh smell. The tidal barrier, Brutalist heavy engineering formed into a triumphal arch, leads to a series of retract-able steel bridges, all of them dynamic and interesting, and some of them quite recent. Ships are left on the river, stuck in the mud, cranes arch above it: of all the mari-time cities in this book, this is the first one that has some real stink and rust. Naturally then it must be sanitized, and this is what current plans entail. The abysmal Premier Inn, worse and more drably standardized, if anything, than the Holiday Inn in the centre, would simply not be allowed to be built like this in any other European city of Hull's population and importance; its tacky blue cladding and minuscule windows are two fingers waved in the city's face (and the insult is accepted because, well, what else is going to happen here, we need jobs, at least it's some development, something happening . . .). Some Art Deco brick silos were recently demolished for more of the same, and what is left there of the warehousing and industry looks forlorn, on the way out. It is still a strange and rich townscape, but of a differ-ent sort to the centre. Space has crept in. The silos and

Lifebelt for Premier Inn

overhead bridges of Maizecor, with Proustian-rush-inducing early 1980s lettering immediately sending me back to my Southampton childhood, lead, if you take the right turning, to a neo-Baroque pub and a small council estate.

Hull acquired a bad rep for its council housing, mainly because of an enthusiasm for peripheral estates and system-building, both of which have always been the more questionable side of the otherwise eminently defensible post-war rehousing programme. But this estate has survived, simple brick houses and flats, around a light and graceful 1960s school, but with all the silos and cranes and warehouses just round the corner. It feels like a New Town, not like an inner-city estate, all lawns and front gardens – what people want. And it doesn't feel

desolate or sad, either, but open and optimistic, and everything no more than a stroll away from work. Except
the work isn't there, and there's no other idea for what to
do but force people into endless JobCentre courses, into
'aiming high' as individuals or just ignoring them and
leaving the city to 'managed decline' and encouraging
the smart ones to move to London. This is at least part of
why 67 per cent of voters here wanted to leave the European Union, not necessarily because they wanted to Send
Them Back – although of course some did – but as an
enormous fuck you to a political class that thought they
could abandon at worst, patronize at best, an entire city
and its population like this.

Hull is of course already a city with culture, so its year-
long designation should be uncontroversial. Culture as a
means for 'regeneration' under New Labour was often
connected with the expansion of universities, something
that got called the 'knowledge economy'. It did lead to
some expansion of research and development, and a few
service industry jobs to service the students and staff, so it
was perhaps better than nothing, but you can see how
skin-deep the effect of these measures, when not accompanied by a wider plan for recovery, can be, by getting the
bus out to the University of Hull. The Paragon Interchange is, as mentioned, a paragon – as far as it goes. You
can get a bus from a logical and clear bus station, to destinations which all seem to terminate in either the word
'estate' or 'ASDA', but the privatized bus network itself is
rudimentary, if regular. Public transport outside London
and, to a degree, Glasgow, Manchester and Newcastle is
predicated on the belief that only people who live in a city

are going to travel on it. Getting to the university on the number 5 bus, having never been there before, turned out to be more difficult than expected, given that none of the stops have names on, let alone the announcements standard on London buses or Manchester trams. What made this especially sad was that I'd recently spent a few days in Rostock, an economically depressed, heavily bombed East German Hansa port smaller than, but otherwise comparable to, Hull. It recently expanded its smooth, fast, elegant and cheap publicly owned tram network with an underground station, putting it on the level of Manchester, and some considerable way above Hull. Suggesting Hull should get similar treatment in a meeting of either town hall or treasury would get you laughed out of town.

After the drive through the relatively affluent pavement cafés (Europe!) and craft beer pubs of Newlands Avenue, and the fifteen-minute walk caused by having got off at the wrong stop, the University of Hull is a pretty standard northern university. There's a neo-Georgian core enclosed by smart Modernist quadrangles by the influential post-war Modernist major-domo Leslie Martin, with at its heart the Brynmor Jones Library. Commissioned, rather puzzlingly given his obnoxiously right-wing politics, by the head librarian, Philip Larkin, himself, it consists of spiky Brutalist storeys cantilevered above an earlier neo-Georgian block, recently supplemented by an inoffensive classical-Modernist new entrance. In here during the City of Culture events was an exhibition of bits and bobs (and especially books) from Larkin's own archive, which led into a selection of the university's very fine art collection. It was all very

Larkin's library

enjoyable and I might have felt better about it had the university been placed, as in Sheffield or Leeds, close to the city centre – but, instead, this leafy, populated, lively world felt most unlike the dockside council estates, where the density of buildings belies a paucity of people. Could 'culture' connect with the rest of the city in a way that made much difference to anyone, beyond encouraging the usual few clever working-class kids to find new and unexpected ways out?

The big industrial hope for Hull pre-Brexit was a wind turbine factory, owned by Siemens, begun in 2011 and opened at the end of 2016. As a nod to this, one of the many public projects of the City of Culture entailed placing one of the blades of these turbines in Queen Victoria Square, where it became an image of abstract industrial might. Surrounding it were the 'public realm improvements' (to use the urbanist jargon) that came with the City of Culture award and its attendant budget – the repair and repaving of many of the city centre streets, and the pedestrianization of some of the squares. Against my reservations, the results are likeable and relaxed, with plenty of benches and places to linger, and with a minimum of fussy street furniture or overbearing public art. The only part of it that felt unnerving was the erection of floodlights, to be shone onto the great civic buildings – they look like giant CCTV cameras (which Hull has plenty of already), overbearingly tall and angular. What was encouraging about the artworks that came with the year-long cultural jolly is that most of them worked with the city, engaging with its spaces and histories. The results didn't feel – albeit to someone from Southampton, that southern city so similar and so different – like they were patronizing or parachuted-in, the cultural equivalent of beaming Alan Johnson down from Millbank to Humberside. That said, the most memorable encounter, when I visited Hull in its City of Culture year was not with a particular artwork, but with a parade to celebrate Hull's Rugby League side winning the Challenge Cup. Seeing these grand squares, made with such pomposity and pride, filled with proud and optimistic people, was thrilling. I wondered what it would have felt like in the Corbyn rallies – much bigger – here a year earlier. Maybe, people must be thinking, maybe the tides will turn?

Maybe Hull's future can be a Norwegian one, where social democracy can flourish far from the ministrations of Jean-Claude Juncker. Maybe. The Tory notion of a

Hull are the champions

post-Brexit UK as rotting Victorian Singapore, low-tax and entrepreneurial, can mean less than nothing for Hull, but any sort of 'Lexit' future, where all the contradictions of Brexit will get resolved in the favour of the working class of Humberside, stumbles at some early and huge hurdles – such as, what to do with all the EU money that has been often the only thing between the city and total collapse. In August 2017, the entrance to Hull marina was decorated, in an act of locking the stable door after the horse had definitely bolted, with the flags of the EU and, numbered out in flowers, the year '2017'. From here you can get a boat to Rotterdam, and from there take a few trains, go on a few walks, and find that almost anywhere else in Northern Europe is proof that Hull's fate wasn't inevitable. Maybe in the future, though, we can go beyond managing an inherently unjust system more justly, with better transport, cleaner streets and nicer buildings. For the social democrats of Northern Europe, that's as good as we'll ever get – the peak of human achievement, beyond which lies uncharted and frightening territory. Maybe in Hull they'll have some ideas about what lies beyond.

BIBLIOGRAPHY

This is not a scholarly book, and accordingly I've not felt the need to footnote it or provide proper references. However I've had to consult a large quantity of books in the course of writing this one, the most useful of which are listed below.

On 'Europe'

Anderson, Perry, *Passages from Antiquity to Feudalism* (Verso, 1974)

—, *Lineages of the Absolutist State* (Verso, 1974)

—, *The New Old World* (Verso, 2009)

Balakrishnan, Gopal (ed.), *Mapping the Nation* (Verso, 1996)

Bickerton, Chris, *The European Union: A Citizen's Guide* (Penguin Books, 2016)

Braudel, Fernand, *Civilisation and Capitalism, 15th–18th Century*, vol. 1: *The Structures of Everyday Life: The Limits of the Possible* (Collins, 1981)

Federici, Silvia (ed.), *Enduring Western Civilization: The Construction of the Concept of Western Civilization and Its 'Others'* (Praeger, 1995)

Flassbeck, Heiner and Costas Lapavitsas, *Against the Troika: Crisis and Austerity in the Eurozone* (Verso, 2015)

Frank, Andre Gunder, *Capitalism and Underdevelopment in Latin America: Historical Studies of Chile and Brazil* (Pelican, 1971), for the description of Portugal's relation to Britain

Judt, Tony, *Postwar: A History of Europe since 1945* (Vintage, 2010)

Luxemburg, Rosa, *The National Question: Selected Writings* (Monthly Review, 1976)

McEvedy, Colin, *The New Penguin Atlas of Recent History* (Penguin Books, 2002)

McNeill, Donald, *New Europe: Imagined Spaces* (Hodder Arnold, 2004)

Pyzik, Agata, *Poor But Sexy: Culture Clashes in Europe East and West* (Zero, 2014)

Sand, Shlomo, *Twilight of History* (Verso, 2017)

Taylor, A. J. P., *Europe: Grandeur and Decline* (Penguin Books, 1990)

Ugrešić, Dubravka, *Nobody's Home* (Telegram, 2007)

Wilson, Andrew, *Belarus: The Last European Dictatorship* (Yale, 2011), for the line about perceptions of 'Europe' in Belarus

On European Architecture, Modernism and Urbanism

Adam, Robert, *The Globalisation of Modern Architecture: The Impact of Politics, Economics and Social Change on Architecture and Urban Design since 1990* (Cambridge Scholars, 2012)

Banham, Reyner, *Age of the Masters: A Personal View of Modern Architecture* (Icon, 1975)

Bergdoll, Barry, *European Architecture 1750–1890* (OUP, 2000)

Charley, Jonathan, *Memories of Cities: Trips and Manifestoes* (Ashgate, 2013)

Colomina, Beatriz, *Privacy and Publicity: Modern Architecture as Mass Media* (MIT Press, 1996)

Colquhoun, Alan, *Modern Architecture* (OUP, 2002)

Frampton, Kenneth, *Modern Architecture: A Critical History* (Thames & Hudson, rev. edn 2007)

Hall, Peter, *Good Cities, Better Lives: How Europe Discovered the Lost Art of Urbanism* (Routledge, 2013)

Irving, Mark (ed.), *1001 Buildings to See before You Die* (Cassell, 2012)

Johnson, Philip and Henry-Russell Hitchcock, *The International Style* (W. W. Norton & Co., 1997)

Kidder Smith, G. E., *The New Architecture of Europe* (Penguin Books, 1962)

Mordaunt Crook, J., *The Dilemma of Style: Architectural Ideas from the Picturesque to the Post-Modern* (John Murray, 1989)

Murphy, Douglas, *The Architecture of Failure* (Zero, 2012)

—, *Last Futures: Nature, Technology and the End of Architecture* (Verso, 2016)

Overy, Paul, *Light, Air and Openness: Modern Architecture between the Wars* (Thames & Hudson, 2007)

Pevsner, Nikolaus, *An Outline of European Architecture* (Penguin Books, 1990)

—, *Pioneers of Modern Design* (Penguin, 1991)

— and J. M. Richards (eds.) *The Anti-Rationalists* (Architectural Press, 1973)

Rasmussen, Steen Eiler, *Experiencing Architecture* (MIT Press, 1964)

Rossi, Aldo, *The Architecture of the City* (MIT Press, 1982)

Spencer, Douglas, *The Architecture of Neoliberalism: How Contemporary Architecture Became an Instrument of Control and Compliance* (Bloomsbury, 2016)

Tafuri, Manfredo, *Architecture and Utopia: Design and Capitalist Development* (MIT Press, 1976)

— and Francesco Dal Co, *Modern Architecture* (Rizzoli, 1987)

Vasudevan, Alexander, *The Autonomous City: A History of Urban Squatting* (Verso, 2017)

Weber, Max, *The City* (Free Press, 1966)

On Particular Places, Cities and Countries

Alexeyeva, Linda and Grigory Ostrovsky, *Lvov: A Guide* (Raduga, 1987)

Amar, Tarik Cyril, *The Paradox of Ukrainian Lviv: A Borderland City between Stalinists, Nazis, and Nationalists* (Cornell UP, 2015)

Ascherson, Neal, *The King Incorporated: Leopold II and the Congo* (Granta, 1999)

Biris, Manos and Maro Kardamitsi-Adami, *Neoclassical Architecture in Greece* (Getty, 2004)

Broughton, Hugh and Melanie Ashton, *Madrid: A Guide to Recent Architecture* (Batsford, 1997)

Burniat, Patrick et al., *Modern Architecture in Brussels* (L'Editions de l'Octogone, 2000)

Cabrero, Gabriel Ruiz, *The Modern in Spain: Architecture after 1948* (The MIT Press, 2001)

Campbell, Barbara-Ann, *Paris: A Guide to Recent Architecture* (Batsford, 1997)

Casey, Christine, *The Buildings of Ireland: Dublin* (Yale UP, 2005)

Connah, Roger, *Finland: Modern Architectures in History* (Reaktion, 2006)

Darley, Gillian, *Factory* (Reaktion, 2003)

Etienne-Steiner, Claire, *Le Havre: Auguste Perret et la Reconstruction* (L'Inventaire, 1999)

Ghirardo, Diane, *Italy: Modern Architectures in History* (Reaktion, 2013)

Grafe, Christoph, *People's Palaces – Architecture, Culture and Democracy in Post-War Western Europe* (Architectura & Natura Press, 2014)

Güell, Xavier and Carlos Flores, *Architecture of Spain 1929–1996* (Caja de Arquitectos, 1996)

Hultin, Olof et al., *The Complete Guide to Architecture in Stockholm* (Arkitektur Förlag, 2009)

Ivanovski, Jovan et al., *Findings: The Macedonian Pavilion at the 14th International Architecture Exhibition* (Youth Cultural Centre Skopje, 2014)

Jäggi, Max et al., *Red Bologna* (Writers and Readers, 1977)

James-Chakraborty, Kathleen, *German Architecture for a Mass Audience* (Routledge, 2000)

Jones, Adrian and Chris Matthews, *Towns in Britain* (Five Leaves, 2014)

—, *Cities of the North* (Five Leaves, 2016)

Kopleck, Maik, *Munich, 1933–1945* (Christoph Links Verlag, 2007)

Kulić, Vladimir et al., *Modernism In-Between – The Mediatory Architectures of Socialist Yugoslavia* (Jovis, 2012)

Mathieson, David, *Frontline Madrid: Battlefield Tours of the Spanish Civil War* (Signal, 2014)

Mazower, Mark, *Salonica, City of Ghosts: Christians, Muslims and Jews 1430–1950* (Vintage, 2006)

Meyhöfer, Dirk, *Hamburg: Der Architekturführer* (Verlagshausbraun, 2007)

Mijalkovic, Milan and Katharina Urbanek, *Skopje, the World's Bastard: Architecture of the Divided City* (Wieser, 2011)

Miller Lane, Barbara, *Architecture and Politics in Germany 1918–1945* (Harvard UP, 1985)

Museum Het Schip, *On the Waves of the City: An Amsterdam School Cycling Tour* (Het Schip, 2009)

Neave, David and Susan, *Pevsner City Guide: Hull* (Yale UP, 2010)

Neuvonen, Petri et al., *Vyborg, Architekturnii Putevoditel'* (SN 'Vyborg', 2008)

Powers, Alan, *Britain: Modern Architectures in History* (Reaktion, 2007)

Rogers, Richard and Mark Fisher, *A New London: Two Views* (Penguin Books, 1992)

Wagenaar, Cor, *Town Planning in the Netherlands* (010, 2010)

Widenheim, Cecilia and Eva Rudberg (eds.), *Utopia and Reality: Modernity in Sweden, 1900–1960* (Yale UP, 2002)

ACKNOWLEDGEMENTS

A great many people helped me with understanding individual places, or invited me to them. Below is a list of everyone whom I haven't forgotten – apologies to those I have, and to those I have not for any implication at any point that they are responsible for the content, particularly the errors. So, thank you Martina Angelotti, Yiannis Baboulias, Aisling O'Beirn, Michel Chevalier, Valeria Costa-Kostritsky, Amanda De Frumerie, Brian Dillon, Vladimir Deskov, Mary Douglas, Robert Doyle, Jools Duane, Maxim Edwards, Alfonso Everlet, Tom Gann, Iskra Geshoska, Leo Hollis, Goran Janev, Daniel Jewesbury, Adrian Jones, Emilia Kaleva, Maros Krivy, Tor Lindstrand, Declan Long, Rikke Luther, Patrick Lynch, Chris Matthews, Will Mawhood, Jonathan Meades, Robin Monotti, Douglas Murphy, Daniel Muzyczuk, Natalia Neshevets, Lora Nicolaou, Christian Victor Palmer, Cigi Danica Pavlovska, Mark Price, Tihana Pupovac, Oleksiy Radynski, Helen Runting, Biljana Savic, Joakim Skajaa, Dubravka Sekulic, Niki Seth-Smith, Matt Tempest, Jacques Testard, Francesco Tenaglia, Lydia Thompson, Noam Toran, Daniel Trilling, Elena Trubina, Aneta Vasileva, Mait Väljas, Tim Verlaan, Christian Wertschulte, Tom Wilkinson. Special thanks are due to Agata Pyzik, with whom I did much of the earlier travel in this non-chronological book and whose opinions on 'Europe' and its construction have been invaluable from start to finish;

and to my father, with whom I enjoyed my first Top European City Breaks.

Porto, Leipzig, Łódź, Vyborg, Aarhus, Bergen, Randstad and Hull were written solely for this book, but it is essentially an anthology. Early versions of Brussels and Hamburg were originally published on the blog 'Sit Down Man, You're A Bloody Tragedy'. Versions of Split, Bologna, Thessaloniki, Sofia, Le Havre, Munich, Meuse–Rhine, Nicosia, Madrid, Stockholm and Narva were originally published in slightly different form as the appallingly named 'Eurovisionaries' in the *Architects' Journal*. These were the idea of Rory Olcayto, and for that reason I owe the idea for this book to him, for which he has my deepest gratitude. Versions of Skopje appeared in 'Guardian Cities', with thanks to Chris Michael and Mike Herd; Lviv, in the *Calvert Journal*, with thanks to Arthur House; Dublin in *Crisis Jam*, with thanks to Angela Nagle; and Arborea in *Wallpaper*, with thanks to Ellie Stathaki.

Many thanks as always to Tom Penn, for good counsel and fine editing. I am very grateful to CW, who doesn't want to be thanked.

INDEX

Index